"This book is a great introduction to and refutation of wokeness—what Shenvi and Sawyer define as 'the contemporary cultural expression of critical theory.' To put it more plainly, this book is about race, gender, and sexuality—what our culture would have us believe about all three, and, by contrast, what the Bible teaches about each. With clear writing, careful research, and calm evaluation, Shenvi and Sawyer have provided an articulate and accessible resource that will serve students, schools, pastors, and churches—and really, any Christian living in the West—for years to come. If someone asks me, 'What is wokeness and what is wrong with it?' this is the first book I'll recommend."

Kevin DeYoung, senior pastor, Christ Covenant Church, Matthews, NC; Associate Professor of Systematic Theology, Reformed Theological Seminary, Charlotte, NC

"If you think wokeness is gone, you need to think again. The effects of wokeness (i.e., critical theory) remain in the culture and church. Shenvi and Sawyer masterfully explain how we got to our cultural moment and how to think biblically about race, sexuality, and gender. *Post Woke* offers practical steps for raising discerning kids and lovingly engaging our neighbors in meaningful conversation. This is on my must-read list for every Christian."

Sean McDowell, PhD, apologetics professor at Biola University; author or editor of over 20 books; popular YouTuber

"Many people claim that the church should stay out of politics. So what happened? Politics become a 'protected category'—if one could classify something as political, then the church would stay silent. As Shenvi and Sawyer show, that is not an option for us anymore—not if we want to be salt and light in the world. The problem is that most churchgoers are still blind to the spiritual implications of these so-called political topics that are redefining Christian morality. In *Post Woke,* Shenvi and Sawyer show exactly how objective truth, the nuclear family, gender, and sexuality were all removed from acceptable pulpit topics and relegated to the political arena. We can't refute what we don't understand. But once we understand? Game on."

Hillary Morgan Ferrer, founder/president of Mama Bear Apologetics; primary author/editor of *Mama Bear Apologetics* and *Mama Bear Apologetics Guide to Gender and Sexuality*

"Even though the excesses of the various social and political tendencies often referred to as wokeness seem to have subsided in the last year or two, Christians should not be complacent: Many of the social problems that made such impulses plausible still remain, and without a robust understanding of the flaws in critical theory and the Christian view of man, we remain vulnerable to the resurgence of radical ideologies. In this book, Shenvi and Sawyer offer a clear, thoughtful guide to the intellectual roots and cultural dynamics of critical theoretical discussion of such things as race and gender and provide calm, well-reasoned Christian responses that readers will find helpful as they think through these issues for themselves. A very fine book."

Carl R. Trueman, visiting professor,
Center for Citizenship and Constitutional
Government, University of Notre Dame

"This is truly a great book. For the first time, I felt as if I understood the attraction of wokeism and why Christian young people buy into its agenda, often believing it is consistent with Scripture. We all know brokenhearted parents whose children have been swept away by seductive cultural currents, and they will not accept superficial answers to their questions. In this book, the authors present critical theory very fairly and then answer it carefully with Scripture.

"Read this book like I did, with a pen in hand, rereading certain paragraphs to get the full impact of their argument. When you are finished you will be prepared to dialogue with those who confront you with a whole range of critical theories and you will help them better understand where they took a wrong turn. Best of all, you will be better equipped to point them confidently to the Scriptures as the source of all moral, cultural, and spiritual truth."

Erwin W. Lutzer, pastor emeritus,
Moody Church, Chicago

"In *Post Woke*, Shenvi and Sawyer cut through cultural confusion with biblical conviction, exposing the theological and moral bankruptcy of contemporary critical theory. They offer much-needed clarity on race, gender, and sexuality—boldly rejecting the false notion of 'gay Christianity' while holding fast to the gospel's call to repentance and faith. Accessible yet theologically robust, this book will equip both leaders and laypeople to stand firm in truth and love in a world that has lost both."

Dr. Christopher Yuan, speaker; author of *Holy Sexuality and the Gospel*; creator of The Holy Sexuality Project video series on biblical sexuality and gender (holysexuality.com)

"I love it when books slap me in the face with clarity and conviction, making me think harder, not just nod along. This is one of those books. Shenvi and Sawyer admirably tackle the tangled web of wokeness with a rare mix of intellectual precision, humility, and genuine compassion. They don't use the term *wokeness* as a cheap insult, but as a helpful description to explain a cultural moment many are struggling to understand. No longer can we send our kids to college without this ideology being shoved in their faces. No longer can we turn on the TV or scroll through social media without encountering the very issues exposed in this book. The cultural current is strong, and it's everywhere. We need to be prepared. This book offers a much-needed flashlight in the cultural fog."

Melissa Dougherty, apologist and author of *Happy Lies*

"Christians today sense a need to think carefully about wokeness but often feel confused or uncertain about how to go about this. Shenvi and Sawyer offer a nuanced, careful, and biblically faithful account that all Christians will benefit from reading. They don't strawman contemporary critical theory, and they are careful not to overreact in their thinking. They also bring forceful critique against the acidic aspects of this ideology. Regardless of where you fall in this discussion, you will find much wisdom and insight in this fair-minded book."

Gavin Ortlund, president, Truth Unites; author, *Why God Makes Sense in a World That Doesn't*

NEIL SHENVI & PAT SAWYER

POST WOKE

HARVEST APOLOGETICS
An Imprint of Harvest House Publishers

Cover design by Bryce Williamson and Kyler Dougherty

Cover images © Arthit_Longwilai, koosen, Wachiwit, Nipon Chinnueng / Getty Images

Interior design by KUHN Design Group

For bulk, special sales, or ministry purchases, please call 1-800-547-8979.
Email: CustomerService@hhpbooks.com

Post Woke

Published by Harvest House Publishers
Eugene, Oregon 97408
www.harvesthousepublishers.com

ISBN 978-0-7369-9283-1 (pbk)
ISBN 978-0-7369-9284-8 (eBook)

Library of Congress Control Number: 2025936302

Printed in the United States of America

25 26 27 28 29 30 31 32 33 / BP / 10 9 8 7 6 5 4 3 2 1

Worthy are you to take the scroll
and to open its seals,
for you were slain, and by your blood
you ransomed people for God
from every tribe and language and people and nation.

Revelation 5:9

God created man in his own image, in the
image of God he created him;
male and female he created them.

Genesis 1:27

The Groom
"Like a lily among the thorns,
so is my darling among the young women."

The Bride
"Like an apple tree among the trees of the forest,
so is my beloved among the young men.
In his shade I took great delight and sat down,
and his fruit was sweet to my taste."

Song of Solomon 2:2-3 (nasb)

If anyone is in Christ, he is a new creation.
The old has passed away; behold, the new has come.

2 Corinthians 5:17

CONTENTS

1

THE GREAT AWOKENING

In the mid-2010s, America underwent a profound religious awakening. Prophets and evangelists rose up to condemn the wickedness of our society. They called for repentance and a changed life. Acolytes wept openly as they confessed their sins, begged for forgiveness, and tearfully promised to do better. Bestseller lists were dominated by devotional material and weighty tomes written by longtime believers. Fortune 500 companies around the world brought in consultants to nurture the spiritual life of their employees. Enthusiastic believers displayed their creedal commitments on yard signs, social media profiles, and resumés. While the movement's initial fervor may have cooled, we still live in a time of religious revival.

But that religion isn't Christianity.

The prophets and evangelists who toured the country and railed against its wickedness were not preachers like John Wesley or George Whitefield; they were activist-scholars like Robin DiAngelo and Ibram X. Kendi. They did not call Americans to repent for their idolatry, greed, or adultery, but for the sins of "whiteness" and "structural oppression." Bookstores didn't do a brisk business in Bibles or Charles Spurgeon devotionals but sold millions of copies of books like *Me and White Supremacy* or *Why I'm No Longer Talking to White People About Race*. Companies didn't recruit new chaplains, but did hire hordes of Diversity, Equity, and Inclusion consultants. Yard signs didn't proclaim "I believe in one God, the Father almighty, maker of heaven and earth, of all things visible and invisible." Instead, they announced "In This House, We Believe Black Lives Matter. Women's Rights Are Human Rights. No Human Is Illegal. Science Is Real. Love Is Love. Kindness Is Everything."[1]

But, despite the differences between Christianity and the Postmodern Religion of Social Justice, we should recognize that the "Great Awokening" was indeed a spiritual affair.[2] People were being called out of an old way of life and into a new one, with a new set of commitments, values, and practices. Though the cultural winds may be shifting, many of the Great Awokening's converts are still clinging to their faith with all the tenacity of true believers.

This book is our attempt as evangelical Christians to explain what happened (and is still happening) to our culture and to equip people to push back against it by reasserting a biblical perspective of race, gender, and sexuality. We want to show people not only how wokeness gets these topics wrong, but how the Bible gets them right.

WOKENESS IN THE WILD

Let's begin with the Great Awokening itself. What did it look like on the ground? What are some of the cultural artifacts demonstrating the spiritual fervor that gripped large parts of the United States and the world for at least a decade? A comprehensive list would fill an entire book, but a few representative examples should suffice.

In 2020, the Smithsonian Institute's National Museum of African American History and Culture published an infographic listing the "Aspects and Assumptions of Whiteness and White Culture in the United States."

These included:

- "Emphasis on the Scientific Method"
- "Objective, rational linear thinking"
- "Cause and effect relationships"
- Concepts like "plan for the future" and "delayed gratification"
- Patterns of communication like "Be polite."[3]

After a public outcry, the Smithsonian removed the chart, but in early 2025, its website still featured an entire page on "whiteness" that explained concepts like "white privilege," "internalized racism," and "white fragility." It also featured a video of critical race educator Robin DiAngelo explaining that her "psychosocial development [as a White person] was inculcated in the water of white supremacy... a system in which whiteness and white people are central and seen as inherently superior [to] people of color."[4] After reading this material, it's natural to ask questions like, Is politeness really an element of whiteness? Were most people in 2020 taught to believe that Whites are inherently superior? And what are statements like these doing on the website of a taxpayer-funded national museum?

Over the course of the Great Awokening, the usage of phrases like *systemic racism* and *white supremacy* skyrocketed at major newspapers like *The New York Times*, *The Washington Post*, and the *Los Angeles Times*, more than quadrupling in the space of a few years.[5] Viral articles featured headlines like:

- "Straight Black Men Are the White People of Black People"[6]
- "Can My Children Be Friends With White People?"[7]
- "Why Can't We Hate Men?"[8]

- "I'm a Trans Man. I Didn't Realize How Broken Men Are"[9]
- "How White Women Use Strategic Tears to Silence Women of Colour"[10]
- "The Most Dangerous Threat to America? White Male Entitlement"[11]
- "The Dad Who Gave Birth: 'Being Pregnant Doesn't Change Me Being a Trans Man'"[12]
- "How White Women Use Themselves as Instruments of Terror"[13]

Once again, it's natural to ask: Do these articles offer accurate perspectives on race or gender or basic biology?

While race was obviously a central concern during this period, the Black Lives Matter organization was representative of the broader social justice movement in linking race to gender and sexuality. BLM was founded by three Black women, two of whom identify as queer. Despite its focus on race, the group's statement of beliefs made multiple, explicit references to gender and sexuality, stating:[14]

> We make space for transgender brothers and sisters to participate and lead.
>
> We are self-reflexive and do the work required to dismantle cisgender privilege and uplift Black trans folk, especially Black trans women who continue to be disproportionately impacted by trans-antagonistic violence.
>
> We foster a queer-affirming network. When we gather, we do so with the intention of freeing ourselves from the tight grip of heteronormative thinking...

Clearly, the founders of BLM saw some deep connection between race, gender, and sexuality. But why? Aren't these categories very different?

The 2018 Netflix reboot of the kids cartoon *She-Ra and the Princesses of Power* featured numerous LGBTQ characters, relationships, and plots. According to *Rolling Stone*, the show's executive producer, Noelle Stevenson (a gay woman who later began to identify as nonbinary and who now uses male pronouns), "steeped the world of the She-Ra reboot in queerness" such that it "features multiple side characters in same-sex relationships, characters who flout traditional gender roles, and even a nonbinary character."[15] Does sexuality really need to be a major theme in kid's cartoons?

Controversy surrounding J.K. Rowling, the billionaire author of the Harry Potter series, provided another example of the progressive consensus on sexuality and gender identity. In December 2019, Rowling ignited a firestorm on social media when she tweeted out her support for British consultant Maya Forstater, who was penalized for her belief that trans women (i.e., biological men who identify as women) are, in fact, men. Rowling wrote: "Call yourself whatever you like. Sleep with any consenting adult who'll have you. Live your best life in peace and security. But force women out of their jobs for stating that sex is real? #IStandWithMaya #ThisIsNotADrill."[16]

The backlash was tremendous. The stars of the Harry Potter movies responded independently but with nearly identical language:[17]

- "Transgender women are women." (Daniel Radcliffe, who played Harry Potter)
- "Trans people are who they say they are." (Emma Watson, who played Hermione Granger)
- "Trans women are women. Trans men are men." (Rupert Grint, who played Ron Weasley)
- "Transwomen are women." (Bonnie Wright, who played Ginny Weasley)

- "Trans women are women, trans men are men." (Eddie Redmayne, who played Newt Scamander)

Rowling wrote a follow-up article stating that, as a survivor of domestic violence and sexual assault, she could not support legislation that would allow biological men access to women's prisons or homeless shelters.[18] She detailed how she had talked extensively to transgender people, supported their choices, and had no animosity toward them. All to no avail. Why? Is it really a cancellable offense to suggest that male rapists should not be housed in women's prisons?[19] Apparently, yes.

Despite increasingly fervent and unbalanced manifestations of wokeness in our culture, some conservatives were insisting in early 2023 that we'd hit "peak woke," presumably because they assumed things couldn't possibly get any worse. For those who dreamt that wokeness was in decline, progressive responses to the Hamas terrorist attacks of October 7, 2023, provided a rude awakening.

While most Americans were still reeling at the news that Hamas, a terrorist organization that currently governs the Gaza Strip, had killed hundreds of Israeli civilians in a coordinated surprise attack, a number of groups immediately voiced their support for Palestinians and even for Hamas. For instance, Black Lives Matter Grassroots issued a "Statement in Solidarity With the Palestinian People," declaring that "we must stand unwaveringly on the side of the oppressed," and that "we see clear parallels between Black and Palestinian people."[20] Black Lives Matter Chicago tweeted out an image of a paraglider with the text "I stand with Palestine" (Hamas had used paragliders to launch their attack).[21] Slow Factory, a progressive organization with more than 600,000 followers on Instagram, posted a statement claiming that "Free Palestine is a Feminist issue. It's a reproductive rights issue. It's an Indigenous Rights issue. It's a Climate Justice issue, it's a Queer Rights issue, it's an Abolitionist

Issue."[22] And, most astonishing of all, a group called Queers for Palestine appeared at many rallies waving signs indicating their support for the Palestinians, despite the fact that homosexual activity is illegal in Gaza and that Islamic culture tends to be extremely hostile to homosexuality, to put it mildly.

These radical attitudes were widespread, especially among young people. In December 2023, a Harvard-Harris Poll surveyed 2,034 registered voters about their perspectives on various political topics. Pollsters explained: "There is an ideology that white people are oppressors and nonwhite people and people of certain groups have been oppressed and as a result should be favored today at universities and for employment." They then asked respondents: "Do you support or oppose this ideology?" Among seniors over age 64, 81 percent answered "oppose" and 19 percent answered "support." The numbers among young adults ages 18-24 were almost completely reversed: 21 percent answered "oppose" and 79 percent answered "support." In other words, the overwhelming majority of young people explicitly subscribed to an oppressed-oppressor ideology.

A follow-up question asked: "Do you think that Jews as a class are oppressors and should be treated as oppressors or is that a false ideology?" Again, there was a stark generational divide. Only 9 percent of seniors agreed that Jews should be treated as oppressors, while 91 percent disagreed. In contrast, 67 percent of young adults agreed that Jews should be treated as oppressors, while only 33 percent disagreed.[23]

Support for radical gender ideology also showed few signs of dwindling. On December 6, 2023, the official X (formerly Twitter) account of the Democratic National Convention posted a graphic that said, "Protect Trans Kids. Protect Trans Kids. Protect Trans Kids. Protect Trans Kids. Protect Trans Kids," with the explanation "Unlike Republicans, we stand with trans kids across the country."[24] That year, the Netflix preschool cartoon series CoComelon Lane featured a song entitled "Just Be You." In it, a preschooler named Nico who has two gay fathers is confused about how to dress when he gets his pictures taken. At one point in the song, he puts on a dress and a tiara and dances for his fathers, who encourage him to "just be you."[25] A 2023 Gallup poll found that 22.3 percent of Generation Z adults (born between 1997 and 2012) identify as LGBTQ+ compared to 9.8 percent of Millennials (born between 1981 and 1996), 4.5 percent of Generation Xers (born between 1965 and 1980), and only 2.3 percent of Baby Boomers (born between 1946 and 1964).[26]

Not only is the rising generation embracing the ideas of queer theory, it is also increasingly intolerant of anyone who rejects them. A 2023 survey found that 27 percent of college students (and 36 percent of liberal college students) believe that a college professor or course instructor should be reported to the university for making the statement "Biological sex is a scientific fact. There are two sexes, male and female."[27]

With all that said, the re-election of President Donald Trump in 2024 was indeed a serious setback for woke ideology. Once in office, President Trump immediately issued numerous executive orders that were intended to root wokeness out of the government and other institutions. These included EO 14187, "Protecting Children from Chemical and Surgical Mutilation"[28]; EO 14188, "Additional Measures to Combat Anti-Semitism"[29]; EO 14190, "Ending Radical Indoctrination in K-12 Schooling"[30]; and EO 14201, "Keeping Men Out of Women's Sports."[31]

However, Christians should not assume that wokeness will simply vanish. Consider just a few post-election examples. On February 14, 2025, *The New York Times* published an article entitled "As a White Man, Can I Date Women of Color to Advance My Antiracism?," in which a "straight white dude" with "very progressive beliefs" asked the paper's resident ethicist whether it was permissible for him to "prioritize dating women of color" to "combat implicit bias."[32] On February 26, 2025, less than a year after the United Methodist Church lifted its prohibitions on gay clergy and same-sex marriage, it announced a three-year plan to train congregations to "welcome the gifts of LGBTQ clergy" and to promote "intersectional justice."[33] On June 7, 2025, *USA Today* published an op-ed declaring: "There is no scientific evidence that transgender women athletes have a physical advantage over cisgender women athletes."[34]

The younger generation has been steeped in woke ideology for a decade. Current high school and college students will graduate and will bring their deeply held beliefs with them when they become our nation's next crop of lawyers, doctors, company executives, judges, educators, politicians, campus ministers, and pastors. Moreover, even if the Overton window[35] shifts rightward and woke ideology becomes less acceptable and normalized in general society, it will still continue to affect individuals. Thus, Christians will need to be hypervigilant in detecting its influence and exceedingly prayerful in understanding the most effective ways to fight it and keep it out of our families and churches. No matter how the culture changes, we will always need to anchor our understanding of race, gender, and sexuality in the Bible.

As we'll show in this book, the cultural phenomenon most people know as *wokeness* has its roots in a body of scholarship known as the critical tradition and in an area of knowledge known as critical theory, which traces its origins to the writings of Karl Marx. We understand that the word *woke* has sometimes been abused by conservatives, who employ it to malign any movie, advertisement, song, or remark they dislike, no matter how benign it actually is. However, many progressives and even academics self-identified as woke prior to 2019, so it did not always have negative connotations. Moreover, we will use the terms *woke* or *woke ideology* or *wokeness* descriptively, not pejoratively, to refer to the contemporary cultural expression of ideas rooted in the decades-old philosophical and sociological framework of the critical tradition.

To avoid arguing over semantics, we will often substitute the neutral term *contemporary critical theory* to describe the ideas that undergird wokeness. In the end, however, it is immaterial whether we use the label *wokeness* or *contemporary critical theory* or *critical social justice* or *cultural Marxism* or *postmodern Neomarxism*. Something was and is clearly going on in our culture, and we should try to understand it.

WHY CHRISTIANS SHOULD CARE

Public manifestations of contemporary critical theory may go viral and end up featured by social media accounts like Libs of TikTok, but all of us are likely to be impacted at a personal level as well. This is certainly the case with us. Before either of us began writing or speaking publicly about contemporary critical theory, we were seeing its ideas unfold in our everyday lives.

For example, Pat's PhD is in the critical tradition. In one of his graduate classes, there was a notable degree of verbal tension between some of the students. Pat suggested the class explore and agree on some core values to guide discussions, such as being other-oriented and courteous. This suggestion provoked the ire of some of his classmates. In their minds, Pat—as a White male—was trying to control the speech, and therefore the mouths, and therefore the bodies of minoritized students, particularly Black females. They assumed he was trying to weaponize "politeness" to mute the voice and temper the expressions of frustration of those who had been treated in racist and bigoted ways. Even an attempt to promote open dialogue was viewed as a patriarchal, white-supremacist bid for power.

Below, we provide additional, specific, real-world examples that demonstrate the perniciousness of woke ideology. We omit identifying information and alter names. Our goal is to provide anonymity for those who are referenced while also warning professing Christians who believe there is "nothing to see here" when it comes to the deleterious influence of critical social theory and the woke perspectives derived from it.

Here are a few stories that we've lived through:

George is a neighbor with a teenage son, Caleb, who began to identify as a woman after leaving for college. Though he was raised in a Christian home, Caleb walked away from the faith and pursued a life that wreaked emotional havoc on the rest of his family. While his family shows great concern and love for him, and prayerful engagement in how he is doing, he can't seem to grasp how showing up at his family's and friends' special occasions in a dress, high heels, and makeup might draw undue attention to himself and dampen the festivities. Nor can he seem to understand that the abnormality of his behavior ought to be a red flag to himself that his gender dysphoria is something to be treated instead of trusted.

Julia is the daughter of close friends, who grew up in a loving Christian home. As a young girl, she made a profession of faith and had a childhood that revolved around homeschool, family devotions, and a Reformed church. She maintained her profession and commitment to orthodoxy through her undergraduate studies at a Christian university. However, in her secular graduate program, she was introduced to the critical tradition, and her commitment to sound doctrine began to fade. It was ultimately displaced as she bought into the lie of queer theory. She cut off her parents and siblings, leaving them devasted and heartbroken.

Danielle is an old friend who went to a very conservative church for years and became enamored with critical social justice and antiracism. She came to embrace whiteness discourse and aspects of third-wave feminism and vocally value-signaled her allyship with the marginalized through woke yard signs and condescending social media posts. As with many who value woke perspectives, an inflated sense of self-importance began to define her as she seemed to believe she was "doing the work" while others weren't.

Jamal was a fellow small-group member who was derailed by Trump's 2016 election. He adopted a social binary (oppressor/oppressed) model as a way to see Whites and Blacks in society. Being a Black man married to a White woman, division ensued. He left his majority White church and began to pull away from family members.

Bill and Lauren had been fellow church members for more than ten years when they began to espouse antiracism discourse that coincided with radical changes in their cultural and political expressions. They started to explore churches they believed would be more sympathetic to their evolving views while simultaneously becoming activist oriented in their disdain for Trump and their zeal for Biden and then Harris. The husband, a former office-bearer in the church, eventually announced that he was deconverting from Christianity and that he should best be understood as an atheist or secular humanist.

Some of these stories are so extreme they may sound fictional. Sadly, they aren't. These are incidents we've witnessed firsthand. They have affected us in real ways. We take no pleasure in recounting these situations and are heartbroken for these people. We have prayed for them many times, and in some instances, we have met with them and pleaded with them to return to their senses and to Christ. Yet these stories need to be shared because they are all too common and are manifestations of a disease that, if left untreated, will endanger the souls of real people.

Woke ideas are not pure, scholarly abstractions. They are being put into practice in our workplaces, in our schools, and in our churches. Therefore, it's crucial for Christians to understand the ideology we're confronting so that we can push back against it.

CONTRAST WITH *CRITICAL DILEMMA*

Post Woke is a follow-up to our previous book *Critical Dilemma: The Rise of Critical Theories and Social Justice Ideology—Implications for Church and Society.*[36] However, this book is neither an abridged version nor a sequel. In other words, we did not merely condense *Critical Dilemma.* Nor did we assume that readers have already read *Critical Dilemma* and have been eagerly awaiting the next installment, like *Star Wars* Episode 17 fans waiting for Star Wars Episode 18 to drop.

Instead, we intend *Post Woke* to be a standalone resource that is equally valuable to people who are entirely new to this discussion and to people who have been following our work for years. So what specifically distinguishes this book from *Critical Dilemma*?

First, *Critical Dilemma* was accessible but intentionally academic, containing almost 800 footnotes and references to over 200 primary sources. While this approach was—and still is—needed, *Post Woke* is written for a broader audience. Readers who are intimidated by the thought of hacking their way through a dense, 500-page forest of citations will hopefully find the concise approach of the present work more manageable.

Second, *Post Woke* is focused less on the esoteric theories that undergird wokeness and more on its everyday expression in the real world. You are less likely to encounter a co-worker quoting Michel Foucault than an HR manager who wants to know your pronouns. We therefore aim to show how woke ideas show up "on the ground" by offering numerous examples, anecdotes, case studies, hypothetical situations, and even diagrams.

Third, *Critical Dilemma* was a resource for anyone—Christian or non-Christian—who wanted to understand what wokeness is, where it came from, and how to respond to it. Indeed, several of our endorsers were secular scholars who disagreed with our evangelical beliefs but who appreciated the book simply because it provided a thorough and compelling overview of contemporary critical theory.

However, *Post Woke* is more specifically written for a Christian audience. That's not to say it will be incomprehensible to non-Christian readers, but we will assume a basic, shared Christian theological framework that we did not assume in *Critical Dilemma*.

Fourth, *Post Woke* is meant to be practical. Readers expressed great appreciation for the action steps we offered in one of the final sections of *Critical Dilemma*. You will find many more recommendations scattered throughout this book, as well as an entire chapter dedicated to reaching your children, co-workers, neighbors, and pastors. We want you to walk away from our book not only with new knowledge, but with a plan of action.

Finally, and most importantly, *Post Woke* articulates a biblical perspective on race, gender, and sexuality. Yes, we offer very clear and unequivocal refutations of woke ideology. But we also offer constructive proposals for tackling controversial topics. We don't merely want Christians to stop thinking about race, gender, and sexuality in terms of critical theory. Instead, the focus of the present work is how Christians should think about these topics in terms of what the Bible says about God, humanity, sin, and salvation.

ROADMAP

Our book is organized as follows:

In chapter 2, we explain how we got here. Why is race still such a polarizing social issue? Where did the #MeToo movement come from, and why was it so popular? How do our impulses toward compassion and the culture's growing secularization affect the uptake of woke ideology?

In chapter 3, we provide a very brief overview of what we call *contemporary critical theory*, the set of academic ideas upstream from wokeness. We sketch a brief history of the critical tradition, from Karl Marx and Antonio Gramsci to Kimberlé Crenshaw and Judith

Butler. We then demonstrate how these ideas express themselves in three major subdisciplines—critical race theory, feminism, and queer theory—and show how they explain various manifestations of wokeness within our culture today.

Chapter 4 is a primer on basic logic. We highlight informal fallacies and rhetorical strategies like the motte-and-bailey, equivocation, and others, which frequently show up in discussions about social justice.

Chapter 5 offers a broad critique of contemporary critical theory, focusing on questions like "What is oppression?," "What is justice?," and "How do we know the truth?" We explain how the Bible answers these questions and how biblical answers conflict with the answers provided by contemporary critical theory.

In chapter 6, we begin by explaining what critical race theory is and why it fundamentally conflicts with Christianity. We then lay out a biblical framework for understanding race, asking questions like "What is race?," "Is America racist?," and "Are people of color oppressed?" Because some Christians have overreacted to the errors of critical race theory by questioning the idea that racism is a biblical category, we also explain why racism is indeed a sin rooted in ethnic partiality, which the Bible explicitly rejects.

Chapter 7 demonstrates that feminism is a critical social theory like critical race theory or queer theory and contrasts feminists' understanding of gender with a Christian understanding of gender. We then address biblical gender roles, and the concepts of hierarchy and authority in the Bible. Finally, we show that while the Bible does obviously condemn sexual assault and domestic violence, critical theory can warp our understanding of concepts like abuse and moral agency.

The topic of sexuality is covered in chapter 8. Queer theory, which applies a critical framework to the subject of sexuality and gender identity, is wholly incompatible with a biblical sexual ethic. We answer questions like "How should Christians think about transgenderism?," "Are people 'born gay'?," and "Does love require affirmation?"

Chapter 9 opens with general guidance for having hard conversations. We then explain how Christians like us, who are concerned about woke ideology, can reach our children, our neighbors, our schools, our workplaces, our pastors, and the dissident right.

Finally, our conclusions are presented in chapter 10.

Each of these chapters can be read largely independently of the others. For instance, if you've already read *Critical Dilemma*, you can probably skip chapters 3 and 5, even though both contain a fair amount of new information not presented in our previous book. Alternatively, if you're unfamiliar with critical theory, but do have a grasp of basic logic, you could skip chapter 4 and come back to it later. Or, if you're somewhat familiar with critical theory and are primarily interested in race, you could begin with chapter 6. However, the book does follow an overall logical sequence, so if you're new to this subject or want to understand all the connections we make between critical theory and progressive views on social issues, we recommend reading it cover to cover.

THE NEED FOR ENGAGEMENT

In summary, wokeness is a powerful force shaping our culture. *Wokeness* is not merely a slur, a baseless accusation lodged by conservatives who—at best—are indifferent to and—at worst—complicit in injustice, racism, and misogyny in our society. Neither is it a nebulous, incomprehensible collection of progressive slogans and social justice vibes. Rather, it is the popular expression of a coherent, comprehensive view of reality that emerged from a particular stream of scholarship known as critical theory.

Given the proliferation of false and unbiblical views of race, gender, and sexuality that are pervasive in our culture, Christians can no longer stay above the fray. Instead, we must seek to understand this new worldview and respond with a distinctly biblical, Christian perspective on ideas that are increasingly shaping the minds and imaginations of our co-workers, friends, and children.

2

HOW WE GOT HERE

In the aftermath of the 2008 election of President Barack Obama, some commentators announced the arrival of a "post-racial America." They believed that we had finally put behind us our awful legacy of chattel slavery and Jim Crow and had become a country where, at least to a great extent, we judged people not by the color of their skin, but by the content of their character.

The aggressive women's liberation movement of the 1970s had also largely died down. Nineteen ninety-two was dubbed the Year of the Woman because of the election of prominent women to Congress, including Dianne Feinstein, Barbara Boxer, and Carol Moseley Braun. Anita Hill's testimony during Clarence Thomas's Supreme Court confirmation hearing renewed concerns about sexual harassment, but the term *postfeminism* had already been adopted to describe the way in which the rising generation took for granted the achievements of their feminist forebears. By the 2000s, seeing women like Hillary Rodham Clinton or Sarah Palin in high government offices was commonplace.

Finally, the gay liberation movement that had begun in the 1960s after the Stonewall Riots had gone mainstream but still faced notable cultural resistance. In 1996, Republican Representative Bob Barr sponsored the Defense of Marriage Act, which defined marriage as the union of one man and one woman. It was passed with the support of large majorities of both Republicans and Democrats (including future President Joseph Biden) and was signed into law by Democratic President Bill Clinton. In 2008, California passed Proposition 8, which amended the state constitution to stipulate that "only marriage between a man and a woman is valid or recognized in California."[1] President Barack Obama and Senator Hillary Clinton both publicly supported traditional marriage through 2008.

For these reasons, a cultural prognosticator could have been forgiven for failing to predict the tremendous cultural upheaval that would take place in the 2010s and 2020s. Today, large segments of the US react with horror at beliefs that were commonplace just two decades ago. Many people believe that colorblindness is not only naïve and impractical, but racist. The #MeToo movement, the Women's March, and the 2022 Dobbs decision that overturned *Roe v. Wade* have reenergized feminism. The national legalization of same-sex marriage under *Obergefell* was followed by an immediate cultural push for the normalization of transgenderism, to the point that many people today—including Supreme Court Justice Ketanji Brown Jackson—have trouble answering the question "What is a woman?"[2]

The breakneck speed of cultural transformation had a side effect that can easily be overlooked: a palpable generational divide. Boomers and Gen-Xers (those born between 1946–1964 and 1965–1980, respectively) have witnessed these changes as adults. Even Millennials (born between 1981–1996) can remember growing up in a world that made assumptions other than those made today. But to Zoomers—Gen Z (born between 1997–2012) and to Gen Alpha (born after 2012)—things look vastly different.

The very oldest Zoomer was 11 when President Obama began his first term and was only 18 when same-sex marriage was legalized. Many in the younger generation have no idea that anything has changed in our culture. This is the only world they've ever known. In the same way that teenagers are "digital natives" who grew up with touch-screens, social media, and iPhones, they are also "woke natives" who grew up thinking that the cultural innovations of the Great Awokening were normal and indisputable.

The following chapter attempts to bridge this generational divide by asking, "How did we get here?" As it turns out, the ideas of the Great Awokening go back decades, even centuries, and are rooted in deeply human, and sometimes even praiseworthy, impulses. Before we get to anything praiseworthy, though, we must have a reckoning with America's racist past because our nation's lamentable racial history is one of the main reasons that critical theory gained a foothold in our culture.

WHY TALK ABOUT RACE?

We suspect that many Christians say little about our country's racial history and present-day racial discrimination because they fear that dwelling on these issues will lead people to embrace critical race theory. In fact, the opposite is likely to be the case. If the church refuses to talk about racial disparities, congregants may turn to progressive sources that will explain them wholly through the paradigm of systemic oppression. If Christian parents don't speak candidly and clearly about these issues, our children may by exposed to them for the first time in high school or college. When that happens, they may begin to ask why they were never taught about these realities and may begin to question everything they've learned. Children who have experienced racism but haven't been taught to see the spurious reasoning in critical race theory's solutions may find themselves attracted to its faulty analysis. The upshot is that a failure to talk about race can make people more, not less, susceptible to the unbiblical narratives we're trying to shield them from.

For this reason alone, we ought to be willing to be honest about our country's past and present. As Christians, we know that our citizenship is ultimately not in the United States; it is in heaven (Philippians 3:20). As much as we love our country, we know that it is temporary. It is not our ultimate home. Its history is strewn with triumphs and tragedies, freedom and oppression, justice and injustice, just like the history of every nation in the world.

But a better reason to think carefully about race is simply the desire to love our neighbors. Loving our neighbors includes understanding their perspective, knowing their history, and seeking their good. We may (and indeed should!) come to the conclusion that conservative policies are generally more conducive to the good of our neighbors than progressive ones. However, we should come to that conclusion after, not before, taking the time to understand why race was and is a constant source of tension in our society.

RACE IN AMERICA

The great English Particular Baptist Charles Spurgeon repudiated slavery in his famed "red-hot letters" to America, in which he wrote that slavery is a "crime of crimes, a soul-destroying sin, and an iniquity which cries aloud for vengeance."[3]

In keeping with Spurgeon's sentiment, we affirm that slavery and Jim Crow were high evils. Abominations. The racism that animated both is still with us. Racial bigotry is a pronounced perversion, a direct and blasphemous assault on the *imago Dei*. Next to elective abortion, slavery is the United States's (both prior and after her formal founding) second greatest sin. Two-hundred and fifty years of slavery,[4] a hundred years of Black Codes, Jim Crow, and lynching, and its continued reality until this present moment ensure racism's noteworthy place among our nation's greatest evils.

According to Harvard historian Henry Louis Gates Jr., from the early 1500s to 1866, the Transatlantic slave trade was responsible for shipping 12.5 million African slaves to the New World (North America, the Caribbean, and South America).[5] Of the 12.5 million, nearly two million perished along the way due to the barbaric conditions of the main segment of the voyage, what came to be known as the horrific Middle Passage.

The Middle Passage

In his acclaimed slave narrative *The Interesting Narrative of the Life of Olaudah Equiano: or, Gustavus Vassa, the African,* Olaudah Equiano offers a sobering and gut-wrenching firsthand account of the horror of the Middle Passage. He states,

> The closeness of the place, and the heat of the climate, added to the number in the ship, which was so crouded [sic] that each had scarcely room to turn himself, almost suffocated us. This produced copious perspirations, so that the air soon became unfit for respiration, from a variety of loathsome smells, and brought on a sickness among the slaves, of which many died, thus falling victims to the improvident avarice, as I may call it, of their purchasers. This wretched situation was again aggravated by the galling of the chains, now become insupportable; and the filth of the necessary tubs [toilets for a large group], into which the children often fell, and were almost suffocated. The shrieks of the women, and the groans of the dying, rendered the whole a scene of horror almost inconceivable.[6]

If you want to understand what slavery was like in America, you should incorporate the writings of actual slaves in your study. We suggest you read Equiano's work, as well as the slave narratives of Frederick Douglass and Harriet Jacobs.

For another firsthand account of the Middle Passage, we turn to Dr. Alexander Falconbridge. Falconbridge, who was White and free, served as a surgeon on a number of slave ships. His job was simply to keep the slaves alive, to keep them from dying during the journey. Dead slaves were bad for business. They hurt the bottom line. Falconbridge was one of many such doctors employed by the slavers to keep their product in good enough shape to be sold when they made it through the Middle Passage to the New World.

Thankfully, some of the doctors who traversed the Middle Passage, including Falconbridge, were sobered by the experience and came to see the evil of slavery. Falconbridge ended up meeting anti-slavery campaigner Thomas Clarkson, and soon joined the Anti-Slavery Society, a British abolitionist group. In his efforts to combat slavery, Falconbridge wrote a book titled *An Account of the Slave Trade on the Coast of Africa.* In it, he described his experience of the Middle Passage. He stated,

> The hardships and inconveniences suffered by the Negroes during the passage are scarcely to be enumerated or conceived...But the exclusion of fresh air is among the most intolerable...the confined air, rendered noxious by the effluvia [an unpleasant or harmful odor, secretion, or discharge] exhaled from their bodies and being repeatedly breathed, soon produces fevers and fluxes [abnormal secretions of blood] which generally carries off great numbers of them...The deck, that is the floor of their rooms, was so covered with the blood and mucus which had proceeded from them in consequence of the flux, that it resembled a slaughter-house. It is not in the power of the human imagination to picture a situation more dreadful or disgusting.[7]

Such descriptions are a reminder that hell is littered with those who aided and abetted the Transatlantic slave trade. Of the more than 10 million slaves who made it through the Middle Passage to the New World, approximately 388,000 made it to what is now the United States,[8] with some estimates as high as 474,000.[9]

Slavery

While the experience of slavery was not the same for every slave, the overall experience was fraught with fear, violence, and dehumanization. For 250 years (10 generations!), Blacks were kept from being subjects in their own lives and made to be objects in the lives of their masters.

The physical, psychological, and spiritual toll on God's image bearers, many of whom were his sons and daughters, was incalculable. Consider this description from abolitionist Theodore Dwight Weld, from his book *American Slavery as It Is: Testimony of a Thousand Witnesses*, published in 1839:

> [Slaves] are treated with barbarous inhumanity; that they are overworked, underfed, wretchedly clad and lodged, and have insufficient sleep; that they are often made to wear round their necks iron collars armed with prongs, to drag heavy chains and weights at their feet while working in the field, and to wear yokes, and bells, and iron horns; that they are often kept confined in the stocks day and night for weeks together, made to wear gags in their mouths for hours or days, have some of their front teeth torn out or broken off, that they may be easily detected when they run away; that they are frequently flogged with terrible severity, have red pepper rubbed into their lacerated flesh, and hot brine, spirits of turpentine, &c., poured over the gashes to increase the torture; that they are often stripped naked, their backs and limbs cut with knives, bruised and mangled by scores and hundreds of blows with the

> paddle, and terribly torn by the claws of cats, drawn over them by their tormentors; that they are often hunted with blood hounds and shot down like beasts, or torn in pieces by dogs; that they are often suspended by the arms and whipped and beaten till they faint, and when revived by restoratives, beaten again till they faint, and sometimes till they die; that their ears are often cut off, their eyes knocked out, their bones broken, their flesh branded with red hot irons; that they are maimed, mutilated and burned to death over slow fires.[10]

We note, any so-called professing Christian slaveholder who participated in or oversaw such barbarity and never came to thorough-going repentance marked by a full-stop cessation of such activity is paying for his sins in hell at this very moment. An existence that is proving to be worse, much worse (remarkably), than that of the slaves who were under his charge.

Jim Crow

Thankfully, slavery based on race finally came to an end in America in 1865. Tragically, slavery is still alive in the United States via human trafficking, both sex trafficking and labor trafficking. Much preventative and advocacy work is needed on both these fronts. Notwithstanding, slavery as an institution and socially accepted enterprise was abolished in 1865 with the ratification of the Thirteenth Amendment to the Constitution.

Unfortunately, this action, as important and as profound and necessary as it was, did not secure equal status and equal rights for Blacks. For the next 100 years (four generations!), until the Civil Rights Movement in the mid-1960s, Blacks would continue to be profoundly (and legally) marginalized. Almost immediately after the Thirteenth Amendment, individual states began to enact laws known as Black

Codes, which radically discriminated against Blacks and dramatically curtailed their newfound freedom. Black Codes deprived Blacks of the right to vote, the right to own and carry weapons, the right to serve on juries, and the right to own, rent, or lease land. Moreover, these codes established punitive labor contracts that restricted and cheated Blacks of their rightful wages.[11]

The Reconstruction Act of 1867 and the ratification of the Fourteenth Amendment (citizenship, equal protection, and due process) helped to offset some of the effect of Black Codes, but it wasn't nearly enough. When Reconstruction officially ended in March 1877, many states were primed to double down on their racism and bigotry toward Blacks by enacting a series of discriminatory laws known as Jim Crow, which were designed to radically disenfranchise Blacks in manifold ways in society. The *Plessy v. Ferguson* US Supreme Court decision rendered in 1896 affirmed the constitutionality of "separate but equal" facilities, effectively fortifying Jim Crow's stranglehold on Blacks in US society for the next 70 years. Here are a few examples of Jim Crow laws that underscore the legal (*de jure*), racist partiality that once dominated the United States.[12]

From Alabama:

- **Nurses:** No person or corporation shall require any white female nurse to nurse in wards or rooms in hospitals, either public or private, in which negro men are placed.
- **Restaurants:** It shall be unlawful to conduct a restaurant or other place for the serving of food in the city, at which white and colored people are served in the same room, unless such white and colored persons are effectually separated by a solid partition extending from the floor upward to a distance of seven feet or higher, and unless a separate entrance from the street is provided for each compartment.

From Florida:

- **Intermarriage:** All marriages between a white person and a negro, or between a white person and a person of negro descent to the fourth generation inclusive, are hereby forever prohibited.
- **Education:** The schools for white children and the schools for negro children shall be conducted separately.

From Georgia:

- **Burial:** The officer in charge shall not bury, or allow to be buried, any colored persons upon ground set apart or used for the burial of white persons.
- **Parks:** It shall be unlawful for colored people to frequent any park owned or maintained by the city for the benefit, use and enjoyment of white persons...and unlawful for any white person to frequent any park owned or maintained by the city for the use and benefit of colored persons.

From Virginia:

- **Theaters:** Every person...operating...any public hall, theatre, opera house, motion picture show or any place of public entertainment or public assemblage which is attended by both white and colored persons, shall separate the white race and the colored race and shall set apart and designate... certain seats therein to be occupied by white persons and a portion thereof, or certain seats therein, to be occupied by colored persons.

Jim Crow was a heinous evil. No doubt, many professing Christians who championed Jim Crow found themselves on the wrong side of

God's judgment as they went from this life into the next. Rhetoric regarding "blind spots" and men being "men of their times" won't suffice. Christians must reject such spurious justifications. As we have argued elsewhere, "Concerted efforts to put dehumanizing infrastructures in place to systemically and systematically strip an entire 'race' of people of their God-given humanity and inalienable rights is worthy of stern, undiluted condemnation."[13]

Two draconian efforts that led to massive disenfranchisements of Blacks were redlining (affecting medical, banking, insurance, and housing opportunities) and the refusal of local and state institutions to apply the federally mandated benefits of the GI Bill to more than one million Black servicemen.

In addition to legal discrimination, Jim Crow created an environment where mob power ran unchecked and the sadistic practice of lynching became a fixture of the time. Arthur F. Raper's invaluable work on lynching underscores its demonic influence. Raper begins with the "Toll of the Mob," where he asserts, "The fact that a number of the victims were tortured, mutilated, dragged, or burned suggests the presence of sadistic tendencies among the lynchers."[14]

The Civil Rights Movement

Thankfully, the legal regime of Jim Crow was slowly eroded over the course of the twentieth century by various landmark Supreme Court decisions and legislation.

For example, in 1948, in *Shelley v. Kraemer*, the Supreme Court ruled that restrictive housing covenants, which prohibited the sale of houses to non-Caucasians and thereby promoted housing segregation, were unconstitutional.[15] In 1954, the court's 9-0 ruling in *Brown v. Board of Education* decision overturned the court's 1896 *Plessy v. Ferguson* decision, which had permitted racial segregation on the grounds of "separate but equal." In their unanimous decision, the justices wrote that "in the field of public education the doctrine of 'separate but equal' has no place. Separate educational facilities are inherently unequal. Therefore [segregation] deprived [students] of the equal protection of the laws guaranteed by the Fourteenth Amendment."[16] Interracial marriage bans were struck down nationwide in 1967 with the US Supreme Court's *Loving v. Virginia* ruling.[17]

Two major pieces of civil rights legislation were passed under the Johnson administration: the Civil Rights Act of 1964 and the Voting Rights Act of 1965. While *Brown v. Board* prohibited government facilities from participating in segregation, the Civil Rights Act also forbade discrimination "on the ground of race, color, religion, or national origin" at all "public accommodations," thus ending practices like the racial segregation of restaurants and movie theaters. The Voting Rights Act prohibited the administration of literacy tests and other methods that had been used to disenfranchise Black voters.

Public opinion shifted in concert with, and in response to, these legal changes. For example, in 1969, 56 percent of non-White adults and only 17 percent of White adults approved of interracial marriage. Those numbers climbed steadily over the next few decades until they reached 96 percent and 93 percent, respectively, in 2021.[18]

All of these changes may seem like ancient history, but they occurred within the lifetimes of people who are still alive today. Presidents Bill Clinton, George W. Bush, Donald Trump, and Joseph Biden *were all in their twenties* before the Supreme Court made any of the landmark decisions mentioned above. President Barack Obama was born prior to both the Civil Rights Act and Voting Rights Act and two years before Martin Luther King Jr. delivered his famous *I Have a Dream* speech in Washington, DC.

Therefore, while it's good and proper for us to celebrate the overturning of Jim Crow laws, it's important to retain some historical perspective. Although slaves were first brought to the Americas in the 1500s, the date of 1619 is typically offered as the beginning of American slavery, which remained legal for two-and-a-half centuries. Legal segregation persisted for another century. It would be preposterous to think that the damage done to the Black community by 350-plus years of discrimination could vanish instantaneously.

In fact, we know that prejudice against Blacks still exists. For example, in 2003, sociologist Devah Pager performed an analysis of multiple experiments conducted over several decades to probe racial discrimination in hiring. She found that, even controlling for factors like education, age, and experience, White applicants received roughly 35 percent more interview callbacks than Black applicants, and that percentage hadn't changed in 30 years.[19]

In another famous example, in 2004, researchers sent pairs of identical resumés to a variety of companies, except that the applicant had either a stereotypical White name (like Greg or Emily) or a stereotypical Black name (like Jamal or Lakisha). Again, resumés with White names received roughly 50 percent more callbacks than resumés with Black names.[20]

Surveys also show the persistence of racial discrimination, even within the church. Although acceptance of interracial marriage is at an all-time high in the US at large, it is significantly lower among White evangelicals. Christian sociologist Bradley Wright found that in 2008, "43% of [White] evangelicals opposed a close relative marrying a Black person."[21] Although the numbers have improved, Baptist pastor and political scientist Ryan Burge found that in 2021, 20 percent of White evangelicals still said they would oppose a close relative marrying a Black person.[22]

Finally, tremendous racial disparities still exist between Whites and Blacks. In 1860, the wealth disparity between Whites and Blacks was almost 60:1. By 1900, it had dropped to 11:1, and by 1960, it reached 8:1. It fell to a minimum of 5:1 around 1990, but has stagnated since then and has even risen slightly in recent years.[23] Blacks are disproportionately incarcerated relative to Whites. Although Blacks make up roughly 14 percent of the US population, they make up roughly 33 percent of inmates in state and federal prisons.[24] When it comes to education, the 2017–2018 high school graduation rate for Blacks was 79.0 percent compared to 89.1 percent for Whites, 81.0 percent for Hispanics, and 92.2 percent for Asians.[25] In 2021, 23.3 percent of Blacks had a bachelor's degree or higher, compared to 37.3 percent of Whites, 18.4 percent of Hispanics, and 55.8 percent of Asians.[26] In terms of health care, Blacks are more likely to be uninsured than Whites, have a life expectancy that is roughly five years less than Whites, and have an infant mortality rate that is twice that of Whites.[27]

One important caveat: Progressives tend to interpret *all* these racial disparities as the result of "systemic racism." We reject this view and will discuss it more in chapters 5 and 6. However, this perspective does not mean that we should ignore these disparities, especially as Christians! Blacks were legally oppressed for centuries in our nation. Because they are currently experiencing deficits over a wide range of categories, we ought to ask: (1) what are the causes?, and (2) regardless of our skin tone, how can we help?

SEXUAL ABUSE

The #MeToo movement is another major reason that woke ideology struck many in the church as not only plausible but revelatory and necessary.

On October 15, 2017, actress and activist Alyssa Milano tweeted, "If all the women who have been sexually harassed or assaulted wrote 'Me too' as a status, we might give people a sense of the magnitude of the problem."[28] Her post prompted millions of engagements on social media, in which women (and men) recounted harrowing stories of sexual assault and harassment at work, at home, and even at church.

The fallout was dramatic and global. A 2018 *New York Times* article listed hundreds of powerful men who were fired from their jobs, lost roles, or even faced criminal charges, including journalist Mark Halperin, comedian Louis C.K., Senator Al Franken, and news anchor Matt Lauer.[29] Among the many horrifying stories that came to light were revelations regarding Hollywood producer Harvey Weinstein, who personified the kind of vicious, powerful male predator that #MeToo opposed.

Weinstein was the cofounder of Miramax and rose to prominence within the film industry, winning an Oscar for *Shakespeare in Love* as well as Tony Awards for *The Producers* and *La Cage aux Folles*. For years, he had been dogged by accusations of sexual harassment, sexual assault, and rape.[30] Typically, women claimed that Weinstein had offered to advance their careers in exchange for various sexual acts. He not only used his money and power to pressure women into sex but also to cover up their allegations and to reach legal settlements with women whose allegations included "sexual harassment and unwanted physical contact."[31]

As the #MeToo movement picked up steam, more and more women came forward, including well-known actresses like Gwyneth Paltrow, Angelina Jolie, Lauren Holly, and Lupita Nyong'o.[32] Weinstein was fired from numerous boards and barred from multiple professional associations. Grand jury indictments and criminal trials followed. On February 24, 2020, a jury found Weinstein guilty of third-degree rape and he was sentenced to 23 years in prison. On December 20, 2023, he was found guilty of a different rape and was sentenced to another 16 years in prison.

Although Weinstein was eventually punished, it would be wildly irresponsible to claim that his sentencing primarily showcased the success of the criminal justice system. Rather, #MeToo activists were right to recognize that—to the contrary—it demonstrated decades of systematic failure. How was a serial abuser and rapist allowed to operate for decades at the highest levels in his industry? Why was he able to avoid justice for so long? Why were women's claims not heard, not believed, or not taken seriously? These are wholly legitimate questions, especially for Christians who believe that rape is a horrific sin, one that—like murder—merited the death penalty in ancient Israel (Deuteronomy 22:25-27).

If Weinstein's case were exceptional or isolated, it might be dismissed as a footnote. But the significance of the #MeToo movement was in the sheer number of stories of sexual harassment and assault that inundated social media for months and even years. #MeToo opened the floodgates. The raging torrent was not confined to Hollywood or to the corporate world, but broke through the doors of the church as well.

On November 21, 2017, a month after Milano's viral #MeToo tweet, Emily Joy Allison, an evangelical Christian and graduate of Moody Bible College, tweeted, "When I was 16 years old I was groomed for abuse by a man in his early 30s who was a 'youth leader' in my evangelical megachurch Northwoods Community Church in Peoria, IL." She and her friend Hannah Paasch launched the #ChurchToo hashtag and solicited similar stories.[33] They came pouring in and are recounted in books like Allison's *#ChurchToo*[34] or Ruth Everhart's *#MeToo Reckoning*.[35] Both books repeat stories of women (and men) who experienced sexual harassment, assault, and rape at the hands of professing Christians within a Christian environment. Worse yet, they tell of how these events were ignored, covered up, or quickly papered over in the name of "unity" and "forgiveness."

Allison's and Everhart's books are noteworthy because they don't focus on big-name pastors or Christian speakers who have been accused of sexual misconduct. Rather, they tell the stories of everyday churchgoers who faced abuse. The ubiquity of these experiences was one reason that #MeToo struck a chord with so many. However, that was not the only factor. The popularity of #MeToo was also due to its emphasis on victim credibility and power dynamics.

The #MeToo movement shined light on the difficulty that many victims face in convincing authorities, or even friends and family members, that abuse actually occurred. In her memoir *How Much Is a Girl Worth?*, lawyer and evangelical Christian Rachael Denhollander recounted how she was repeatedly sexually abused as a 15-year-old gymnast by Dr. Larry Nassar.[36] Her parents believed her accounts, but she had trouble convincing anyone else of the assaults until a local newspaper ran a story more than a decade later about sexual abuse and coverups within the USA Gymnastics organization. Denhollander came forward publicly to accuse Nassar in 2016, over a year before the advent of #MeToo. Dozens of other survivors followed suit. Nearly two decades after Denhollander's abuse, Nassar was convicted of multiple charges, including possession of child pornography and sexual assault, and was effectively sentenced to life in prison. Michigan State University also agreed to a $500 million settlement for its role in covering up Nassar's crimes.[37]

In contrast to the skepticism or even hostility that sexual assault victims often face when telling their stories, #MeToo accepted them unreservedly. Hashtags like #BelieveWomen proclaimed activists' commitment to embracing women's testimony. For people who had kept their own pain bottled up because of their fears of being disbelieved, this mantra was empowering.

#MeToo was also concerned with how power affects personal and institutional responses to sexual abuse. Christians can, rightly, bristle at the phrase *power dynamics*, given how it is used to justify all kinds of fallacious arguments and unbiblical claims. But the idea that power can be used to circumvent accountability and corrupt justice is hardly the invention of Marxists; it is a thoroughly biblical idea. The Bible warns that "a bribe blinds the eyes of the wise and subverts" (Deuteronomy 16:19) and condemns leaders who "despise justice and pervert all that is right" by "judg[ing] for a bribe...teach[ing] for a price, and...practic[ing] divination for money" (Micah 3:9-11). Narrative portions of the Bible, like Ahab's murder of Naboth (1 Kings 21) or Joab's murder of Abner (2 Samuel 3) or Amnon's rape of Tamar (1 Samuel 13), also show how the powerful can misuse their power to evade justice. In the same way, actions today that would instantly land a poor man in prison are ignored when they're committed by a powerful politician or a wealthy businessman.

These same power dynamics can shield or even enable sexual abuse. Imagine a simple example. A poor, single mother with three kids has just gotten a job that she desperately needs as a secretary for the owner of a small business. If he can fire her at his discretion, how likely is she to complain if he makes sexually inappropriate jokes at her expense? How much discomfort or even abuse will she endure before she quits? Now imagine the situation is different and the female owner is being sexually harassed by her male secretary. Obviously, the outcome is very different.

Many women have found themselves in these situations, where, for various reasons, they felt pressured to keep silent. Is it any wonder that seeing society finally recognize this pressure felt liberating?

In chapter 6, we'll have more to say about the problems of the #MeToo movement's framing of these issues. For example, as part of their #MeToo activism, both Everhart and Allison have rejected a traditional biblical sexual ethic and have embraced LGBTQ+ affirming theology. Allson went even farther, embracing abortion, extramarital sex, and "ethical nonmonogamy" (e.g., adultery). After leaving evangelicalism, she deconstructed her faith to the extent that she no longer says the creeds at the "very small, very gay Episcopal church" that she attends.[38] Similarly, a laudable openness toward women's testimonies does not mean that women's testimony should be treated as infallible or that due process should be ignored. However, our goal in the present chapter is not to point out the problems of the #MeToo movement, but to show why valid concerns over sexual abuse can prime Christians to accept critical theory's analyses of society.

COMPASSION

A third reason that wokeness is appealing is that it presents itself as a compassionate response to suffering and injustice in the world. The instinct to protect the vulnerable is a good and God-given one. Consider some of the commands in Scripture for Christians to show compassion and to care for the needy:

> Open your mouth for the mute, for the rights of all who are destitute. Open your mouth, judge righteously, defend the rights of the poor and needy (Proverbs 31:8-9).
>
> Be merciful, even as your Father is merciful (Luke 6:36).
>
> Put on then, as God's chosen ones, holy and beloved, compassionate hearts, kindness, humility, meekness, and patience, bearing with one another and, if one has a complaint against another, forgiving each other; as the Lord has forgiven you, so you also must forgive (Colossians 3:12-13).

In the Old Testament, the Hebrew words for "compassionate" and "merciful" are used to describe God's own character and disposition. God tells the Israelites not to withhold a poor man's cloak as a pledge because "if [the poor man] cries to me, I will hear, for I am compassionate" (Exodus 22:27). Deuteronomy 32:36 says that "the Lord will vindicate his people and have compassion on his servants." King Hezekiah tells the Israelites that "the Lord your God is gracious and merciful and will not turn away his face from you, if you return to him" (2 Chronicles 30:9). Nehemiah declares "you are a God ready to forgive, gracious and merciful, slow to anger and abounding in steadfast love, and did not forsake them" (Nehemiah 9:17). The psalmist sings that God "has caused his wondrous works to be remembered; the Lord is gracious and merciful" (Psalm 111:4).

Likewise, in the New Testament, Jesus is characterized by compassion (see Matthew 9:36; 14:14; 15:32; 20:34; Mark 1:41; 6:34; 8:2; Luke 7:13) and he uses the word "compassion" in two of his most famous parables to commend a character's attitude or actions. When the Good Samaritan comes across a Jewish man who has been beaten and robbed, he "saw him [and] had compassion. He went to him and bound up his wounds, pouring on oil and wine. Then he set him on his own animal and brought him to an inn and took care of him" (Luke 10:33-34). In the parable of the prodigal son, when the younger brother returns to his father, Jesus says that "while [the younger brother] was still a long way off, his father saw him and felt compassion, and ran and embraced him and kissed him" (Luke 10:22).

Compassion and mercy are not inventions of twenty-first-century progressives; they are divine attributes that Christians are to emulate. They are indispensable characteristics of saving faith (Matthew 25:31-46).

People, especially young people, see the zeal with which social justice activists pursue policies that they view as compassionate. This enthusiasm is compelling and is contrasted with stereotypes of conservative Christians, who are portrayed as callous, complacent, and self-righteous. While the actual empirical data on conservative Christians flatly contradicts this caricature,[39] the false impression that "progressives are compassionate, and Christians aren't" is powerful.

SECULARIZATION

Finally, like Western Europe, the US has been secularizing for decades, albeit at a slower rate. For example, in 1953, a Gallup poll showed that 98 percent of Americans believed in God. By 2011, that number had dropped to 92 percent. It then fell to 81 percent in 2023. Those numbers reflect a generational decline, with 87 percent of seniors professing a belief in God compared to only 68 percent of 18–29 year-olds who profess belief in God.[40]

Church membership has also plummeted since World War II. In the 1950s, roughly 73 percent of US adults were members of a church, synagogue, or mosque. That percentage declined slightly to 70 percent in 2000, but then dropped rapidly over the next two decades, to only 47 percent in 2021.[41]

Finally, fewer and fewer Americans are identifying as Christians while increasing numbers are identifying as having "no religious preference." In the 1950s, well over 90 percent of Americans identified as Christian, and less than 3 percent identified as having "no religious preference." By 2023, only 68 percent of Americans identified as Christians, while 22 percent said that they had "no religious preference."[42]

Of course, none of these numbers represent the actual percentage of practicing, believing Christians in the United States.[43] But they do reflect a cultural shift away from Christianity. This shift is also characterized by a degree of hostility toward the Christian faith that is more pronounced than it has been historically in US society. The Bible and what it teaches is not just wrong, it is evil. While the "negative world" thesis is flawed in certain respects, its overall point and contentions are correct.[44] The cultural capital once afforded to biblical claims regarding morality is waning, and with it common grace.

Christianity, even when it was merely embraced culturally rather than confessionally, provided a structure to most Americans' lives. It offered a metanarrative, an overarching story, by which people made sense of reality. Christianity teaches that the universe was created by a good, just, holy, loving, righteous God, that human beings were made in his image, that we fell into sin and rebellion, that we therefore deserve God's wrath, that God sent Jesus to rescue humanity, that Jesus rose from the dead to reconcile us to God, that he will return one day to bring judgment and salvation, and that we should live the rest of our lives in joyful service to him.

Even if people didn't personally accept the truth of this narrative, it inevitably shaped their imagination. In the same way that

Americans automatically, implicitly accept the goodness of freedom or democracy or individualism because it's baked into our culture, Americans also automatically, implicitly accepted the goodness of a Christian view of life. It provided them with a sense of meaning and purpose, influenced their behavior, and shaped their moral intuition.

The shift away from Christianity toward secularism has therefore left a vacuum in peoples' spiritual lives. Because—as French philosopher Blaise Pascal observed—there is an infinite, God-sized abyss in each person's heart, a culture that has abandoned God will seek for a God-substitute. People didn't cease to be religious; they merely replaced one religion with another. In the 1960s and 1970s, as Christian profession declined, some turned to Eastern religions or to New Age practices to find meaning and purpose. Others turned to sexual expression and hedonism. Others to materialism and consumerism.

However, during the last decade, social justice and critical theory have filled this religious void. Again, at this point, we aren't levelling this charge as an indictment of critical theory but merely as an explanation for why it has become so popular. Everyone craves meaning, purpose, morality, and community. We want to feel that we are doing good in the world. Contemporary critical theory channels that energy and directs it down the path of activism.

HOW DOES WOKENESS HAPPEN?

Thus far, we've summarized some of the appeals of wokeness. It takes racism and sexism seriously. It highlights shameful, but unfortunately very real, episodes in our nation's past. It calls attention to widespread racial disparities and present-day mistreatment of women. It expresses love and concern for the vulnerable. It repudiates oppression and injustice. It positions itself as compassionate. It fills the spiritual void left by the cultural displacement of Christianity. And it provides people with a secular metanarrative that offers them meaning, purpose, moral commitments, and community.

Based on these observations, let's sketch a hypothetical account of how a college freshman comes to embrace wokeness:

> Emily grew up in a conservative Christian home and attended an evangelical church with her family throughout her childhood. She was homeschooled by her mom, who gave up her career as a nurse when she had children. Their curriculum was based on a classical model of education that focused on the great works of Western literature. Emily's circle of friends consisted entirely of other Christian homeschoolers and members of her church youth group. The radio in the car was usually tuned to the local Christian station or to conservative talk radio. She volunteered every week at a homeless shelter for women and children, and planned to major in social work in college so that she could continue caring for the vulnerable.
>
> Her first semester as a freshman at a state university was overwhelming. She met her roommate, who was a nominal Muslim, and several other students on her floor, who came from a variety of religious backgrounds. During orientation week, she signed up with several student groups, including Students for Justice, which had a large display on domestic violence. She also quickly joined a local evangelical campus ministry but had a more difficult time finding a local church that belonged to her denomination.
>
> As a social work major, Emily was required to take Introduction to Sociology. Her class used Andersen and Collins's anthology *Race, Class, and Gender* as one of its texts. She was exposed to the idea that our society is suffused

by systems of power that include racism, sexism, classism, ageism, and heterosexism. She was especially struck by Marilyn Frye's essay on oppression that compared sexism to a wire birdcage. Each single wire looks harmless and inconsequential, but they form an impenetrable network that traps women within an oppressive system. Emily thought of her mother's decision to quit her job while her father continued to work.

The class also read excerpts from Eduardo Bonilla-Silva's *Racism Without Racists*, and Emily learned about the tremendous racial disparities between Blacks and Whites for the first time. She was shocked to read the racially insensitive statements made by many Whites in the book and began to recall, with a sense of shame, how she'd occasionally heard similar statements made by her own friends at home.

When she attended the first Students for Justice meeting, she was excited to meet other freshmen who shared her passion for helping battered women. One of her fellow students mentioned that homeless LGBTQ+ youth are especially vulnerable to violence due to their experience of "intersectional oppression." The group leader then talked about a trip to a local shelter for Pride night, where the students would wear safety pins to show their solidarity with the LGBTQ+ community and would cook dinner for residents. Emily was torn because her parents had raised her with a biblical view of sexual ethics but had also taught her that caring for the poor and vulnerable is a Christian duty.

That night, she and her roommate had dinner at a cooking co-op. A group of upperclassmen had rented an apartment off campus, where they shared grocery bills and took turns cleaning. They were very friendly, were fellow social work majors, had a close-knit community, and all shared a passion for progressive politics. Several were in same-sex relationships.

The next week, Emily shared some of what she was learning in class with a campus minister. He immediately warned her about the dangers of cultural Marxism and told her that "social justice" was a godless ideology that no Christian should support. When she asked for resources, he recommended a YouTube video. When she pressed him on the question of racial disparities, he said that he was colorblind and that sociology was incompatible with the Bible. She went home confused.

A month later, Emily was becoming more agitated and disillusioned with her Christian upbringing. She had learned in class how large swaths of the church had supported slavery. When she searched online, she discovered that her home church's denomination had been created in defense of slavery, something she'd never known. According to her professor, its founders had appealed to White, Eurocentric, male interpretations of Scripture to justify their beliefs. Emily's Students for Justice group had continued to volunteer at the women's shelter, and she had encouraged Christian friends to come, but they had nervously refused. She was making many new friends at the co-op and had decided to join it the following year.

Two weeks later, Emily's mother called her to see how she was doing. She had had a frustrating day. A friend at Students for Justice had learned that she had been homeschooled and began asking her about her experience. When he discovered that she identified as an evangelical, he began peppering her with questions, most of them related to gender and sexuality. He was appalled by her beliefs and told her that he attended a progressive church nearby that was LGBTQ+ affirming. When her mother asked her what was wrong, Emily at first said nothing, and then finally blurted out her disillusionment with their church's denominational history. Emily's mother became defensive and insisted "all that was a long time ago."

"But how do we know we're not wrong about other things, like how we treat gay people?" demanded Emily. Her mother didn't answer, and instead, started asking Emily about whether she had joined a church.

Emily hung up.

The story above is fictional but it fits many of our actual experiences with Christian students on secular college campuses. Incoming freshman with traditional Christian beliefs are already under intense cultural pressure to compromise on their beliefs about gender and sexuality. They often find that their education with respect to race and history was deficient.

They wake up to real injustices they may not have confronted before. They discover that many non-Christian students are kind, caring people. They form friendships and find community that they didn't experience within the church. They appreciate the zeal and compassion of campus activists who seem to genuinely care about the poor and the marginalized.

All of this makes wokeness seem attractive. Moreover, their parents, pastors, and concerned Christian friends may not be equipped to understand the ideas that they're being exposed to. Our goal in this book is to provide compassionate clarity. If you find yourself being tugged toward woke ideas, we'll explain exactly what they are and what you're getting into. If you want to help others resist wokeness in our culture, we'll show you how. We want all Christians to think biblically about topics like race, gender, sexuality, and justice. Doing so will help us to love God with all our minds and love our neighbors as ourselves.

3

WOKENESS AND CONTEMPORARY CRITICAL THEORY

Imagine a teenage atheist whose mission in life is to undermine Christianity. After almost 30 minutes of intensive research on Google, he walks into the nearest church and declares, "Christianity is a fraud! Did you know that the Bible originally wasn't even written in English? And why do Christians eat bacon? Also, the earth isn't flat. Checkmate!"

It's unlikely that our zealous but confused young firebrand will be very successful at deconverting Christians because he hasn't taken the time to grasp even the basics of the religion he's critiquing.

In the same way, Christians who want to push back against wokeness need to begin with a basic understanding of the ideas that are driving it. In this chapter, we'll explain the origins of wokeness, its fundamental outlook on reality, and how it is applied to topics like race, gender, and sexuality.

A VERY BRIEF HISTORY OF CRITICAL THEORY

Wokeness—as it is expressed in our culture today—is rooted in an area of knowledge known as critical theory, which stretches all the way back to the writings of Karl Marx. In fact, as Dr. Bradley Levinson affirms, "Karl Marx invites consensus as a 'true' critical theorist. Indeed, for many, he alone inaugurates the critical tradition."[1] Dr. Stephen Bronner adds, "Critical theory was conceived within the intellectual crucible of Marxism."[2] Marx was consumed with the problem of economic inequality. Why does poverty exist? Why are working conditions so miserable? Why is there such a huge gap between the rich and the poor?

Marx answered these questions by formulating a grand theory of history. According to Marx, history unfolded in a series of epochs characterized by which groups controlled the "means of production," the ability to produce material goods. Capitalism was merely the latest epoch of history, in which the bourgeoisie (the owning class) ruled over the proletariat (the working class). The structure of society, its values and norms, its religion, its art, and its dominant ideology were byproducts of this fundamental economic relationship.[3] For Marx, the economic structure of a society determined its other characteristics.

To appreciate Marx's perspective, imagine an outside consultant trying to understand the characteristics of an auto-parts company. At first, he might be puzzled by the company's values, norms, and office culture. Why do employees get an entire week off in February? Why do they wear colorful shirts with large numbers on their backs every Friday? Why is the break room television always tuned to ESPN? These phenomena have nothing to do with the company's official mission statement or the demands of the automotive industry. Rather, they are explained by the fact that the company's owner is a huge football fan. The company's culture reflects the owner's values and will change only when he sells the company.

Analogously, according to Marx, a capitalist nation's values, culture, and religion will always reflect capitalism and will change only when the means of production are no longer controlled by capitalists.

Marx predicted (and encouraged) imminent revolution among the working class that would lead to a classless communist utopia. Yet capitalism was still flourishing around the world even decades after Marx died. Why?

To answer this question, neo-Marxists increasingly focused on ideology as an obstacle to the liberation of the working class. For example, Italian neo-Marxist Antonio Gramsci argued that the working class not only failed to recognize its own oppression, but actually consented to its own oppression. Bourgeois values so suffused culture that the working man came to see his poverty and powerlessness as natural, normal, and even unavoidable. He absorbed the ideology of his oppressors, coming to believe that capitalism was a just, fair, and even God-ordained system and that it was his best chance at social and economic advancement.[4]

Similarly, the philosophers and sociologists of the Frankfurt School expanded Marx's narrow focus on economic oppression to include other, more subtle forms of oppression. They believed that man needed to be liberated not only from poverty, but from the tyranny of the "culture industry" and the conformity induced by mass media.[5] In 1937, Max Horkheimer first introduced the term *critical theory* to label this approach to social analysis. Whereas traditional theory was satisfied with simply describing the world, critical theory was fundamentally committed to changing it.

When the members of the Frankfurt School fled the Nazi regime in the 1930s, they found a home at Columbia University. In the decades that followed, critical theory grew and expanded, spinning off entirely new disciplines like cultural studies, critical legal studies, and critical pedagogy. In all its iterations, critical theorists are concerned with power: Who has power and who doesn't? How is power used to justify existing social arrangements? How is power subtly present in the ideas and norms that are taken for granted within society?

Two recent branches of the critical tradition are especially relevant to contemporary culture: critical race theory and queer theory.

Critical race theory (CRT) emerged in the late 1980s and early 1990s as an offshoot of critical legal studies.[6] Critical legal theorists argued that human law was not a set of abstract principles rooted in either divine law or natural law, but rather was a mechanism by which the ruling class maintained its power. Critical race theorists shared this perspective,[7] but were critical of critical legal theorists' tendency to embrace colorblind analyses of the law. In contrast, critical race theory insisted that a proper understanding of American law had to include the ways in which law was a mechanism by which the *White* ruling class maintained their *racial* power within society.

Derrick Bell, the first tenured Black law professor at Harvard, is considered the godfather of CRT.[8] In his scholarship, Bell challenged standard civil rights narratives and questioned whether school integration was actually optimal for Black students. He also famously suggested that racial progress occurred not when Whites were morally persuaded to act, but rather when White self-interest happened to align with Black liberation, a concept he called "interest convergence."[9]

Bell's students, including Kimberlé Crenshaw and Mari Matsuda, followed in his footsteps, applying a critical lens to the workings of race and law in America. For the first few years of its existence, CRT was largely confined to the legal academy. However, a major turning point occurred in 1995 when Gloria Ladson-Billings and William Tate published a paper entitled "Toward a Critical Race Theory of Education."[10] Over the course of the next decade, CRT spread to many other fields, leading critical race theorist Angela Harris to write that CRT had "exploded from a narrow subspecialty of jurisprudence chiefly of interest to academic lawyers into a literature read in departments of education, cultural studies, English, sociology, comparative literature, political science, history, and anthropology around the country."[11] Even more importantly, the ideas of CRT have been mainlined to the masses via mandatory DEI (Diversity, Equity, and Inclusion) trainings, classroom exercises, and bestselling books like Robin DiAngelo's *White Fragility* and Ibram X. Kendi's *How to Be an Antiracist*.

Queer theory also emerged in the 1990s. If Derrick Bell was the godfather of CRT, then French philosopher Michel Foucault was the godfather of queer theory. Foucault was fascinated by the idea that knowledge itself is a form of power. He embraced what he called "archaeology" and "genealogy" as tools to expose how truths we now take for granted are actually social constructs that justify existing social structures. In particular, his *History of Sexuality* was an influential account of how sexual norms had evolved over the centuries.

The term *queer theory* was coined by Teresa de Lauretis in 1991. Along with the postmodern and poststructuralist theorizing of Michel Foucault and Jacques Derrida, queer theory inherited the critical perspective of the second-wave feminism of the 1960s and the radicalism of the gay liberation movement of the 1970s. Queer theorists challenged the way that gender and sexuality were conceptualized. Just as American society was marked by racial beliefs that normalized and naturalized whiteness to the detriment of people of color, they believed that it was also marked by beliefs about gender and sexuality that normalized and naturalized the gender binary and heterosexuality in a way that marginalized LGBTQ people.

Two texts are particularly important for understanding queer theory: Gayle Rubin's 1984 essay "Thinking Sex"[12] and Judith Butler's 1990 book *Gender Trouble*.[13]

Rubin's "Thinking Sex" is considered one of the seminal works of gay and lesbian studies and queer theory. In it, she argues that sexuality, like gender, is socially constructed and that social stigma surrounding everything from homosexuality, to prostitution, to pedophilia, to bestiality is based on false notions of natural, God-ordained sexual norms.

Butler's main contribution to queer theory was the concept of *gender performativity*. Butler, following in the footsteps of second-wave feminists, believed that gender is distinct from sex. However, she went even farther. For Butler, "gender is performative," and consequently "it follows that the reality of gender is itself produced as an effect of that performance."[14] In other words, Butler believed that gender is a role we play as we act out certain social expectations.

Like critical race theory, queer theory has escaped the confines of academia and now routinely informs the thinking of educators, psychologists, therapists, counselors, politicians, and even doctors. While virtually no one outside of the academy has read Butler or Rubin, the proliferation of new gender and sexual identities, pronoun hospitality, the invention of new pronouns, and the creation of new Pride flags can be traced back to their ideas.

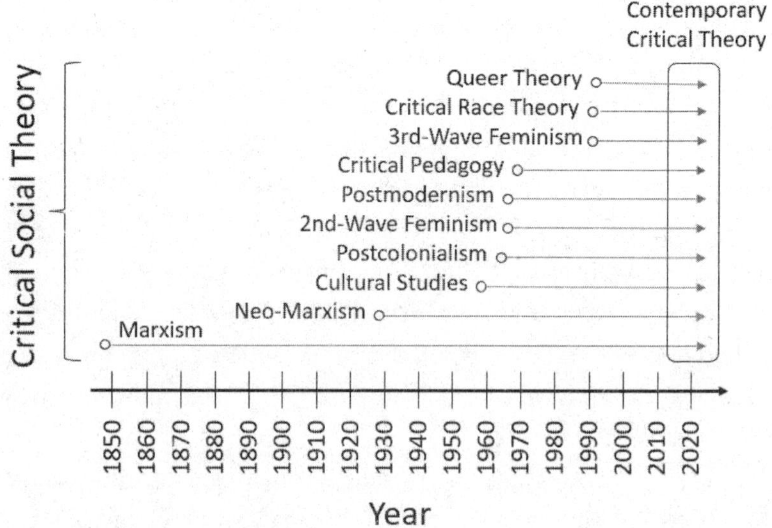

Figure 1—A timeline of the critical tradition

From a historical perspective, the critical tradition can look incredibly complex (see Figure 1). It spans a century and a half, encompasses numerous subfields, and includes the work of thousands of scholars. How, then, is it possible to say anything concrete about so diverse a field? Is it possible to offer a singular Christian assessment of critical theory any more than it's possible to offer a singular Christian assessment of psychology or agriculture or sports?

One factor helps focus our consideration of critical theory as a contemporary phenomenon: intersectionality.

The term *intersectionality* was coined by critical race theorist Kimberlé Crenshaw in two seminal papers published in 1989 and 1991.[15,16] While intersectionality can be narrowly understood as the claim that our identities are complex and can't be reduced to a single axis like race or class or gender, Crenshaw has a far broader conceptualization in mind. Crenshaw's understanding of intersectionality is that axes of identity are hierarchical, inseparable, and interlocking.

First, Crenshaw does not merely believe that we belong to multiple social categories, but that each category entails a hierarchy. Crenshaw writes:

> ...the following analogy can be useful in describing how Black women are marginalized in the interface between antidiscrimination law and race and gender hierarchies: Imagine a basement which contains all people who are disadvantaged on the basis of race, sex, class, sexual preference, age and/or physical ability. These people are stacked—feet standing on shoulders—with those on the bottom being disadvantaged by the full array of factors, up to the very top, where the heads of all those disadvantaged by a singular factor brush up against the ceiling.[17]

In other words, men are advantaged over women, Whites over

people of color, young people over the elderly, and heterosexuals over homosexuals.

Second, Crenshaw insists that these identity categories are inseparable and laments both feminists who focus solely on gender and antiracists who focus solely on race. In both cases, she contends that the use of a single lens obscures the way in which Black women are uniquely oppressed and marginalized, even within progressive movements.

Finally, Crenshaw not only wants us to integrate our theoretical analyses of race and gender and sexuality, but also our activism. In other words, she does not believe that we should dismantle racism only, but that we must dismantle all hierarchies, including those based on class, gender, sexuality, and physical ability. In *Words That Wound*, she and her coauthors write:

> Critical race theory works toward the end of eliminating racial oppression as part of the broader goal of ending all forms of oppression. Racial oppression is experienced by many in tandem with oppressions on grounds of gender, class, or sexual orientation. Critical race theory measures progress by a yardstick that looks to fundamental social transformation. The interests of all people of color necessarily require not just adjustments within the established hierarchies, but a challenge to hierarchy itself.[18]

Crenshaw's formulation of intersectionality was a watershed moment within the critical tradition because it provided a framework that not only allowed but demanded the integration of various subdisciplines. Consequently, many texts on critical pedagogy discuss class and gender.[19] Texts on queer theory often consider race and other aspects of identity contextualized by privilege and oppression.[20] Texts on disability studies regularly consider the intersections of race, class, and disability[21] and at times have whole chapters dedicated to disability and intersectionality.[22] In the minds of critical theorists, all these subjects are inextricably intertwined.

For this reason, we will spend the remainder of the chapter explaining the ideas at the heart of what we call *contemporary critical theory*. In other words, standing on this side of the intersectional revolution, we can ask: What are the core ideas that unify the work of contemporary critical race theorists, queer theorists, critical pedagogues, critical social justice scholars, and intersectional feminists? What are the ideas that undergird woke activism both in the academy and on the ground?

THE FOUR PILLARS OF CONTEMPORARY CRITICAL THEORY

Contemporary critical theory is rooted in four core ideas: the social binary, hegemonic power, lived experience, and social justice, which are drawn from the critical tradition in the academy. Let's consider each of those in turn.

The Social Binary

The *social binary* is the idea that society can be divided into oppressor groups and oppressed groups. In their book *Is Everyone Really Equal?*, Robin DiAngelo and Özlem Sensoy write: "For every social group, there is an opposite group...the primary groups that we name here are: race, class, gender, sexuality, ability status/exceptionality, religion, and nationality."[23]

Oppressor groups are also referred to as *dominant groups* or *agent groups* or *advantaged groups* or *privileged groups*, while oppressed groups are referred to as *subordinate groups* or *targeted groups* or *disadvantaged groups* or *marginalized groups*. Table 1 illustrates this framework.

Per the concept of intersectionality, a person who belongs to multiple oppressed groups experiences greater oppression than a

Identity Marker	Type of Oppression	Oppressor Group	Oppressed Group
Race	Racism	Whites	People of color
Class	Classism	The rich	The poor
Biological sex	Sexism	Men	Women
Sexuality	Heterosexism	Heterosexuals	Homosexuals
Gender identity	Cisgenderism	Cisgender people	Transgender people
Physical/mental ability	Ableism	The able-bodied	People with disabilities
Age	Ageism/Adultism	Adults	The elderly/ children
Religion	Religious oppression	Christians	Non-Christians
Colonial status	Colonialism	Colonizers	Indigenous people
Skin color	Colorism	Light-skinned people	Dark-skinned people

Table 1—The social binary of oppressor and oppressed groups

person who belongs to only one. Hence, contemporary critical theorists would claim that a rich, able-bodied straight White woman is indeed oppressed with respect to her gender, but that her experience of oppression is quantitatively and qualitatively less than that of a poor, disabled, Black lesbian.

While the oppressive ladder posited by the social binary is intuitive to many progressives, it may strike many conservatives as bizarre or even delusional. Walk down the street in most American cities, and you will not routinely encounter overt racism much less overt racial tyranny, injustice, and violence. Enter the average mall, or restaurant, or swimming pool, or gym and you'll see people of all ethnicities, ages, genders, and classes interacting freely and unselfconsciously (or at least appearing to do so). Indeed, many people from minoritized groups themselves will be puzzled. "I'm a woman," they'll say. "In what sense do men oppress me?" Or "I'm an African immigrant. I own my own company. Why should I think of myself as marginalized?"

Here, we need to understand the second major idea of critical theory: oppression through ideology, or what critical theorists call *hegemonic power*.

Hegemonic Power

According to contemporary critical theory, oppression is not just a matter of cruel treatment, overt injustice, and tyranny. Rather, oppression is ideological in nature. According to critical theorists, the ruling classes—whether Whites, or men, or heterosexuals, or Christians, or the able-bodied—impose their values and norms on the rest of society in a way that justifies their own power, privilege, and dominance. Again, listen to Sensoy and DiAngelo: "*Hegemony* refers to the control of the ideology of a society. The dominant group maintains power by imposing their ideology on everyone."[24]

For example, critical theorists believe that men impose their beliefs about male superiority on culture in a way that appears to us to be natural, objective, neutral, rational, or even God-ordained. We are taught in subtle ways to value masculine characteristics, qualities, attributes, and ways of thinking. Strength is masculine; weakness is feminine. Intellect is masculine; emotion is feminine. Reason is masculine; intuition is feminine. These patriarchal value judgments are then used to justify the social dominance of men. We think that men deserve to be in charge because they're stronger, smarter, more intellectual, and more rational. Even women are brainwashed into the patriarchy via television, movies, fairy tales, cultural tropes, and thousands of subtle messages that suffuse our daily experience.

According to contemporary critical theorists, hegemonic narratives that prop up the privilege of Whites (through white supremacy), men (through patriarchy), heterosexuals (through heteronormativity), cisgender people (through cisgenderism), Christians (through Christian hegemony), and able-bodied people (through ableism) likewise shape our consciousness in ways that barely register to us.

Movie buffs may recall an exchange from the 2000 blockbuster *The Matrix*. The protagonist Neo is desperate to know what "the Matrix" is and asks his mentor Morpheus. Morpheus replies that the Matrix is all around them. It looks ordinary and mundane but has been carefully constructed to blind them to the reality that they are slaves trapped in an artificial world built by their overlords.

Critical theorists believe that our culture's hegemonic narratives function like the Matrix. These narratives lead us to believe that society is basically fair and make us unable to imagine alternative social arrangements that would liberate and empower us. We consent to our own oppression, never knowing that we are slaves.

So how do we escape these insidious, oppressive narratives that are deeply embedded within society? Through the third central idea of contemporary critical theory: lived experience.

Lived Experience

Those of us who spend too much time on social media have probably seen the hashtags #BelieveWomen or #BelieveAllWomen or #BelieveBlackWomen. Some people use these phrases to simply urge us to take reports of sexual abuse and harassment seriously. But others take a more radical view, arguing that women in general and Black women in particular have a clearer view of the sexism that suffuses our society. This perspective is rooted in standpoint epistemology, the view that our knowledge is deeply shaped by our social location (i.e., the position we occupy in society with respect to power and privilege).[25]

Standpoint epistemology teaches that members of dominant groups have a single consciousness. They can see society only through the ruling class's lens. In contrast, members of oppressed groups have a *double consciousness*. Not only are they expected, like all of us, to see society through the dominant group's lens, but they can also see society through the lens of their own lived experience. This dual awareness gives them greater insight into power dynamics, social injustice, and oppression than those of us who are privileged. In this context, #BelieveAllWomen means that women have inherent authority to speak to issues of sexual oppression and that men should therefore defer to their testimony rather than questioning it.

But can we really "believe all women"? For example, how can we believe both women who embrace feminism and women who reject feminism?

Critical theorists' solution to this conundrum turns on their understanding of hegemonic power. Recall that they believe we've all been conditioned into dominant white supremacist, patriarchal, heterosexist, ableist norms. Thus, both men and women are socialized into patriarchal beliefs. However, through their lived experiences, some women can achieve what is called a "critical consciousness" or "liberatory consciousness." Only such women are able to truly grasp the oppressive structures that surround them, and these are the women we should believe when it comes to patriarchal oppression.

Likewise, standpoint epistemology would enjoin us to "look to the margins" when it comes to racial injustice, heterosexism, ableism, ageism, and a host of other structural oppressions. We are not merely to take the testimony of the oppressed into consideration. Rather, we are to center it and valorize it. As Ijeoma Oluo writes, "If you are looking for a simple way to determine if something is about race[:] It is about race if a person of color thinks it's about race."[26] We should also be hesitant to subject the beliefs of oppressed people to the scrutiny of supposedly objective evidence and Western standards of rationality. After all, what we consider to be objective and rational are precisely those criteria which the ruling class has created to justify its own dominance!

This way of thinking is not restricted to academia; it has also found its way into the evangelical church. For instance, Latasha Morrison is the founder of a Christian racial reconciliation ministry called Be the Bridge, whose document "16 Bridge-Building Tips for White People" offers several textbook examples of standpoint epistemology. It advises Whites:

> 7. Don't explain away a POC's [i.e. person of color's] experience of oppression. They are the expert on their own experience. Don't play devil's advocate or provide an alternative explanation for what happened. Take their word for it.
>
> 9. Don't demand proof of a POC's lived experience or try to counter their narrative with the experience of another person of color.
>
> 11. Do not chastise POC (or dismiss their message) because they express their grief, fear, or anger in ways you deem "inappropriate."...Provide space for POC to wail, cuss, or even yell at you.[27]

As absurd and deleterious as these guidelines are to genuine social cohesion, where every group is valued and has the opportunity to flourish, these guidelines make perfect sense if Whites are naturally blind and ought to defer to the special insight of people of color.

Social Justice

Finally, the end goal or telos of critical theory is and has always been *social justice*, which contemporary critical theorists define in terms of dismantling the systems and structures that perpetuate the social binary. For example, Mary McClintock explains that social justice is "the elimination of all forms of social oppression," where "social injustice takes many forms [and] can be injustice based on a person's gender, race, ethnicity, religion, sexual orientation, physical or mental ability, or economic class."[28]

Whereas classical Marxists believed that class inequality could be remedied only by reshaping the material structure of society (i.e., by changing who controlled the means of production), critical theorists believe that social inequality can be remedied only by reshaping the ideological structure of society (i.e., by changing the dominant narratives promulgated by the media, education, and the government).

Social justice is then primarily achieved by deconstructing the taken-for-granted norms, values, symbols, and narratives from which the ruling class derives its power. In their place, new norms, values, symbols, and narratives are constructed, which transfer cultural power from the oppressor group to the oppressed group. For example, the "myth of meritocracy" is debunked and shown to be an excuse that justifies the economic dominance of straight White men. In its place, critical theorists erect a narrative of systemic bias that is responsible for the disparities we see today. Similarly, the myth of "American greatness" is debunked and shown to be a mechanism by which European settlers justified slavery and the genocide of indigenous peoples. In its place, critical theorists tell a story of cruelty, greed, stolen land, and oppression whose legacy shapes everything around us.

To be clear, none of these narratives are entirely true and none are entirely false. We do not live in a perfect meritocracy. Nor do we live in a racist, sexist dystopia. US history is not one of unbroken greatness nor is it one of unbroken depravity. History and sociology and economics are messy, just like human beings. But the story told by critical theorists is necessarily simplistic because its primary purpose is not accuracy but activism. Indeed, the idea of neutral scholarship that has a purely disinterested, objective perspective is—in the minds of critical theorists—an impossibility. Critical theorists' scholarship is, and has always been, directed toward human liberation via deconstruction of the oppressive hegemonic norms under which we all live.

Once we understand the four pillars of contemporary critical theory, many otherwise-incomprehensible cultural artifacts will suddenly make sense.

Why do we see groups like Queers for Palestine and social media accounts proclaiming that "Reproductive Justice is Palestinian Justice"?[29] Aren't LGBTQ people far more accepted in Israel then in Palestine? What does abortion have to do with the Arab-Israeli conflict? The answer is that once Israel is positioned as a colonialist oppressor, contemporary critical theory demands intersectional solidarity, which includes positioning an abjectly evil terrorist group (Hamas) as an oppressed victim in need of defending, no matter how obscene, perverted, grotesque, and blatantly foolish such a position is. According to contemporary critical theory, to fight colonialism is to fight racism is to fight sexism is to fight heterosexism is to fight ableism and on and on.

Why are we told to "center Black voices" but are also told not to listen to Black economists like Thomas Sowell or Glenn Loury? Because, as former *New York Times* journalist Nikole Hannah-Jones tweeted, "There is a difference between being politically Black and being racially Black...We all know this and should stop pretending that we don't."[30] Black conservatives have not yet achieved a critical consciousness that allows them to see the ways they've been oppressed by the White ruling class. Therefore, according to contemporary critical theory, they are still captive to White supremacist narratives and shouldn't be relied on as authorities.

Why do the American Medical Association[31] and the American Psychological Association[32] insist that gender is a socially constructed category that isn't rooted in sex? Why does the ACLU deny that transgender women (i.e., biological men who identify as women) have an advantage when competing in women's sports?[33] Don't even high school students learn about chromosomes? Does it take an advanced degree (or perhaps the lack of one?) to recognize that the average 6'3" biological man is a danger to the average 5'5" woman in a game of rugby? Progressive opinions make far more sense when we recognize that queer theory views the gender binary as an arbitrary and oppressive social construct that must be dismantled to liberate LGBTQ+ people.

Years ago, after Neil gave a talk on critical theory at a local state university, his host remarked, "Once you see it, you can't unsee it." He was right. A working knowledge of critical theory is vital for understanding the ideas driving many of our elite institutions.

CONTEMPORARY CRITICAL THEORY EXPRESSED

The four pillars of contemporary critical theory explained above provide a framework for understanding various critical social theories today. For example, CRT applies the four central principles of contemporary critical theory to race, contemporary feminism applies them to gender, and queer theory applies them to gender identity and sexuality.

In chapters 6, 7, and 8, we'll provide more details about how Christians should think about these fields and topics. But below, we'd like to illustrate just how well CRT, feminism, and queer theory map onto the fourfold framework we laid out in the last section.

First, CRT, feminism, and queer theory all affirm the social binary. Within CRT, Whites are the oppressor group, while people of color (Blacks, Asians, Hispanics, Native Americans, and so forth) belong to oppressed groups. Occasionally, critical race theorists will add a third, intermediate category for biracial people or "assimilated people of color."[34] Nonetheless, the polarity between oppressed and oppressor is clear.

Feminism views men as the oppressor group, while women are the oppressed group. A major point of contention within the feminist movement, especially in the last ten years, has been over the status of transgender people: If a biological male identifies as a woman, is he a woman? Most contemporary feminists would say yes, but a vocal minority of feminists (known pejoratively as TERFs or trans-exclusive-radical-feminists) disagree, either because they believe that sex-based rights are important or because they believe that a lifetime of gendered oppression renders a biological woman's experience different than that of a trans woman (i.e., a man who identifies as a woman).

Queer theorists accept the feminist characterization of men as an oppressor group and women as an oppressed group, but go farther, categorizing heterosexuals as oppressors and LGBTQ+ people as oppressed. Occasionally, the binary is drawn between straight and queer, where *queer* is a catchall term that includes an ever-expanding array of new gender identities.

Second, CRT, feminism, and queer theory affirm that oppression is an artifact of the hegemonic power of oppressor groups. For critical race theorists, Whites assert hegemonic power through white supremacy, which is understood not in terms of white ethnonationalist hate groups, but as a "powerful ideology [which] promotes the idea of whiteness as the ideal for humanity."[35] For feminists, men assert hegemonic power through the patriarchy, the norms and structures that support male dominance. For queer theorists, straight people—especially straight men—impose their rigid ideas about gender and sexual categories through heterosexism and the gender binary.

Third, CRT, feminism, and queer theory affirm the importance of lived experience. CRT believes that the hegemonic narrative of white supremacy blinds Whites to their racial privilege. In contrast, people of color recognize the many ways in which the majority culture marginalizes them and thus can come to a better understanding of racism and racial inequality.

Feminism criticizes appeals to "reason" and "objectivity" as masculine modes of thought. As Margaret Andersen and Patricia Hill Collins write in their anthology *Race, Class, and Gender*, "the idea that objectivity is best reached only through rational thought is a specifically Western and masculine idea, one that we will challenge throughout this book."[36] For feminists, intuition, communality, and "embodied knowledge" are also important sources of truth.

Queer theory elevates lived experience to an even greater degree, because "gender identity" is based on wholly subjective feelings that can only be known by the individual. As Carl Trueman writes in his book *The Rise and Triumph of the Modern Self*, transgenderism is predicated on the idea that "the reality of the body is not as real as the convictions of the mind" such that "psychology trumps biology."[37] Not only is a person's lived experience the best way to know about their gender identity, it is literally the only way to know their gender identity. And once they come to see themselves as queer, they also become aware of the ways in which society forces them into restrictive gender roles and categories.

Finally, CRT, feminism, and queer theory all aim at liberation and social justice. Critical race theory aims to dismantle the systems, structures, and ideologies that produce unequal outcomes for Whites and people of color. Feminism's goal is to dismantle the patriarchy. Queer theory attempts to dismantle the gender binary and traditional cultural mores surrounding sexuality.

	CRT	**Feminism**	**Queer Theory**
1. The social binary	Whites/ People of color	Men/Women	Straight/Queer
2. Hegemonic oppression	White supremacy	Patriarchy	Heterosexism, Cisgenderism
3. Lived experience	Voice of color	Embodied knowledge	Gender identity
4. Social justice	Racial justice	Gender justice	Queer liberation

Figure 2—How the four pillars of contemporary critical theory are expressed in various critical social theories

Figure 2 compares these three fields using the framework we provided for understanding contemporary critical theory. This comparison is important, because many Christians naively believe that critical race theory and feminism and queer theory are entirely unrelated disciplines. That's incorrect for many reasons. Here are two.

First, these theories share a nearly identical belief structure because they were all birthed out of the critical tradition. In other words, they are all ideological cousins. They developed under different conditions and in different contexts, just as you and your biological cousin were raised in different families. But their ideological resemblance is no more accidental than the physical resemblance of the members of your extended family. Indeed, we could perform the same exercise with other critical social theories like postcolonial theory, fat studies, or disability theory. All of them fit naturally into the same basic framework of (1) social binary, (2) oppression through hegemonic power, (3) lived experience, and (4) social justice. While we recognize that various critical social theories speak to more than just these four ideas, nevertheless, these four ideas are pertinent to each of them and to the critical tradition as a whole. And it is these four ideas that are having the greatest impact on society and the church.

Second, as we mentioned earlier, even if critical race theory, critical pedagogy, queer theory, postcolonial theory, feminism, and disability theory had emerged entirely independently of one another, intersectionality knit them together into a single garment. Contemporary critical theorists do not merely suggest, but demand, that we view the social world in terms of a system of interlocking oppressions that cannot be pulled apart and analyzed separately. In the words of Harper et al., "CRT…consistently challenge[s]" the idea that "one can fight racism without paying attention to sexism, homophobia, economic exploitation, and other forms of oppression or injustice."[38]

Again, we cannot stress this point enough: Christians who think they can apply CRT to race alone while ignoring class and gender and sexuality are repudiating not only the spirit but the letter of CRT (see more in chapter 6). Moreover, we see this synergy constantly expressed in both the culture and in the church.

UNDERSTANDING CULTURE THROUGH CRITICAL THEORY

Occasionally, we're asked why we spend so much time (or any time, really) trying to explain the ideological foundations of wokeness to Christians. They'll ask, "Who cares about Antonio Gramsci or Kimberlé Crenshaw or Judith Butler? Why should we spend our time trying to decipher word salads tossed together by progressives? Isn't it obvious that a little common sense is all it takes to dismantle these ideas?"

This is a frequent but mistaken response.

The errors of wokeness are *not* obvious to many people, which is why these ideas have such a grip on our society.

Moreover, what we take as common sense is shaped by our worldview, our upbringing, and our social circles. Thus, if you encounter people who do not share your commonsense notions of race, class, and gender, you'll have to find another way to explain the errors of wokeness to them.

If you're a parent with college-age kids, they may come home with their heads crammed full of cutting-edge critical social theory. Therefore, it's vital that you have at least some understanding of these ideas and can explain why they're wrong.

Finally, understanding critical theory has tremendous explanatory power—that is, it has the ability to explain many otherwise incomprehensible phenomena.

For example, in 2021, the Education Trust-West organization published a guide entitled "A Pathway to Equitable Math Instruction—Dismantling Racism in Mathematics Instruction,"[39] which provided a "framework for deconstructing racism in mathematics" and offered "essential characteristics of antiracist math educators and critical approaches to dismantling white supremacy in math classrooms by making visible the toxic characteristics of white supremacy culture" (p. 1). These characteristics included "Perfectionism," "Worship of the Written Word," "Paternalism," "Either/Or Thinking," "Fear of Open Conflict," "Individualism," and "Objectivity" (p. 5). Antiracist math educators were urged to "center ethnomathematics" and to "[i]dentify and challenge the ways that math is used to uphold capitalist, imperialist, and racist views" (p. 9). According to the document, "white supremacy culture shows up in math classrooms" when "there is a greater focus on getting the 'right' answer than understanding concepts and reasoning" (p. 66). While the authors conceded that many math problems do have right answers, they stated that "upholding the idea that there are always right and wrong answers perpetuate [sic] objectivity as well as fear of open conflict," both of which they identify as elements of "white supremacy culture in organizations" (p. 66).

Most readers are bewildered when they encounter these claims. What is ethnomathematics? Are Chinese math teachers complicit in white supremacy culture when they insist that there are always right and wrong answers to math problems? Do they fear open conflict because they are perpetuating whiteness? What is wrong with individualism and objectivity? Instead of dismissing this entire document as incoherent nonsense, we can make sense of it if we understand contemporary critical theory.

Contemporary critical theorists believe that all knowledge is socially constructed such that objectivity is an illusion. Whiteness is an ideology rather than a skin color, and it subtly pervades American culture. Thus, concepts like "either/or thinking" and "individualism," which appear to many as race-neutral, are actually manifestations of whiteness. On their view, dismantling racism does not just require us to reject overt discrimination, but all the subtle ways in which racism is concealed, even in ostensibly race-neutral disciplines like math.

Or consider the idea, advanced by some conservatives, that wokeness is really just about hatred toward Whites. That hypothesis doesn't explain why so many advocates for woke ideas like Robin DiAngelo or Tim Wise are themselves White. Nor does it explain why wokeness is a global phenomenon, affecting people in places like Switzerland, Singapore, Kenya, and India, where racial tension is either far less prevalent or nonexistent compared to the US. Nor does it explain why gender and sexuality play such a prominent role in woke activism.

The reality is that wokeness is like a virus that adapts to its host. It identifies the most salient social problem in each society and then uses that as a beachhead for marshaling an assault on the ruling class. In the US, racial conflict is preeminent. In Kenya, intertribal conflict is the central issue. In India, it's caste or the legacy of colonialism. If you think wokeness is just about anti-White resentment, you'll be unable to explain why it's making inroads in African or Asian nations, where the population is 99 percent non-White.

Or how do we reconcile the constant chatter about "lived experience" and "centering marginalized voices" with many progressives' dismissive attitude toward conservatives? Why are pro-life women ignored or even openly despised by feminists? Why do we see White progressives lecturing Black conservatives on "how race actually works in the US"?

These phenomena make perfect sense once you understand the concept of false consciousness. The lived experience of marginalized people is authoritative *if they have achieved a liberatory consciousness*. But if they fail to recognize their own oppression, then they are still blinded by the patriarchy, by white supremacy, by heterosexism, and by ableism. Thus, their internalized oppression means that they will simply parrot the talking points of the ruling class. In contrast, a White woman like Robin DiAngelo can charge tens of thousands of dollars to explain white fragility to the United Methodist Church because, by acknowledging her white privilege, she can see the inner workings of America's racial hierarchy.

In conclusion, in this chapter we've explained the history of critical social theory and the basic ideological framework into which all critical social theories fit. Critical race theory and queer theory are the two most prominent and influential critical theories in our culture today, but others are influential to varying degrees in particular environments. For example, young teachers can expect to be introduced to the critical pedagogy of Paulo Freire and Henry Giroux during their education. Adoption agencies and social workers will be exposed to cultural studies. Health care workers may encounter the assumptions and vocabulary of fat studies in their training. And anyone in the corporate world may face mandatory diversity training, which will draw heavily on all of the above.

Put succinctly, contemporary critical theory is everywhere. We can't avoid it, so our only choice is to engage it. But before we do, we need to be equipped with a biblical worldview and the ability to reason well. We'll talk about the latter in the next chapter.

4

THINKING WELL, THINKING BIBLICALLY

Both of us homeschooled our children. Part of their curricula involved training in formal and informal logic. They pored over textbooks, memorized tables, and learned how to decipher esoteric symbols that look like they belong in a Dungeons and Dragons rulebook. For obvious reasons, the classes were intimidating. "Are we ever going to use this?" is a question that hovered in their minds as they struggled to work through the end-of-chapter exercises.

However, logic is simply the discipline of thinking well. Consequently, whenever you think accurately about any subject, you are making use of logic, even if you don't realize it. Managing your schedule requires logic. Balancing your budget requires logic. Driving on the interstate requires logic (unless you're from New Jersey). In the same way, when you figure out how to arrange the chairs into rows for your Sunday school class, you're doing number theory, and when you bake a cake, you're doing chemistry, whether you know it or not. Logic is built into the fabric of our universe because God is a rational being who designed an ordered universe that reflects his wisdom.

Most importantly, studying the Bible requires logic. Whenever you try to understand Paul's reasoning in Romans 1–5 or follow Jesus' debates with the Pharisees or parse the different arguments for or against some eschatological view (i.e., some perspective on the end times), you're employing logic. In fact, you're using logic as you're reading this sentence! In communication theory it's part of the *decoding* process the receiver of the communication employs. Assigning meanings to words and then stringing those meanings together to apprehend what the author is saying requires multiple applications of logic.

In this chapter, we'll show why an understanding of logic is so important for dealing with contemporary critical theory. As it turns out, activists who are steeped in the ideas of contemporary critical theory often rely on poor or muddled thinking in their analyses of social problems. Of course, anyone can employ bad reasoning. However, contemporary critical theory is especially prone to certain fallacies, for reasons that we'll explain below. In particular, we'll illustrate specific informal fallacies with examples relevant to social justice activism, showing exactly where each argument goes wrong.

BULVERISM

What It Is

Oxford scholar and Christian apologist C.S. Lewis coined the term *Bulverism* in an essay from his book *God in the Dock*. In that essay, he mused on how atheists attempt to debunk belief in God by appealing to wish fulfillment. "Of course you believe in God," says the atheist, "because he is a psychological projection of your need to feel loved. He is a coping mechanism arising from a guilty conscience. He is the result of wish fulfillment that arises from your desire to escape death." Lewis pointed out that the atheist had committed a common but disastrous logical blunder in making such claims. Lewis wrote:

> Suppose I think, after doing my accounts, that I have a large balance at the bank. And suppose you want to find out whether this belief of mine is "wishful thinking." You can never come to any conclusion by examining my psychological condition. Your only chance of finding out is to sit down and work through the sum yourself. When you have checked my figures, then, and then only, will you know whether I have that balance or not. If you find my arithmetic correct, then no amount of vapouring about my psychological condition can be anything but a waste of time. If you find my arithmetic wrong, then it may be relevant to explain psychologically how I came to be so bad at my arithmetic, and the doctrine of the concealed wish will become relevant—but only after you have yourself done the sum and discovered me to be wrong on purely arithmetical grounds. It is the same with all thinking and all systems of thought. If you try to find out which are tainted by speculating about the wishes of the thinkers, you are merely making a fool of yourself. You must first find out on purely logical grounds which of them do, in fact, break down as arguments. Afterwards, if you like, go on and discover the psychological causes of the error.
>
> You must show *that* a man is wrong before you start explaining *why* he is wrong. The modern method is to assume without discussion *that* he is wrong and then distract his attention from this (the only real issue) by busily explaining how he became so silly.[1]

Lewis is correct. Bulverism is fallacious. Even if someone does have an ulterior motive for making some claim, it does not follow that this claim is false.

The kind of cynicism that Bulverism demands is a universal acid that will ultimately dissolve and deconstruct all truth claims. If we are permitted to dismiss the truth of a claim on the grounds that the person making the claim has some hidden desire that supposedly motivates the claim, what claim will emerge unscathed?

Do you believe that God exists? That's just wish fulfillment.

Do you believe that Jesus existed? That's because you're a Christian. If you admitted that he's a myth, your world would crumble.

Do you believe that the earth is a sphere? Ha! No wonder! You're probably getting kickbacks from Big Geography lobbyists.

Do you claim that 2 + 2 = 4? That's because you're a mathematician; you have to say that or you'd lose your job.

While anyone, regardless of their ideological leanings, can engage in Bulverism, it is almost unavoidable to those who embrace contemporary critical theory. Recall that the critical tradition, stretching all the way back to Marx, has always insisted that people were socialized into a "false consciousness" by being immersed in the ideology of the ruling class. Thus, in modern times, Whites are blinded by the system of white supremacy that dominates our country. Men are blinded by the patriarchy. Straight people are blinded by heterosexism and cisgenderism. The rich are blinded by capitalism and classism.

Given this foundational assumption, contemporary critical theory *can't avoid* appealing to Bulverism to explain the dissent of straight White men:

"Of course Whites don't believe in systemic racism; it's invisible to them! They have both conscious and subconscious reasons to deny the existence of a system that advantages them."

"Of course men don't believe in the patriarchy! It has so colonized their minds that they can't see it. Admitting that they are oppressors would require them to give up their privilege."

"Of course straight people don't believe trans women are women. They are used to living in a world that valorizes their own gender identity."

But what happens if a conservative Black woman rejects the idea of systemic racism or the patriarchy or transgenderism? Again, critical theory supplies the answer: She is suffering from internalized oppression. She has imbibed the norms and values of the ruling class and has not yet attained a critical consciousness. Her beliefs can also be explained away as manifestations of her proximity to power.

Critical theory therefore enshrines Bulverism, a fallacious form of reasoning, at the very heart of its approach to knowledge. Its pronouncements become unchallengeable. No matter who you are, your claims can be dismissed either as an attempt to protect your privilege or as a symptom of your internalized oppression. In both cases, the critical theorist effectively bypasses any engagement with your arguments and can ignore any evidence you might present in defense of your claims. Your identity alone is sufficient to show that your beliefs are false.

How to Respond

As we've seen, Bulverism is so foundational to contemporary critical theory that it often won't be perceived as a fallacy at all. The belief that our culture is suffused with oppressive narratives that dictate what we believe and what we can know is not seen as corrosive anti-knowledge but as a mark of sophistication. Several responses are possible, all of which aim to expose the dangers of this way of reasoning.

First, try explaining why Bulverism is a flawed approach to knowledge. If your interlocutor is a Christian, citing C.S. Lewis's use of the term and his explanation of it may be useful. It may also be useful to point out how this approach to knowledge will undermine basic Christian doctrine. For example, if a Christian endorses Bulverism, what will they say when a progressive tells them "You only believe in the Trinity because you've been brainwashed into White Western theological norms," or "You only believe that Jesus died for your sins because you feel guilty about all the sins you've committed"?

If your interlocutor is not a Christian, you can point out that this deconstructive approach to knowledge has no stopping point. Do you think that hard work is the key to success? You only believe that because that's an "aspect and assumption of Whiteness," as the Smithsonian Institute recently informed us.[2] Do you think that science is a reliable method for determining truth? That's because you've internalized the discourses of Western patriarchal colonialism. It's easy to get on the train of Bulverism, but much harder to get off.

Alternatively, you could simply accept the accusations made against you, for the sake of argument, and then ask whether your claims are true. For example, imagine you claim that the gender income gap is largely the result of personal choices,[3] and are told, "You believe that only because you want to retain your male power and privilege." You can respond, "Let's grant, for the sake of argument, that you're correct. I am an awful, sexist bigot who is solely motivated by a desire to retain my male power and privilege. Are you now willing to look at the evidence that the gender income gap is largely the result of personal choices?" Of course, they may simply respond, "No, I am not willing to look at the evidence"! But you will have severed the connection between your supposed motivations and the truth of your claim.

Another approach is to turn Bulverism around on your interlocutor, demonstrating how useless it is. The claim "You say that only because you're a straight White male" can be met with a counterclaim: "You say *that* only because you're a critical theorist." Hopefully, your conversation partner will realize that these kinds of schoolyard rejoinders should be left on the playground, where they belong.

MOTTE AND BAILEY

What It Is

The motte and bailey is a rhetorical strategy identified by philosopher Nicholas Shackel in a paper criticizing the methodology of postmodern scholars (see Figure 3).

He describes the motte-and-bailey fallacy in the following way:

> A Motte and Bailey castle is a medieval system of defence in which a stone tower on a mound (the Motte) is surrounded by an area of land (the Bailey) which in turn is encompassed by some sort of a barrier such as a ditch. Being dark and dank, the Motte is not a habitation of choice. The only reason for its existence is the desirability of the Bailey, which the combination of the Motte and ditch makes relatively easy to retain despite attack by marauders. When only lightly pressed, the ditch makes small numbers of attackers easy to defeat as they struggle across it: when heavily pressed the ditch is not defensible and so neither is the Bailey. Rather one retreats to the insalubrious but defensible, perhaps impregnable, Motte. Eventually the marauders give up, when one is well placed to reoccupy desirable land.

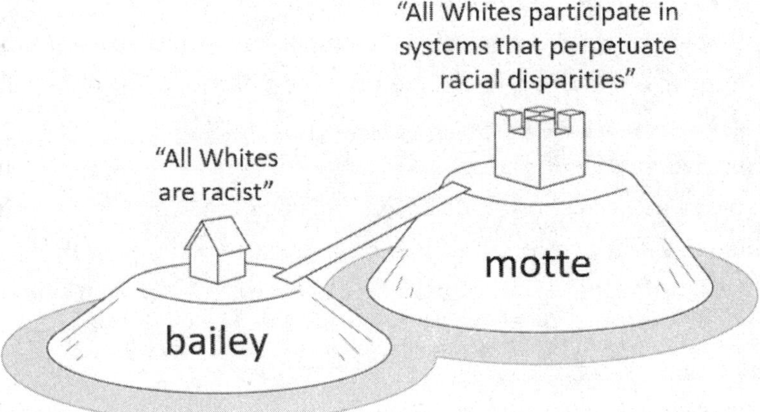

Figure 3—The motte-and-bailey rhetorical technique. When someone's radical, indefensible claim is challenged (the bailey), they can retreat to the more modest, defensible claim (the motte).

> For my purposes the desirable but only lightly defensible territory of the Motte and Bailey castle, that is to say, the Bailey, represents a philosophical doctrine or position with similar properties: desirable to its proponent but only lightly defensible. The Motte is the defensible but undesired position to which one retreats when hard pressed.[4]

In other words, postmodern scholars deploy a motte-and-bailey strategy when they first make an outrageous, indefensible claim (the bailey) and—when challenged—retreat to a commonsense, defensible claim (the motte). Then, once the challenge is repulsed, the scholar continues to make the outrageous claim as if nothing happened.

For example, they might first make a claim like "Truth is a social construct." Then, as soon as they're challenged, they reply, "All I meant was that truth claims are always made in a particular social context." Once the challenger agrees that yes, of course, all truth claims are made in a particular social context and then wanders off, the scholar continues saying, "Truth is a social construct."

We could also call this strategy the "all I meant" strategy:

"When I said that 'men have no advantage over women in sports,' all I meant was that not every man is better at sports than every woman."

"When I said that 'America is racist,' all I meant was that there exist many racial disparities in America."

"When I said that 'science is colonialism,' all I meant was that modern science emerged during the eighteenth and nineteenth centuries at the same time as European colonialism."

How to Respond

We can discern the best response to the motte and bailey by recognizing that the worst response is to attack the motte. In the analogy, the defender built the motte for the express purpose of repelling attacks. To extend the analogy, you could even imagine a cunning nobleman who intentionally lured marauding armies into his town's bailey in order to bombard them with flaming arrows from the impregnable motte.

In the same way, postmodern scholars expect and may even delight to see hapless victims blundering into their bailey while they innocently insist that they were only making the thoroughly pedestrian and commonsense claim in the motte. They may *want* you to throw a fit about their original claim while they quietly retreat to the safety of the fallback claim, making you look irrational and reactionary.

If denying the motte (the modest, defensible claim) is a bad strategy, then the correct strategy is to (1) affirm the motte claim while (2) rhetorically severing the postmodernist's retreat to the motte by exposing the stark difference between the motte and the bailey.

For example, when someone declares that "Science is colonialism" (the bailey), you should preempt their retreat to the motte by saying, "Modern science certainly emerged around the same time as European colonialism. But that's not what you said. Surely, you don't believe that science—which is grounded in objective truth and is therefore the domain of all people and all cultures everywhere—is solely a Western, European endeavor? That claim, the claim you actually made, is nonsensical and is quite dismissive toward non-Western scientists."

Or when someone says, "Men have no advantage over women in sports," you could respond, "Of course, not every man is better at sports than every woman. But surely you don't mean that the *typical* man has no advantage over the *typical* woman! For example, in track events, high school boys routinely outperform female Olympic athletes."[5]

Your goal is to show that the two claims they are trying to conflate are actually extremely different. By doing so, you burn the bridge between the bailey and the motte and force the other person to do battle in the bailey, where they originally planted their flag.

EQUIVOCATION

What It Is

The fallacy of equivocation occurs when the same word is used with two different definitions. Equivocation is similar to motte and bailey in that it relies on oscillating between two different meanings. However, equivocation is often unintentional. Whereas motte and bailey is employed as a deliberate strategy, equivocation can be the result of carelessness, lack of precision, or genuine confusion.

In addition, equivocation is often far more subtle. There is no genuine confusion about the meaning of sentences like "Science is colonialism" or "Men have no advantage over women in sports." These statements are bizarre precisely because all the words being used have agreed-upon meanings. In contrast, equivocation trades on verbal ambiguity.

Consider the following arguments:

"The gender categories of masculine and feminine are social constructs. Therefore, we should not assign gender at birth."

"Racism is a sin. Therefore, we should oppose the systems and structures that constitute racism."

"God is a God of justice. Therefore, Christians should support justice organizations."

We'll unpack each of these statements in later chapters, but here, we simply want to note that there is a subtle shift in meaning between the definitions of words in the first and second sentences listed above. This problem is particularly acute today because progressives have redefined words like *oppression*, *justice*, *gender*, *racism*, *freedom*, *democracy*, *love*, and *bigotry*.

How to Respond

One of the most important steps in any discussion is defining your terms. Don't assume that you and your dialogic partner are using terms in the same way. But also don't assume that the same term is being used in a consistent manner throughout the discussion.

Confusion also arises due to *concept creep*, the way in which a well-defined, narrow understanding of some idea or concept is slowly (and sometimes intentionally) broadened. Take the word *trauma*. Trauma used to refer to a psychological injury caused by an event that would evoke "significant symptoms of distress in almost everyone" and that was "outside the range of usual human experience." But today, trauma can refer to "anything 'experienced by an individual as physically or emotionally harmful.'"[6] Consequently, it becomes very difficult to assess the truth of a statement like "People who experience trauma may require years to fully recover." If trauma here refers to a soldier watching the members of his platoon die in a firefight, then this statement is probably true. But if trauma refers to accidentally reading an unredacted copy of *Little House on the Prairie*, then this statement is false.

In both cases, participants in any discussion should define their terms up front and then ask questions to ensure that each term is used univocally throughout the conversation.

APPEAL TO EMOTION/AD HOMINEM

What They Are

The appeal to emotion and the ad hominem are two distinct fallacies that we will treat together because they're often closely related in discussions about social justice, particularly surrounding issues of gender and sexuality. The appeal to emotion fallacy invokes people's feelings of pity or disgust or compassion or indignation in the place of logical argument. The ad hominem fallacy attacks the arguer rather than the argument. But both fallacies shift the discussion away from the argument itself.

For example, consider the following argument on the subject of gender:

> Premise 1: If gender is rooted in biology, then a person with male biology is a man.

Premise 2: Gender is rooted in biology.

Therefore,

Conclusion: A person with male biology is a man.

This argument is valid (i.e., if its premises are true, then its conclusion is true), so to deny the argument's conclusion, we would have to deny one or both of the premises. For example, in chapter 7, we'll see that queer theorists deny premise 2.

However, rather than denying either premise of this argument, a person employing an appeal to emotion would instead say, "If you claim that a person with male biology is a man, you'll cause great harm to gender nonconforming people. Doesn't your religion teach you to love your neighbor? How could you willfully inflict such suffering on others?" Because Christians are indeed called to love their neighbors and to show compassion toward the suffering, this response is rhetorically powerful. However, it is still logically fallacious. There is no logical argument that proceeds from the premise "This idea causes harm" to the conclusion "This idea is false."

Appeals to emotion are often combined with ad hominem attacks like "only a hateful bigot would make that argument." Again, this claim is untethered to any rational case against the argument or its conclusion. Even if it were true that only a hateful bigot would make an argument rooting gender in biology, that doesn't show that gender is not rooted in biology. All the ill intention in the world doesn't invalidate the laws of logic.

While ad hominems and appeals to emotion can be employed on both sides of the political aisle, critical theory encourages them for two reasons.

First, critical theory elevates lived experience *as a source of knowledge*. Thus, someone's experience of harm from hearing an argument or reading a book or seeing a culturally appropriated Halloween costume gives them knowledge about its oppressive nature. This knowledge is hidden from the person promoting the offending argument, book, or costume.

Second, critical theory denies that logic and reason are neutral. Their supposed neutrality is merely a mechanism by which the ruling class justifies its oppression. Therefore, from the perspective of critical theory, it is true almost by definition that only an oppressor would promulgate certain ways of thinking or would give credence to certain conclusions.

How to Respond

First, keep calm! Responding to insults with insults is not only impermissible for the Christian, but takes the spotlight off the argument itself, which is precisely where it belongs.

Second, point out that actual love is always rooted in the truth. To love someone is to will their good. But we can't will someone's good if we don't know what is truly good. We may have great compassion for a sick patient and a strong desire to help them. But helping them requires us to know what disease is afflicting them. It would be madness for a doctor to say, "I feel deep compassion for your condition. Please tell me which drugs you sincerely believe will make you better, and I will prescribe them to you even if I know they'll kill you." In the same way, a person who offers love at the expense of truth is not truly loving.

Finally, we can respond to ad hominems the same way we responded to Bulverism: by accepting the accusations and then asking again whether our argument is true or false. Simply say, "Let's grant, for the sake of argument, that I am an awful, hateful, miserable misanthropic bigot and that my conclusion causes trauma. Nonetheless, is my argument true or false?"

FALSE DILEMMA

What It Is

A dilemma is a difficult choice between two undesirable alternatives. A false dilemma involves naming only two alternatives when a third alternative exists. A false dilemma is a fallacy because it artificially, though often implicitly, restricts our choices.

Those of us with kids will recognize that they often use false dilemmas to get what they want. "Daddy, you can either buy me a hot dog or I can starve to death." "Mommy, I can either go to the petting zoo or I can be miserable for the rest of my life." The expectation is that because Daddy and Mommy don't want you to starve to death or to be permanently miserable, their only choice will be to hesitantly buy you a hot dog or take you to the petting zoo.

But false dilemmas abound, even amongst scholars. For example, Ibram Kendi insists:

> The opposite of "racist" isn't "not racist." It is "anti-racist." What's the difference? One endorses either the idea of a racial hierarchy as a racist, or racial equality as an antiracist. One either believes problems are rooted in groups of people as a racist, or locates the roots of problems in power and policies, as an antiracist. One either allows racial inequities to persevere, as a racist, or confronts racial inequities, as an antiracist. There is no in-between safe space of "not racist."[7]

Of course, this is a false dilemma. It is entirely possible to be a nonracist who is neither committed to racism nor to Kendi's brand of antiracism.

Similarly, Kendi writes that you either believe, as an antiracist, that "racial discrimination is the sole cause of racial disparities in this country and in the world at large," or you are—at best—an assimilationist racist.[8] Again, there is a third and obviously correct option:

that racial disparities are caused by many factors, including racial discrimination (see more in chapter 6). For now, we will simply observe that false dichotomies can be powerful tools to cudgel people into embracing a particular idea or policy because they reject what they think is the only other alternative.

How to Respond

When offered a false dilemma, respond by presenting a third option. False dilemmas are employed to force us down a path we'd otherwise avoid. We're meant to be so repulsed by one alternative (e.g., racism) that we reluctantly embrace the other (e.g., Kendi's particular version of antiracism). When we realize that we don't have to choose the less bad of two bad options, the dilemma vanishes.

HASTY GENERALIZATION

What It Is

The fallacy of hasty generalization occurs when someone bases a belief or claim on a small number of examples or on a too-limited amount of evidence. Sadly, this is done all the time, including in our national media. People take a handful of incidents and make sweeping, universal claims. During some of the horrible killings of unarmed Black men by police, one was apt to hear that black bodies were falling in the streets, that it wasn't safe for Blacks, especially Black boys or men, to leave their homes. The intimation was that White, racist cops were killing innocent Blacks with impunity.

The reality was/is quite different. White police have millions of interactions with Black people every year, from benign interactions (like waving people through a crowded concert venue, or making eye contact and saying hello at McDonalds), to traffic stops, to investigation of crimes, to arrests. The vast, vast majority happen without incident. Out of those millions of interactions per year, typically less than 30 unarmed Black people are killed by White cops per year. When we factor out those who were either committing a crime and/or attacking the police, the number drops further (literally to just 5 to 15 people per year).[9] Moreover, the ones that could even be possibly racially motivated reduces the number even further. While any innocent death is notably tragic, there is not an epidemic of White racist cops killing unarmed Black people in the US today. Not even remotely.

A few years ago, Pat counterprotested at a rally being held by a soft White power group. He engaged the leader, asking him why he despised Black people and felt they were inferior. The leader rattled off four or five negative anecdotal experiences he and his family had with Black people. Pat then calmly explained to him that he was making an error in logic and engaging in this very fallacy—that his small data set of personal experiences wasn't sufficient to draw a universal perspective about all Black people or Black people as a whole. This seemed to stymie him for a minute, as if he were seeing the point but it did not stick; he ended the conversation abruptly.

How to Respond

First, maintain your composure. People who have succumbed to this fallacy have abandoned logic and are being driven by emotion. Your ability to be emotionally and rhetorically calm will have a soothing effect on your interlocutor. Your non-defensive posture will help de-escalate the conversation and take some of the negative energy out of it, which will make room for some logical considerations.

Next, in a polite and measured tone, explain the fallacy of hasty generalization and the other person's part in it while acknowledging that we all do it at times. This acknowledgment will help them save face and reduce the chance of any new barriers being erected due to embarrassment or being put on the spot.

Finally, try to show them where they have a small data set of negative experiences that has *not* caused them to draw universal negative conclusions. For instance, you could ask them if they have had any negative experiences with White people (or with men or women or tall people or short people). They likely will reluctantly agree. Even if they don't publicly agree, we know they will be thinking about it because we know they likely have had a host of negative experiences with people who are White. Then close the loop and remind them that their negative experiences with a few White people did not color their entire view of White people and that they should afford the same courtesy to Black people.

Whatever the issue may be, ask them questions to understand them better in order to unearth examples in their life where they did not let a small amount of evidence or instances dictate their beliefs and perspectives. Then attempt to exploit that to dislodge them from the hasty generalization in question.

APPEAL TO AUTHORITY

What It Is

Finally, the appeal to authority fallacy justifies some claim on the basis of the supposed consensus of alleged experts. The words *supposed* and *alleged* are crucial because not all appeals to authority are fallacious. For example, if nearly all virologists agree that the common cold is caused by a virus, we are justified in deferring to their authority because (1) there is a real consensus about the cause of the common cold, and (2) we're consulting actual experts in the relevant field. Of course, we ought to recognize that even legitimate experts are fallible and can be wrong even when they unanimously agree. For instance, no matter how many queer theorists tell you trans women are women, they are incorrect. But we are justified in giving at least some credence to scholars who have studied a topic far more than we have.

Unfortunately, appeals to authority often trip up Christians when it comes to critical theory precisely because the subject matter experts are in near-complete agreement. They all believe that critical theory really is the proper way to think about social dynamics, race, gender, sexuality, power, oppression, and justice.

For example, many Christians have come to think that critical race theory is the only way to take race seriously. They believe it is the language and ideology of serious scholars. Therefore, they believe that trying to talk about race without categories like "white privilege" and "intersectionality" is like trying to talk about physics without categories like "atoms" and "energy." Doing so is naïve and unsophisticated at best, foolish and arrogant at worst.

However, in this case, the experts are wrong, and Christians ought to reject critical theory as the only smart, sophisticated way to think about race, class, and gender.

How to Respond

Christians need to avoid two opposite errors: (1) embracing everything secular scholarship tells us, and (2) rejecting everything secular scholarship tells us. Some Christians have a strong desire for approval from the world and especially from the world's intelligentsia. But the Bible warns us, "The fear of man lays a snare, but whoever trusts in the Lord is safe" (Proverbs 29:25). How many of the "assured results of scholarship" from one generation not only contradict historic Christian doctrine, but are debunked and rejected by the very next generation of secular scholars? We should therefore be wary of blindly tethering our beliefs to the pronouncements of the academy.

Alternatively, other Christians seem to despise secular scholarship and have a reflexive disdain for whatever academics believe. However, this posture is also foolish and is almost impossible to maintain consistently in practice. Should we really disregard the counsel of secular structural engineers when we build a hospital parking garage? Should we really ignore the advice of our atheist cardiologist when we have a heart attack? Saint Augustine, the prominent fourth- to fifth-century theologian, warned Christians that non-Christians often have accurate knowledge about the natural world through reason and experience. Therefore, when they hear Christians "talking nonsense on these topics," it discredits Christianity.[10]

We can avoid both these dangers by (1) seeking an accurate understanding of secular scholarship, and (2) subjecting secular conclusions to biblical scrutiny. In our own experience, some non-Christians will indeed despise Christians simply for having true Christian beliefs regardless of how well-articulated and well-informed these beliefs are. However, as Augustine points out, at least some non-Christians are scandalized by Christians who hold false beliefs and have never bothered to correct them.

In the case of contemporary critical theory, Christians will have to be prepared to stand against "expert consensus" on how we should conceptualize race, class, gender, sexuality, physical ability, age, and colonial status. However, we can do so while having a thorough understanding of the claims of contemporary critical theory, accepting them when they are true and offering well-thought-out objections when they are false.

Additionally, there are people with genuine expertise in a field that are challenging their field's conventional wisdom. Their authority in a particular field adds to the credibility of their challenge. This is the case with Pat, who has a PhD in the critical tradition, speaks and writes in the critical tradition, and has been an editorial board member and coeditor of a peer-reviewed education journal in the critical tradition. The present work shows that few academic fields are monolithic, and that genuine critique can come from Christian scholars who are inside, not outside, of the knowledge area they are critiquing.

LOGIC ON FIRE

A basic grasp of logic is important for Christians, especially for those of us trying to understand and engage the ideas of critical theory. In an age of social media, the 24-hour news cycle, infotainment, and political polarization, rhetoric is ubiquitous and critical thinking is rare. We have to learn to cut through the propaganda and subject every claim to careful logical analysis. And once we've understood the underlying argument used to advance some claim, we have to ask whether it is valid and whether its premises are compatible with biblical teaching.

For those who feel overwhelmed by the task of wading through the verbiage of DEI policies, position statements, and equity task forces, here's a cheat sheet. It lists important steps in evaluating arguments that you can apply anywhere and to anyone, whether they align more with the left or the right:

Step 1: Define your terms. How is each word being used? Is it being used consistently, or does its meaning change from one sentence to the next (or within the same sentence!)? Is each definition narrow and precise or broad and nebulous?

Step 2: Identify premises. What are the core assumptions at the heart of the argument? Are there any hidden premises, or unspoken assumptions?

Step 3: Test the argument's validity. If the premises of the argument are true, then is the argument's conclusion true? In other words, does the argument's conclusion actually follow logically from its premises?

Step 4: Look for fallacies. Does the argument engage in an informal fallacy such as the ones we've covered in this chapter?

Step 5: Look for reason and objective evidence. Is the argument sound? In other words, are the argument's premises actually true? What surveys, experiments, or other data are cited? Are the argument's premises compatible with the Bible? What passages of Scripture are cited, if any? What passages of Scripture contradict the argument's premises?

We can run through this checklist with any argument, whether it's offered by a politician, a guidance counselor, an activist, or a pastor. And one final important piece of advice is this: slow down. Take the time to actually understand the argument being made. Ask questions. Ask for clarification. Your goal in a discussion should not be to score before the shot clock runs out or to dunk on your opponent to the raucous applause of your fans. Your goal should be to discover the truth.

We understand why some Christians feel ill-equipped to wade into a discussion about critical theory. The secular academy, especially in the humanities, has largely embraced it. Politicians, CEOs, and media personalities repeat its talking points. Activists spout unfamiliar jargon, cite French philosophers with unfamiliar names, and confidently expound on "white ways of being" and "gender performativity." Christians who instinctively recognize that these ideas are fundamentally wrong sometimes feel like they're taking crazy pills.

We're here to encourage you: Don't be intimidated. Many of these arguments do not stand up to scrutiny.

Be humble. Be willing to learn. Be willing to listen.

But also be confident. Think clearly and biblically. Push back on bad ideas. The emperor has no clothes.

5

CHALLENGING CONTEMPORARY CRITICAL THEORY

In the previous chapter, we provided a basic introduction to logic and common logical fallacies. In this chapter, we'll turn to contemporary critical theory, the framework we discussed in chapter 3. Then, in chapters 6 through 8, we'll address the subjects of race, gender, and sexuality. In each chapter, we'll provide a more detailed description of the critical social theory corresponding to each of these subjects, but our main emphasis will be how these topics should be viewed from a biblical perspective. It's not enough for us to simply criticize bad ideas. We should also offer positive alternatives rooted in Scripture.

Too often, when young Christians listen for voices speaking about racism or sexism or sexuality, the only voices they can find—and certainly the loudest ones on offer—come from the secular left. Some Christians may even lament the fact that they have to use secular material discussing these subjects. But if they can't find anything written from a Christian perspective, they may feel that anything—however flawed—is better than nothing.

Because this chapter will critique contemporary critical theory as a whole, we'll start with the biggest question of all: What is reality like?

WHAT IS REALITY LIKE?

Christian philosophers have long made use of the concept of *worldview* to refer to our fundamental view of reality. A worldview answers all of the big and unavoidable questions of life: What are human beings? What is the fundamental problem with the world? How can that problem be fixed? What is our purpose in life? What happens when we die?

A Christian worldview answers these questions based on what the Bible teaches. What are human beings? We are God's creatures, made in his image and likeness. What is the fundamental problem with the world? Our first parents, Adam and Eve, rebelled against

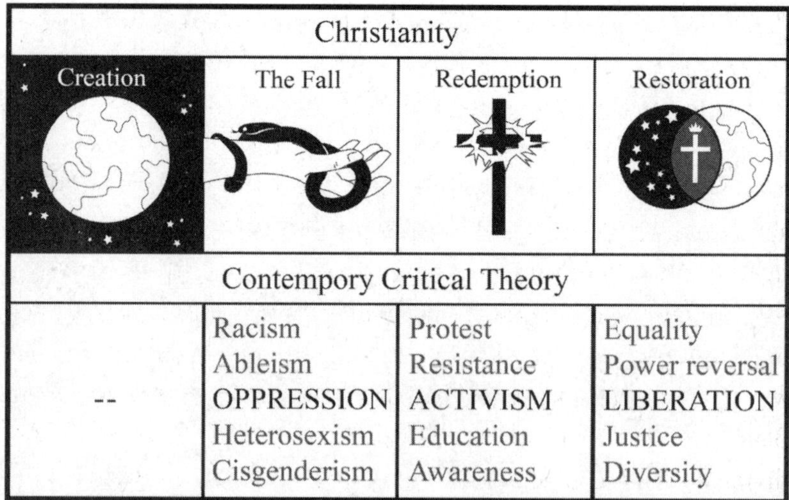

Figure 4–Christianity and contemporary critical theory as metanarratives

God and the world fell into sin and death. How can that problem be fixed? God sent his son Jesus Christ to live a sinless life, die in our place, and rise from the dead to rescue us. What is our purpose in life? To glorify God and enjoy him forever. What happens when we die? We will each stand before God, either to face his wrath in hell or to be welcomed into his presence.

Another way to view Christianity is as a metanarrative, a grand story of reality (see Figure 4). The Christian view of reality is told in four acts: creation, fall, redemption, and restoration. God created the universe and everything in it, including human beings, and pronounced it very good. But we fell into sin and death. So God sent Jesus to redeem us through his death and resurrection. And one day, Jesus will return and will restore all things.

Contemporary critical theory offers answers to these same worldview questions but tells a very different story about reality.

What are human beings? We are members of various oppressed and oppressor groups locked in a battle for dominance. What is the fundamental problem with the world? Some groups have hegemonic power and impose their oppressive narratives on society. How can that problem be fixed? Through political activism and social transformation. What is our purpose in life? To work for the liberation of oppressed groups. What happens when we die? We don't know and it doesn't matter. What matters is liberation in this world. Claims about an afterlife are a mechanism by which the ruling classes distract us from alleviating oppressive conditions in the present.

Contemporary critical theory also offers us a metanarrative, but one without a creation element. If we were created in any sense, it was by the hegemonic narratives that constructed us as male or female, Black or White or Hispanic or Asian, rich or poor, able-bodied or disabled. There was no singular fall, but throughout history, the ruling class has oppressed others and has manipulated social relationships for its advantage. The solution is not redemption, but activism.

We should stand in solidarity with the oppressed, divest ourselves of privilege, and work for our own liberation. The end goal is not the new heavens and the new earth, but the earthly promised land of diversity, equity, and inclusion.

The first and most obvious problem with contemporary critical theory, then, is that it functions as a worldview, a comprehensive lens through which we interpret reality. But it's impossible for two worldviews to peacefully coexist in our lives. They will constantly be competing for our allegiance.

A person trying to embrace Christianity and contemporary critical theory at the same time is like a diplomat trying to work for both the United States and communist Russia at the height of the Cold War. In every armed conflict, in every trade dispute, in every border negotiation, he will have to prioritize the interests of one country or the other. His loyalty will be divided, and at every moment, both countries will be vying for dominance in his mind and heart.

One common response is that Christians can embrace contemporary critical theory while still retaining Christian doctrinal commitments because the former can be embraced merely as an analytic tool. While we agree that select insights of contemporary critical theory may be true and even helpful to Christians, its overall project and outlook cannot be embraced because it is decidedly not merely an analytic tool. Contemporary critical theory makes claims about identity, morality, justice, and day-to-day experience. By its very nature, it seeks to colonize more and more of our mental landscape. Like Christianity, it doesn't want to be compartmentalized and confined to one narrow jurisdiction. It is not content to be applied only to race or only to gender or only to class or only to sexuality or only to education or only to mental health or only to the humanities. To adapt a saying from Dutch theologian Abraham Kuyper, "There is not a square inch in the whole domain of our human existence over which critical theory does not cry, Mine!"

To those who still hold out hope that contemporary critical theory can be domesticated, the remainder of this chapter will show how it is opposed to Christianity in four major areas: the nature of oppression, the nature of our identity, the nature of justice, and the nature of truth.

WHAT IS OPPRESSION?

We're often asked, "What is the fundamental error of critical theory? What is the fountainhead of all its many incompatibilities with Christianity?"

The answer is its understanding of oppression.

As we mentioned in chapter 3, critical theorists have redefined the word *oppression* to refer not only to overt acts of cruelty and tyranny, but also to the ways in which the ruling class uses ideas to justify its own dominance within society. Critical theory views norms as arbitrary constructs used to maintain the status quo and to create oppressive hierarchies.

What is entirely missing from this understanding of oppression is the idea that some norms are grounded in God's commands. This omission is a necessary outworking of critical theorists' non-theistic view of reality. If there is no God, then there can be no God-ordained norms; therefore, all norms are imposed on us by those with hegemonic power. We should note not all critical theorists are atheists or agnostics. Syncretism, cognitive dissonance, and inconsistencies abound. Our point is simply that God is not a part, a category, or an aspect of the discipline and worldview of critical theory.

Of course, *some* norms are indeed oppressive, such as the practice of *sati*, the now-abandoned Hindu practice of widow-burning, or Chinese foot-binding, or Aztec human sacrifice, or chattel slavery in the United States. But Christians must reject the premise that all hierarchies are arbitrary or that all norms are oppressive.

While the Bible provides us with numerous examples of God-ordained hierarchies (we'll talk more about this in chapter 7), one should be wholly uncontroversial: the authority that parents do and should have over their children. God commands parents to love their children, care for them, and discipline them. Parents have God-ordained authority over their children, but children do not have God-ordained authority over their parents. There is indeed a power imbalance, yet this imbalance is natural, healthy, and even crucial for the children's safety, development, and well-being. Yes, parental authority can be abused, as all authority can. But giving a three-year-old or even a thirteen-year-old authority over her parents would be terrible for both the parents and for the child.

Yet critical theorists do in fact problematize parental authority. In their paper "Understanding and Fighting Sexism: A Call to Men," Peter Blood, Alan Tuttle, and George Lakey write:

> People are just beginning to have a glimpse of what oppression based on age involves...Children [are] considered helpless, dependent, and cute—creatures to be cherished and taken care of, but not full human beings to be deeply respected and trusted with significant power. They experience 10-15 years of unpaid labor and brainwashing in our current form of education.[1]

This claim is not bizarre or inexplicable; it is the logical outworking of critical theory's beliefs about power, oppression, and hierarchy. Activists ruthlessly apply this corrosive, deconstructive approach to everything from gender to criminal justice to health care, with disastrous results.

The fundamental incompatibility of Christianity's and critical theory's views of oppression is most apparent when we apply it to God himself. If oppression occurs whenever those in authority use their power to impose their norms and values on the rest of us in a way that justifies their dominance, then who is the ultimate Oppressor? God himself. As a student told Pat in a class discussing hegemonic power, "God is the great Oppressor." The Bible is one long hegemonic discourse justifying God's sovereignty over us. In it, he issues commands that are binding on all people across time, space, and culture. He claims not merely to be good and righteous, but to be the standard by which goodness and righteousness themselves are judged. God commands us to internalize these claims. We are to set our minds and hearts on God's law and to view his commands as good and natural. To a critical theorist, this is the very essence of hegemonic power and oppression.

WHAT IS OUR IDENTITY?

The next area in which contemporary critical theory conflicts with Christianity has to do with identity. All of us inevitably ask questions like, Who am I? How do I see myself? How do I see others?

The fundamental difference is that critical theory sees our identity as primarily horizontal, whereas Christianity sees it as primarily vertical. In other words, for critical theorists, our identity comes primarily from our relationship to other people. For Christians, our identity comes primarily from our relationship to God.

Critical theorists believe that virtually every aspect of our identity is collective and socially constructed. Our race is socially constructed. Our gender is socially constructed. Our class is socially constructed. Even our status as able-bodied or disabled is socially constructed.

When critical theorists make claims like these, they generally recognize that there is an objective truth about our skin color, or our biology, or our income, or our physical ability. In other words, they would acknowledge that some people have dark skin or XX chromosomes or a six-figure income or two legs. When they speak about the social construction of these categories, they are referring to the social meaning that our culture assigns to these empirical facts.

For instance, why do we classify some people with dark skin as "Black"? After all, some people who are raced as Black have lighter skin than some people who are raced as White. And where did these categories come from? Historically, why was there an ongoing debate about whether Mexicans or Indians should be classified as White? And if White and Black merely refer to skin color, why are certain stereotypes associated with the categories of White and Black in US society today? And why are the same stereotypes not found in other societies?

Similarly, critical theorists would argue that the categories of "able-bodied" and "disabled" are socially constructed. Certainly, biological differences exist between people. One person may have lost a leg while another has not. But the Paralympic Games show that some amputees are actually faster and stronger than others who have not lost limbs. Why classify the former as "disabled"? Moreover, we do not view some biological differences as disabilities. We don't consider a fair-skinned person to be "disabled" even if they have a higher risk for skin cancer than a dark-skinned person. Why? Some people experience anxiety around disabled people and talk more slowly to them, even if their disability has nothing to do with their mental acuity. Consequently, the social meanings we impute to the categories of abled/disabled do not flow necessarily from empirical facts about physical abilities.

Additionally, critical theorists believe that some identities are differently valued by society. The fundamental dichotomy between dominant and subordinate identities is the basis for the social binary that we discussed in chapter 3—e.g., Whites are a dominant/agent/oppressor group, and Blacks are a subordinate/target/oppressed group.

Thus, critical theorists do not merely want us to adopt a collective identity, but to view ourselves as part of various collectively oppressed (or oppressor) groups. Identifying as Black is insufficient. Each Black person needs to embrace blackness as an oppressed identity category that is the basis for their political activism. Likewise, critical theorists argue that Whites need to accept that they are part of an oppressor group, not because of anything they have necessarily done personally, but because of the social meaning of whiteness in our society.

For example, in the 1989 paper "White Privilege and Male Privilege," in which she coined the term *white privilege*, Peggy McIntosh laments: "My schooling gave me no training in seeing myself as an oppressor, as an unfairly advantaged person, or as a participant in a damaged culture. I was taught to see myself as an individual whose moral state depended on her individual moral will."[2] She wants fellow White people to understand why they are "justly seen as oppressive, even when we don't see ourselves that way."

In her best-selling book *White Fragility*, Robin DiAngelo writes:

> ...a positive white identity is an impossible goal. White identity is inherently racist; white people do not exist outside the system of white supremacy...I strive to be "less white." To be less white is to be less racially oppressive.[3]

For McIntosh, DiAngelo, and many others, it is not merely enough to have a racial identity. We must also internalize a racial identity that is tied to our status as either an oppressor or the oppressed.

In contrast, Christians believe that the primary component of our identity is vertical, not horizontal. We are all God's creatures and our vertical relationship with him takes precedence over our horizontal relationship with other people. Consequently, human beings are fundamentally united across lines of race, class, and gender in at least three ways.

First, we are all united in the *imago Dei* (Genesis 1:27). All of us bear God's image and therefore possess inalienable value and dignity, whether Black or White, male or female, young or old, rich or poor.

Second, we are all sinners who have rebelled against God and deserve his wrath (Romans 1:18; 3:23). Therefore, we can never look at another person as wholly "other." In our sinful nature, we deserve nothing but judgment and condemnation.

Third, we all need the salvation offered by Jesus Christ alone: "There is one mediator between God and men, the man Christ Jesus" (1 Timothy 2:5-6). There is not one rescuer for Jews and another for Gentiles, one for men and another for women, one for Africans and another for Europeans. There is only one Savior: Jesus of Nazareth, the Messiah.

These three doctrines of human solidarity deeply undermine contemporary critical theory because they unite human beings across lines of race, class, and gender. Moreover, these doctrines are not mere abstractions. The local church, in the most concrete possible way, shows us that God's kingdom runs roughshod over the social divisions that fracture the world outside. Within the church, we are called into intimate fellowship with people who do not share our race, class, or gender. We are to view one another not just as associates or even friends, but as family. We recognize, of course, that the church has failed miserably at times to live up to its ideal and calling; nevertheless, its ideal and calling remain and will be fully realized in the life to come (Revelation 5:9; 7:9).

Finally, accepting critical theory's view of identity would be devastating to the church because it would divide the body of Christ into oppressor Christians and oppressed Christians. Women or people of color or disabled people or the poor would be encouraged to constantly be on the lookout for slights, microaggressions, or subtle power differentials. Men, Whites, the able-bodied, and the rich would be encouraged to constantly be self-conscious, hypersensitive, and anxious. There is no better way to breed suspicion, resentment, strife, and dysfunction among God's people. Where we have seen churches embrace intersectionality and CRT, we have seen disaster.

The first-century church was no stranger to actual ethnic conflict and outright oppression. When the New Testament was written, the Roman Empire had subjugated and oppressed the Jewish nation for more than a century. Jewish groups like the Zealots wanted to throw off Roman tyranny while Rome responded with brutality. Jews and Gentiles (i.e., non-Jews) were divided by religion, custom, culture, language, and mutual hostility. Into this world of violent conflict, the apostles announced the good news of peace between God and man, and then peace between Jew and Greek, slave and free, male and female—peace purchased by Christ once and for all on the cross.

Listen to what Paul wrote in Ephesians 2:12-16:

> Remember that you [Gentiles] were at that time separated from Christ, alienated from the commonwealth of Israel and strangers to the covenants of promise, having no hope and without God in the world. But now in Christ Jesus you who once were far off have been brought near by the blood of Christ. For he himself is our peace, who has made us both one and has broken down in his flesh the dividing wall of hostility by abolishing the law of commandments expressed in ordinances, that he might create in himself one new man in place of the two, so making peace, and might reconcile us both to God in one body through the cross, thereby killing the hostility.

For Paul, the unity of the church was not merely an aspirational goal, but a present reality.

Critical theory wants the church to be one more battleground on which the world's political and cultural conflicts can be fought. But God insists that the church should be a place where God's people can escape the cruelty, hatred, and enmity of the world and find safe haven with our brothers and sisters in Christ.

WHAT IS JUSTICE?

Like *oppression*, the word *justice* is used repeatedly in the Bible. Occasionally, Christians can become so suspicious of our culture's incessant chatter about justice and oppression that we forget the Bible talks constantly about both. Consider just a few of the commands in Scripture.

> "Learn to do good; seek justice, correct oppression; bring justice to the fatherless, plead the widow's cause" (Isaiah 1:17).
>
> "Give justice to the weak and the fatherless; maintain the right of the afflicted and the destitute" (Psalm 82:3).
>
> "He has told you, O man, what is good; and what
> does the LORD require of you
> but to do justice, and to love kindness, and to walk
> humbly with your God?" (Micah 6:8).

Not only are Christians commanded to seek justice, but justice is a divine attribute. In Psalm 89:14, the psalmist declares to God: "Righteousness and justice are the foundation of your throne; steadfast love and faithfulness go before you." Deuteronomy 32:4 affirms: "The Rock, his work is perfect, for all his ways are justice. A God of faithfulness and without iniquity, just and upright is he." And Isaiah calls God "a God of justice" (Isaiah 30:18). Consequently, calls to do justice should immediately resonate with Christians.

But what is justice? *Easton's Bible Dictionary* defines justice as "rendering to every one that which is his due," a phrasing which was popularized by first-century Roman orator Cicero and codified by sixth-century Byzantine Emperor Justinian.[4] This definition makes justice synonymous with fairness or impartiality, a theme that is repeated many times in the Bible (Deuteronomy 1:17; 1 Timothy

5:21; James 2:1-13; cf. Deuteronomy 10:17; Romans 2:11; Ephesians 6:9; Acts 10:34). One verse that captures this definition well is God's command in Leviticus 19:15: "You shall do no injustice in court. You shall not be partial to the poor or defer to the great, but in righteousness shall you judge your neighbor."

Note here that injustice can be committed by showing partiality toward either the poor or the rich. The just judge is one who decides each case on its own merits regardless of the status of the disputants.

In contrast, critical theorists have redefined *justice* or *social justice* to refer to "the elimination of all forms of social oppression," where "social injustice takes many forms [and] can be injustice based on a person's gender, race, ethnicity, religion, sexual orientation, physical or mental ability, or economic class."[5] To a critical theorist, social justice *means* dismantling the systems, structures, and norms that produce or perpetuate the social binary. For example, white supremacy is a system that produces the oppression of people of color, and racial justice *means* dismantling the systems, structures, and norms that produce or perpetuate racial hierarchies. The cisheteropatriarchy is a system that produces the oppression of women and LGBTQ people, and gender justice *means* dismantling the systems, structures, and norms that produce or perpetuate gender and sexual hierarchies in society.

In theory, these two definitions can overlap. When systems and structures encourage or even codify partiality, then biblical justice demands that we dismantle them. For example, in the antebellum South, slavery laws permitted brutal and unjust treatment of Blacks. Today, "reproductive rights" laws permit the murder of the unborn. And although discrimination on the basis of race, sex, ethnicity, and age is *legally* prohibited in the US, individual institutions, in certain instances, have continued to practice *illegal* discrimination by favoring or disfavoring certain groups.

However, in practice, three considerations dramatically limit the extent to which these definitions overlap.

First, the idea of retributive justice, which is prominent in the Bible, is almost entirely absent (and is even problematized) in critical theory. For example, in his essay "Racially Based Jury Nullification: Black Power in the Criminal Justice System" in the anthology *Critical Race Theory: The Cutting Edge*, district attorney Paul Butler argues that "the black community is better off when some nonviolent lawbreakers remain in the community rather than go to prison" and that "criminal conduct among African Americans is often a predictable reaction to oppression." Therefore, he concludes that "it is the moral responsibility of black jurors to emancipate some guilty black outlaws."[6]

In contrast, in the Bible, both divine justice and human justice require the punishment of evil. When God proclaims his name to the Israelites, he highlights his mercy, but also this very attribute of punishing sin:

> The Lord, the Lord, a God merciful and gracious, slow to anger, and abounding in steadfast love and faithfulness, keeping steadfast love for thousands, forgiving iniquity and transgression and sin, but who will by no means clear the guilty, visiting the iniquity of the fathers on the children and the children's children, to the third and the fourth generation (Exodus 34:6-7).

Human rulers are to imitate this attribute of God's justice. Paul explains that every human ruler "is God's servant for your good. But if you do wrong, be afraid, for he does not bear the sword in vain. For he is the servant of God, an avenger who carries out God's wrath on the wrongdoer" (Romans 13:4-5). Any theory of justice that does not include this aspect of punishing evil is therefore deficient.

Second, and even more importantly, because critical theory's understanding of oppression is faulty, its understanding of justice is equally faulty. As we said in the last section, many norms that critical theory views as oppressive are actually good and just from a biblical perspective. For instance, the prohibition of same-sex marriage is viewed as oppressive by queer theorists because it positions homosexuality as inferior to heterosexuality. But, from a Christian perspective, homosexuality *is* inferior to heterosexuality because the former is sinful while the latter is not. Therefore, it is good and just for any society to recognize and encourage traditional marriage while prohibiting same-sex marriage. Yet due to the widespread acceptance of critical theory, this claim is increasingly seen as horrifically regressive and bigoted.

Likewise, queer theory wants to dismantle the gender binary by recognizing the existence of three or more genders on official government forms, on medical records, and elsewhere. They view the gender binary as oppressive because it marginalizes people who do not identify as male or female. Yet again, the gender binary is good and God-ordained. Denying its existence by passing laws that destabilize it in the name of social justice is, in fact, deeply wrong and unjust.

Contemporary critical theory's understanding of social justice and a biblical understanding of justice are not only different, but often contradictory.

Finally, contemporary critical theory's understanding of social justice is often tied to its understanding of equity. Equity used to be a synonym for equality, but—like many words—it has been redefined by critical theorists. Equality refers to treating people equally. But, in the minds of critical theorists, equal treatment is actually unfair and inappropriate when people are unequally situated within society. To remedy the disadvantages that oppressed people face, they should be treated *differently* than privileged people.

The idea that differential treatment can be just is not wholly without merit. For example, many public facilities have reserved handicapped parking spaces so that they are more accessible to people in wheelchairs. No one in his right mind would claim that this accommodation is unfair on the grounds that "we should treat everyone the same and shouldn't exclude anyone from certain parking spaces." In this case, special, exclusive accommodations do seem reasonable so that handicapped people have access to the same opportunities as everyone else.

However, critical theorists generally want to go much further to argue that equity demands different treatment for women, people of color, LGBTQ people, etc. because of the disadvantages they face due to systemic racism, sexism, heterosexism, and other diffuse oppressive systems. This claim is much more dubious. For one, are we really willing to argue that dark skin is analogous to a physical handicap and requires an analogous mitigation at the policy level? Additionally, the construction of a handicap ramp is a discrete, one-time action. Once it is built, access is equalized and the problem is solved. In contrast, the demands of equity are open-ended and never quite seem to be satisfied.

To understand why, we have to probe critical theorists' understanding of equity. While they often insist that equity merely secures equality of opportunity, the correct question to ask is, How can we tell that equality of opportunity has been secured? Their answer is, "When outcomes are equal." Thus, we discover that what was originally billed as equality of opportunity was actually equality of outcome all along.

Ibram X. Kendi makes this understanding explicit in his book *How to Be an Antiracist*. He writes: "Racial inequity is when two or more racial groups are not standing on approximately equal footing [and racial] equity is when two or more racial groups are standing on a relatively equal footing." He presents racial disparities in home ownership as an example of racial inequity. He then explains: "A racist policy is any measure that produces or sustains racial inequity between racial groups. An antiracist policy is any measure that produces or sustains racial equity between racial groups."[7] In Kendi's mind, racial equity will be achieved only when all racial groups have roughly the same level of home ownership.

In other words, social justice requires equity, which requires equality of outcome. The idea that social justice will be attained only when outcomes are equalized is another reason to reject critical theory's definition of justice. Biblically speaking, equal outcomes are not necessarily reasonable, good, or desirable. For example, it would be unjust if athletic competitions were rigged so that every demographic group was equally represented in the winner's circle. Or it would be unjust if unqualified male candidates were routinely promoted over qualified female candidates so that gender parity could be achieved at the highest levels of some profession.

Of course, if we see persistent disparities, that can certainly be an occasion to check that our rules and procedures are truly fair and that no one is being inadvertently disadvantaged. But we can't merely assume that unequal outcomes are always and only the result of injustice. In his book *Disparities and Discrimination*, Black economist Thomas Sowell wholeheartedly rejects the idea that "statistical disparities in socioeconomic outcomes imply either biased treatment to the less fortunate or genetic deficiencies in the less fortunate." He offers numerous examples of group disparities that are the consequence of geography, culture, and a host of other factors, culminating in examples of disparities within families based on birth order. He asks: "If there is not equality of outcomes among people born to the same parents and raised under the same roof, why should equality of outcomes be expected—or assumed—when conditions are not nearly so comparable?"[8] He's correct. While discrimination often leads to disparities, we cannot assume that all disparities are caused by discrimination.

HOW DO WE KNOW THE TRUTH?

The final major way in which contemporary critical theory conflicts with Christianity is in its view of epistemology, or how we know truth.

Critical theory exalts the role of lived experience in acquiring knowledge and is immensely skeptical of claims to objectivity. In their book *Is Everyone Really Equal?*, Sensoy and DiAngelo write:

> [Critical theorists] argue that a key element of social injustice involves the claim that particular knowledge is objective, neutral, and universal. An approach based on critical theory calls into question the idea that objectivity is desirable or even possible...who we are (as knowers) is intimately connected to our group socialization (including gender, race, class, and sexuality)..."*what* you know" is connected to "*who* you are" and "*where* you stand."[9]

In contrast, Christians should demand that our lived experience and any other source of claimed insight be tested against the teaching of Scripture. Moreover, Scripture provides us with objective truth that is available to everyone, regardless of their social location.

Obviously, lived experience can be a source of knowledge, and our prejudices and sin can lead us to misinterpret Scripture. But the limitless and one-sided cynicism of critical theory toward "dominant knowledges" is a gateway to deconstruction.

For example, books like Kristin Kobes Du Mez's *Jesus and John Wayne* and Beth Allison Barr's *The Making of Biblical Womanhood* ask us to question the ways that modern evangelical doctrine is merely an extension of patriarchal power.[10,11] Jonathan Wilson-Hartgrove's *Reconstructing the Gospel* and Joseph Barndt's *Becoming an Antiracist Church* insist that modern evangelicals have a warped understanding of the gospel due to their fealty to "slave-holder religion" and "imperialism."[12,13] Such books rarely, if ever, actually examine the words of Scripture to make these claims. Instead, they simply assert that White male evangelical interpretations have been warped by the social location of White male evangelical interpreters and then equally assert their own interpretation of Scripture.

But how far will this cynicism take us? Why can't we also assert that homophobia and transphobia are responsible for the church's uniform rejection of homosexuality and transgenderism throughout history? Or that the social location of the White male Protestant Reformers invalidates the theology of the Protestant Reformation? Or that the all-male Council of Nicaea was beholden to Roman imperialism and ancient patriarchy and therefore had an incorrect view of theology?

Once we start engaging in Bulverism (see chapter 4), there is no easy stopping point. Even worse, if we hit the brakes at LGBTQ-affirmation or the five solas of the Reformation or Nicene Christianity and insist that the Bible *does* actually affirm traditional marriage or Protestant theology or the deity of Christ, we'll be told that we're still blinded by our privilege and need to center the interpretations of marginalized groups.

Consequently, Christians should reject critical theory's approach to knowledge from the outset. We can be open to the possibility that we're misinterpreting Scripture and self-reflective when it comes to our own blind spots. But we must never assume that one person's interpretation is incorrect and another's is correct merely because of their respective social locations. Using your social location, or background, or personal experience as the lens through which you interpret Scripture is deeply erroneous. It is eisegesis and must be resisted and rejected.

TWO COMPETING WORLDVIEWS

Contemporary critical theory functions as a worldview. It answers *ontological* questions (What does it mean to be human?), *phenomenological* questions (How should we understand our lived experience?), and *epistemological* questions (What is truth and how do we know it?). These are worldview questions. As a result, its fundamental approach to reality is in conflict with a Christian view of reality.

However, even if we were to consider each of the core beliefs of contemporary critical theory independent of the larger framework into which they fit, we'd still find unresolvable conflicts. Not all norms are oppressive. Not all categories are socially constructed. Justice does not require us to abolish all hierarchies. And truth is primarily known through Scripture, reason, and objective evidence, not through lived experience.

For all these reasons, contemporary critical theory and Christianity are fundamentally incompatible. To the extent that we embrace one, we will have to abandon the other. We can't serve two masters.

6

RACE

Over the past decade, the ideas of contemporary critical theory have made significant inroads into the conservative evangelical church. Today, there is reason for cautious optimism, mainly because of Christians' reactions to the excesses of transgender activism. While the average person may have little understanding of critical theory, they sense that something is wrong when doctors begin cutting off the breasts of healthy teenage girls in the name of inclusion.

But if the ideas of critical theory are as toxic as we claim, how did they ever establish a foothold within evangelicalism? In a word: race. Race is a subject with a lengthy and uncomfortable past within the US and among Christians (see chapter 2). There has long been a movement for racial reconciliation within evangelicalism that seeks to address our racial division and pursue unity in Christ. As a result, when the language and ideas of critical race theory began to be smuggled into the evangelical church, well-meaning Christians often didn't notice them or tended to give them a pass. After all, if a patient is dying of cancer, do we really need to be overly scrupulous about the purity of the medicine he's taking? But, as we'll see, sometimes the purported medicine is poison, and the proposed cure is worse than the disease.

CRT AND RACE

Critical race theory (CRT) is one of many critical social theories that fall under the umbrella of critical theory. Because we already sketched the history of CRT in chapter 3, here we'll simply explain the ideas at the heart of CRT. The similarities between CRT and other critical social theories will be obvious and will serve as another reminder that—to a rough approximation—different critical theories apply the same basic framework to particular subjects like race, gender, sexuality, or education.

The four central ideas of critical race theory are (1) the normalcy of racism, (2) the hiddenness of racism, (3) the centrality of lived experience, and (4) the interlocking nature of oppression.

First, critical race theorists believe that racism is normal, permanent, and pervasive. Regarding US society in 1992, the godfather of CRT, Derrick Bell, stated "racism is an integral, permanent, and indestructible component of this society."[1] Whereas the Civil Rights Movement tended to define racism in term of individual racial prejudice, CRT redefined it in terms of systems and structures that produce disparate outcomes, even absent ill intent on the part of any particular person. This conceptualization of racism dovetails well with the popular claim that racism is "prejudice plus power." On this assumption, while people of color can be racially *prejudiced*, they cannot be *racist* because they supposedly lack the collective, systemic power to impose their prejudices on Whites.

Second, critical race theorists believe racism is concealed beneath ideologies like colorblindness, meritocracy, neutrality, and objectivity. They recognize that American society *appears* far more just and fair than it did under Jim Crow or chattel slavery. However, they believe that the appearance of justice disguises mechanisms that continue to perpetuate and ensure the racial status quo.[2] Certainly, they object to institutions that feign objectivity and a commitment to social justice but are implicitly committed to racial hierarchy. However, they are also skeptical that any objective standard of merit actually exists. As critical race theorists Richard Delgado and Jean Stefancic put it: "[F]or the critical race theorist, objective truth, like merit, does not exist, at least in social science and politics. In these realms, truth is a social construct created to suit the purposes of the dominant group."[3]

Third, critical race theory valorizes the lived experience of people of color as critical to understanding racism. In keeping with the central pillars of contemporary critical theory, CRT believes that the hegemonic narrative of white supremacy blinds Whites to their racial privilege. In contrast, people of color can recognize the many ways in which the majority culture marginalizes them and thus can come to a better understanding of racism and racial inequality. This heightened awareness of social reality means that people of color possess innate authority to identify their oppression and speak with a unique "voice of color" when they interpret their experiences.

Finally, critical race theorists believe that racism is only one of many "interlocking systems of oppression" that include sexism, classism, heterosexism, ableism, and ageism. This intersectional sensibility is not some progressive addition to CRT. Rather, it has been a foundational principle of CRT since its advent in the late 1980s. As critical race theorist Khiara Bridges puts it: "intersectionality was not offered as a corrective to CRT; instead, it *is* CRT."[4]

OBJECTIONS TO CRT

Because CRT is a subdiscipline of critical theory, most of the objections we raised in chapter 5 will still apply. However, we'll quickly run through several other criticisms.

First, racism should not be defined as "prejudice plus (systemic) power" precisely because racism is a sin, and sin does not cease to be sin because of our social location. Therefore, playing word games to redefine *racism* so that it can only be committed by Whites is as illegitimate as redefining *adultery* so that it can only be committed by women. Yes, racist acts are more harmful when they are committed by those in power. But they are always sinful no matter who commits them.

Second, while the prejudice-plus-power redefinition of racism entails that no people of color can be racist, some authors go farther and argue that all Whites are racist. For example, Ijeoma Oluo states: "if you are white in a white supremacist society, you are racist. If you are male in a patriarchy, you are sexist. If you are able-bodied, you are ableist. If you are anything above poverty in a capitalist society, you are classist. You can sometimes be all of these things at once."[5] All these claims are incorrect. While it is possible to argue that all human beings have the seeds of every sin in their hearts, it is false to argue that one demographic group is universally guilty of some sin while another is immune to it.

Third, because CRT defines racism in terms of pervasive systems and norms even in the absence of any ill intent on the part of an individual, it has come to encompass all kinds of phenomena that aren't actually racist. In 2019, *Politico* published Reverend William J. Barber's piece "The Racist History of Tipping," which called tipping a "particular vestige of slavery."[6] A *UC-Irvine Law Review* article entitled "The Unbearable Whiteness of Milk" explored "nutritional racism" and "food oppression."[7] A 2020 CNN article listed "everyday words and phrases that have racist connotations" including *Master bedrooms*, *blacklist*, *black mark*, and *grandfathered in*.[8] A 2020 *Scientific American* article explored "The Racist Roots of Fighting Obesity," which argued that "Black women have been specifically targeted" in the "massive public health campaign urging fat people to eat right, eat less and lose weight," and that this concern "reflects the racist stigmatization of Black women's bodies."[9] Problematizing words or phrases, let alone health initiatives, due to their etymology or associations is foolish and will dull people's sensitivity to actual racial prejudice. Ironically, acting as if everything is racist actually *helps* white power and white nationalist groups, which is another strong incentive to reject this thinking and practice. If everything is racism, then nothing is racism.

Relatedly, systemic racism is usually defined in terms of racial disparities in outcomes, rather than in terms of unjust policies. We explained in chapter 5 that this understanding of systemic racism is incorrect. Not all disparities, whether they're related to race or gender or class, are the product of injustice.

Fourth, denying the concept of objective merit will have serious consequences. At a purely material level, it is obviously true that a hard-working, exemplary employee merits a promotion more than the boss's lazy, dishonest son. But at a spiritual level, the concept of objective merit is even more important. We need a Savior precisely because we don't objectively merit God's favor. And Jesus can be our Savior precisely because he did objectively merit God's favor. Take away objective merit and you take away the gospel. Objective merit is sometimes difficult to assess, but we cannot erase the concept itself in order to justify our preferred policies.

Fifth, CRT's claim that there exists a unique *voice of color* that enables non-Whites to see and articulate truths that are hidden from Whites is sometimes applied to the interpretation of Scripture. This is an especially dangerous application of an already-false claim. The meaning of Scripture is found in authorial intent, and authorial intent can be discovered through historical-grammatical exegesis using tools like study, scholarship, and historical research, which are available to all people regardless of ethnicity. Moreover, while lived experience can sometimes give us insight into truth, no one currently has the lived experience of a first-century fisherman like Peter or an eighth-century BC prophet like Isaiah, which might actually help us understand their meaning. Most importantly, the greatest asset for interpreting the Bible correctly is not one's social location, but one's desire to love, honor, and submit to God.

Finally, Christians must wholeheartedly reject a key premise of intersectionality: that racism, sexism, classism, heterosexism, ableism, transphobia, etc. are all inseparable interlocking systems of oppression that must be dismantled simultaneously. Some norms—like heterosexuality, or the gender binary, or particular gender roles—are good, not oppressive. To dismantle them would not be just and liberating, but unjust and harmful.

Although far more could be said about the incompatibility of CRT and Christianity, we don't merely want to critique it. In the remainder of the chapter, we want to offer Christians a biblical way to think about race and to pursue ethnic unity. Sometimes, our arguments will be compatible with CRT. Mostly, they will flatly contradict it. However, we will not appeal to CRT to make our case, which is the crux of the debate over whether CRT contains any true insights that Christians can appreciate. The short answer is, "Yes, it does..." The longer answer is, "...but we don't need CRT to discover them." In other words, God's special revelation in Scripture and the empirical study of history are sufficient to understand race quite apart from any true insights that might be offered by CRT.

WHAT IS RACE?

Race is a social construct. This is indeed a claim that CRT affirms, but it is also the teaching of the Bible. In Acts 17:26, Paul declares that God "made from one man every nation of mankind to live on all the face of the earth, having determined allotted periods and the boundaries of their dwelling place." Hence, the Bible affirms that there is only one race: the human race.

This reality makes racial bigotry not only evil but genuinely stupid. It is hatred of one's own kind. As joint image bearers and sons and daughters of God, racial disunity should then be anathema among Christians. Racial hatred and discord not only have an insidious impact on the individual soul, they also have deleterious effects on our communities and the comportment of our nation (the US).

What we call "race" today is a category that developed during the seventeenth and eighteenth centuries as European explorers encountered new people groups and attempted to classify them. Unfortunately, this exercise was not purely intellectual and morally neutral. The system of race that they developed was meant to justify the dominance of the White race over "inferior" races.

Despite the testimony of the Bible, some Christians are hesitant to affirm that race is a social construct because they worry that gender and sexuality are hiding just around the corner. If we affirm that race is a social construct, won't we be forced to affirm that gender is also a social construct? Moreover, most people recognize the obvious truth that variations in physical appearance related to, say, skin color and hair texture, correlate with ancestry. Therefore, they wonder whether the platitude "race is a social construct" will lead us to deny equally obvious differences between the sexes.

These legitimate concerns can be answered.

It is trivially easy to show that race is qualitatively different than gender. When an interracial couple has a baby, the child will often inherit a mixture of racial characteristics from their parents (e.g., tan skin and curly hair). But the child will not inherit a mixture of gender characteristics. At all. This example also shows that race is truly a spectrum while gender is not. It is possible to be half-Indian or one-quarter White or five-eighths Asian. But it is not possible to be half male, one-quarter male, or five-eighths male.

Furthermore, our ancestry and genes are objective facts, but they also do not challenge the idea that race is a social construct. The simplest proof of this claim is how legal and social definitions of whiteness varied over the course of US history. There were comically tragic court cases in which defendants had to "prove" their race to exculpate themselves from the charge of then-illegal miscegenation (i.e., interracial marriage). Indeed, in 1919, an Indian man argued that he should be permitted to become a naturalized US citizen because his Aryan heritage qualified him as being anthropologically and scientifically "White." His case went all the way to the Supreme Court, which decided against him *on the grounds that race was a "commonsense" legal category, and not a scientific category*![10]

Today, debates (from both the right and the left) over whether Jews or Hispanics or Middle-Easterners qualify as White further demonstrate that race is a social category that is not grounded in biology or in human nature.

That said, it would be equally wrong to conclude that because race is a social construct, race doesn't exist at all. Social categories can still be meaningful and real and can have a profound effect on human behavior.

For example, while someone's age is an objective fact, "child" is a socially constructed category. The legal definition of *child* has fluctuated over the course of US history. In other cultures, the cutoff between child and adult is very different than ours. Moreover, the legal privileges and responsibilities and the social expectations attached to being a child also vary over time and from country to country. Despite these facts, it would be extremely strange to argue that because "child" is a social category whose precise characterization varies from culture to culture, it does not exist at all. Indeed, the Bible itself repeatedly makes distinctions between children and adults (e.g., 1 Corinthians 3:1; 13:11; Ephesians 6:1; 1 John 2:12).

Therefore, Christians should recognize that race is a social construct while also recognizing that it is a real social category.

One additional point: When it comes to discussions of race, it is often more helpful to invoke the biblical category of *ethnos* (a Greek word, which can be translated as "nation" or "people group"), those who share a common language, culture, history, and ancestry. For simplicity, we will refer to this biblical category as an "ethnic group" or an "ethnicity." Using this definition of ethnicity, race is an extremely broad and fluid category that can encompass many different ethnic groups. For instance, a racial category like "Whites" includes the English, the Irish, Czechs, Germans, Italians, and the French, while an ethnic category like "Japanese" roughly specifies a single people group.

WHY IS RACISM A SIN?

Ten years ago, it went without saying that racism was a sin. However, the rise of critical race theory and the ever-expanding redefinition of *racism* have made some Christians cynical. They perceive that charges of racism are being used as cudgels to promote progressive political ideology. The backlash against CRT has become so severe that Christians in some circles are beginning to argue that the concept of racism is a modern invention and should be rejected wholesale as a category.

So what is racism, and why is it a sin?

The short answer is that racism is a form of partiality, and partiality is repeatedly condemned as sinful in the Bible because it is incompatible with God's character (Deuteronomy 1:17; 1 Timothy 5:21; James 2:1-13; cf. Deuteronomy 10:17; Acts 10:34; Romans 2:11; Ephesians 6:9).

However, a racism-skeptic could respond that not all forms of partiality are sinful. God commands us to love all people, but also commands us to have a special love for those nearest to us (Exodus 20:12; Ephesians 5:21–6:8; 1 Timothy 5:8). The racism-skeptic's argument would then run something like this:

> Throughout the Bible we find commands to love and honor certain people above others (our parents, our children, our rulers, our pastors, our church, fellow believers, etc.). None of these commands permit us to hate our neighbor,

> but all of them assume that rightly ordered loves will prioritize those with whom we have a special relationship.
>
> Once we establish that there is a natural and God-ordained hierarchy of loves, the principle of kin-love follows. Our greatest duty is toward our immediate family. Then our duties expand outward to our extended family, our distant relatives, our clan, and our own ethnic group until only later reaching other ethnic groups. Therefore, what people call "racism" is actually a thoroughly biblical and God-ordained hierarchy of loves.

This argument has two main problems.

First, it ignores the fact that race is a social construct, which is why its boundaries constantly vary. Even if we were to construct a hierarchy like the one suggested by the racism-skeptic, how plausible is it to suggest that the lines can be drawn neatly around race categories? For example, does a White American really have a special obligation to love a White farmer in Siberia or a White businessman in Western Turkey? While they (arguably) share the same race, their ethnicities are completely different because they have no common language or culture, and the overlap of their histories and ancestries are vanishingly small.

Conversely, consider the inhabitants of a nation like Colombia, which was the setting of the 2021 Disney film *Encanto*. Reflecting the actual demographics of Colombia, the main character's extended family (the Madrigals) included relatives whose ancestries traced to Europe, Africa, and the Americas, but who had still all presumably lived in Colombia for generations. The Madrigals are bound by the same language, culture, history, and even familial ties. Thus, multiple races can be found within a single ethnicity or even within a single family. And that points toward a second and even greater problem.

Even if we hypothesize that we have some vanishingly small duty toward our entire ethnic group, it pales in comparison to the duty we have toward our actual neighbor. Jesus makes this point in the parable of the Good Samaritan in Luke 10. The Samaritans were the ethnic and religious enemies of the Jews. Yet when a Jewish man is robbed and left for dead, the priest and the Levite—fellow Jews—both pass by him, while the Samaritan shows him extravagant love and compassion. The Samaritan models the neighbor-love that God requires.

Yes, in principle, we are to love all people everywhere. But your neighbor is not "all people everywhere." Neither is your neighbor "only people from your own ethnic group." Instead, your neighbor is anyone along your path, anyone you meet, anyone in front of you at the moment.

Racists justify their ethnic partiality by constructing a completely abstract hierarchy in the name of "rightly ordered loves." But if they fail to love the actual neighbor right in front of them, that failure—ironically—reveals deeply disordered loves. In America in particular, your actual neighbors, your actual classmates, your actual co-workers, are likely to include people of different races. If you are White, to love a White stranger who lives 1,000 miles away from you more than you love the actual Black and Asian and Hispanic people in your neighborhood, workplace, or church is nonsensical. The same argument applies to Blacks, Asians, Hispanics, and every other racial/ethnic group.

Because Jesus used the Golden Rule to explain the command to love your neighbor, a simple test of racism is this: Would you want your neighbor to treat you the way that you treat him? In other words, would you want him to give the job to a less-qualified candidate who shared his ethnicity? Would you want him to ignore you when you visited his church? Would you want him to ascribe negative stereotypes to you because of your ethnicity? Would you want him to withhold his friendship from you?

Racism is not the only sin or the greatest sin, but it is a serious one because, at its heart, it is a violation of the second-greatest commandment.

IS AMERICA RACIST?

It's not at all uncommon to hear claims that America is a racist or white supremacist nation. To understand these claims, we must remember that critical race theorists have redefined the terms *racism* and *white supremacy* to refer to systems and norms rather than to personal attitudes. This distinction is crucial because actual data undermine the idea that personal racial prejudice is common in the United States.

For example, the Policy Institute at King's College, London, analyzed results from a 2022 World Values Survey in a study entitled "Love thy neighbour? Public trust and acceptance of the people who live alongside us."[11] Participants were asked to name groups they would *not* like to have as neighbors. Only 8 percent of Americans said they wouldn't like to have neighbors who were immigrants or foreign workers, and only 3 percent said they wouldn't like to have neighbors of a different race. In both of these categories, the United States was ranked #6 in tolerance out of 24 countries listed. For instance, in Canada, 9 percent of respondents said they wouldn't like to have neighbors who were immigrants or foreign workers, and 4 percent said they wouldn't like to have neighbors of a different race. In Mexico, the numbers were 14 percent and 11 percent. In Russia, the numbers were 32 percent and 16 percent.

Within the United States, surveys similarly fail to show that Whites hold strong anti-Black prejudices. In a 2019 article for *Tablet*, then-graduate student Zach Goldberg analyzed survey data on reported "feelings of warmth" between different racial groups (Whites, Blacks, Hispanics, and Asians).[12] Not surprisingly, members of every racial group rated their feelings of warmth toward their own racial ingroup as higher than their feelings toward racial outgroups.[13] For instance, Blacks had warmer feelings toward other Blacks than toward Whites, Asians, or

Hispanics. However, Whites had the lowest in-group bias, and White liberals actually had warmer feelings toward non-Whites than toward Whites. Political scientist L.J. Zigerell analyzed similar data from 2020 and found that Whites were the only racial group that had virtually no in-group preference, viewing all racial groups with equal warmth, while other racial groups all displayed substantial in-group preferences.[14]

Of course, self-reports can be misleading, and even sincere beliefs don't necessarily translate into action. But the same result also held for behavior under experimental conditions: Zigerell published a meta-nalysis of 17 studies that showed, "For White participants (n=10 435), pooled results did not detect a net discrimination for or against White targets, but, for Black participants (n=2781), pooled results indicated the presence of a small-to-moderate net discrimination in favor of Black targets [i.e., pro-Black discrimination]."[15]

What are we to conclude? As we argued in chapter 2, there is experimental evidence of racial discrimination in some contexts. There is also experimental evidence against racial discrimination in other contexts. Surveys show some people hold negative views of interracial marriage. Other surveys show that Whites report notably less in-group bias than other racial groups. Some people in the US are opposed to living next to immigrants and people of another race. But the overwhelming majority are not. And Americans are significantly less opposed to having immigrant neighbors or neighbors of a different race than citizens of other counties.

Thus, while we can say that racism still exists in America, there is little evidence that America is a racist nation, unless you adopt critical race theory's redefinition of racism, which we reject.

ARE POC IN AMERICA OPPRESSED?

Given our nation's racial history and the reality of present-day racism, many sympathetic Christians may think it reasonable to affirm that people of color are oppressed in our society today. But that claim requires us to jettison the traditional definition of oppression; it isn't true that all or even most people of color in America today experience "unjust or cruel exercise of authority or power."[16] Walk through a mall or spend time at the beach, and you'll find people of all ethnicities relaxing, playing, talking, and enjoying the same activities. The actual day-to-day experiences of the vast majority of Americans are far more affected by socioeconomic factors than by race and could not be characterized as oppression. This claim only makes sense if we see oppression as a largely invisible product of symbols and norms that most people—even its ostensible victims—don't recognize.

Here, someone might respond, "But what about actual injustices that Blacks suffer? For example, we've all seen horrifying videos of unarmed Black men who were killed by police. Doesn't this constitute oppression?"

While we'd readily admit that injustices are committed against individual Black people, the question is whether people of color *as a group* are oppressed. For instance, do Blacks *as a whole* experience oppression at the hands of police? This is certainly a common narrative. For example, after the murder of Ahmaud Arbery, a distraught LeBron James tweeted, "We're literally hunted EVERYDAY/EVERYTIME we step foot outside the comfort of our homes!"[17] Many pundits and celebrities echoed this sentiment to the extent that a *Skeptic* magazine survey found that more than 50 percent of those who self-identified as "very liberal," 26 percent of "moderates," and 22 percent of those who were "very conservative" believed that police killed more than 1,000 unarmed Black men in 2019.[18]

However, this belief is grossly incorrect. According to *The Washington Post*'s database of police shootings, the actual number of unarmed Black men shot and killed by police in 2019 was 13.[19] A second database put the number at 31 when all forms of lethal violence were included, still orders of magnitude smaller than 1,000.[20] Moreover, not even 1,000 shootings would validate the idea that Blacks as a whole experience oppression at the hands of police or that LeBron James's comment has any basis in reality. For comparison, the FBI records that 6,446 Black men were victims of homicide in 2019.[21]

What about the facts that Black men are roughly 2.5 times more likely to be killed by police than White men, and that unarmed Black men are roughly seven times more likely to be killed by police than unarmed White men? Don't these facts clearly demonstrate racism in the use of lethal force? Not necessarily. Blacks are also roughly seven times more likely to commit violent crime than Whites. Thus, the disparity in police shootings is largely explained by a disparity in crime rates; all groups that commit more crime are more likely to have violent encounters with the police.[22]

Another way to challenge this narrative is to simply ask Blacks themselves about their experiences with the police. For example, according to a 2018 Bureau of Justice Statistics report, 21.1 percent of Blacks age 16+ had any contact with the police over the past year, and only 3.8 percent of that group reported experiencing use of force or threat of force, meaning that approximately 0.6 percent of Blacks each year report that they have experienced either force or the threat of force from police.[23] Likewise, the Law Enforcement Epidemiology Project at the University of Illinois, Chicago, estimated that approximately 0.03 percent of Blacks reported being injured by police in 2016.[24] To provide a point of comparison, roughly 2.8 percent of Blacks visited the emergency room in 2019–2020 as a result of traffic accidents.[25] While even a single act of unjustified use of force by a law enforcement officer is wrong, these numbers do not support the idea of an epidemic of police brutality against Blacks.

Moreover, when Blacks are asked how they actually feel about the level of police presence in their neighborhood, there is little evidence that they want it decreased. For example, a 2020 Gallup poll found that 20 percent of Blacks wanted police to spend more time in their area, 19 percent wanted them to spend less time, and 61 percent wanted no change.[26] In 2021, the Detroit Police Department asked citizens how they would feel if police presence were increased in their neighborhood. Fourteen percent of Whites said an increased police presence would make them feel less safe, and 41 percent said it would make them feel more safe. In contrast, only 8 percent of Blacks would feel less safe, and 45 percent would feel more safe.[27] Finally, a 2024 paper surveyed more than 500 White and Black Americans and found that most Blacks wanted to "maintain or increase police patrols" and to "maintain or increase police spending."[28] These results held true whether or not crime declined or any new police reforms were passed.

The only way to reconcile Blacks' self-reporting and expressed desire for increased policing with the narrative that "Blacks are oppressed by police" is to hypothesize that Blacks are victims of a false consciousness that blinds them to the reality of their own oppression. For reasons we've already explained, we reject this view as false and—ironically—as subtly dismissive of Black agency and competence. We should let people think and speak for themselves rather than telling them what they ought to think and say. And when they are asked about their own views, most Blacks do not endorse proposals like abolishing the police or even reducing police presence.

We've spent an extended time on policing merely to point out that popular narratives are often empirically false and that claims of collective oppression often implicitly assume contemporary critical theory's understanding of oppression, which Christians should reject.

SHOULD CHRISTIANS BE COLORBLIND?

Most conservatives today view colorblindness as an unqualified ideal that is the fulfillment of the Civil Rights Movement. CRT's skepticism and—occasionally—outright hostility toward colorblindness has made conservatives even more emphatic that colorblindness is ideal.

In one sense, Christians absolutely ought to be colorblind: We should be impartial, treating everyone with kindness and fairness without regard to their ethnicity. When most Christians think of colorblindness, this is the version they have in mind.

However, colorblindness can sometimes be used to insist that we should ignore race and ethnicity entirely. This approach is incorrect and has no basis in Scripture. There is nothing wrong with having an ethnic identity, and the Bible repeatedly comments on the ethnicity of various figures, sometimes making it a central part of a narrative (Ruth 1:15-16; 1:22; 2:2; 2:21; 4:5; 4:10; Luke 10:25-37; 17:11-19; Acts 2:5-12). Paul himself was Jewish and exulted in his Jewish ethnicity (Romans 9:2-4; 1 Corinthians 9:19-23; Colossians 4:11). So merely noticing and even celebrating our own ethnicity or someone else's is not wrong.

Remember, ethnicity is not merely about the color of our skin. It also encompasses our language, culture, and history. The idea that French people, for example, should not talk about their French heritage in polite company or that the English should have no fondness for cricket or tea is odd.

One obvious reason that people are nervous when it comes to ethnic identity is America's history of racism and white supremacy. However, another major obstacle to reclaiming a positive, biblical understanding of ethnicity is its misuse and weaponization by contemporary critical theory. Critical theorists use ethnicity to attach either oppressed or oppressor labels to certain groups and to impute to them either special knowledge or special blindness. Moreover, critical theory's treatment of ethnicity is unapologetically asymmetric. The ethnicity of Blacks or Hispanics or Asians is lauded, while the ethnicity of Whites is either treated as something shameful or is denied altogether (many CRTs insist that Whites have no ethnicity because it was abandoned in exchange for a false White racial identity).

Admittedly, there is some justification for this asymmetry. For example, in the immediate aftermath of World War II, as the atrocities of the Nazi regime were exposed, it would have been inappropriate to respond to the grief and solidarity of ethnic Jews with a loud affirmation of the goodness of German ethnicity. Yet it would be equally inappropriate, and frankly unsustainable, to insist that Germans can never again identify as Germans or celebrate their cultural heritage. Indeed, any complete suppression of German identity would be likely to generate a backlash and overcorrection that would eventually cultivate an excessive ethnic pride in young Germans who felt unfairly reviled for a history over which they had no control.

We're seeing something similar in the US today. On the one hand, there is an understandable asymmetry between how phrases like "Black is beautiful" and "White is beautiful" are perceived given US racial history. On the other hand, many young White men have grown up in a world which labels them as oppressors for reasons they can't control. Everyone else is encouraged to celebrate their ethnicity, but they cannot. Prestigious job listings openly encourage applications from every demographic group except straight White men. It's therefore unfortunate, but unsurprising, that there are growing numbers of angry young White men who feel that they are now a victim group who can find sympathy and solidarity only in ethnonationalist organizations.

How do Christians untangle this mess?

First, we should reaffirm that ethnicity can legitimately be celebrated by everyone, not only by people of color.

Here, it's important to distinguish race from ethnicity. White and Black can both be racial categories that lump together groups with entirely different ethnicities like Norwegians, Hungarians, and Australians (all "White") or Ethiopians, Liberians, and Namibians (all "Black"). When White and Black are used as *racial* categories, there is little biblical warrant for celebrating either, because that requires us to invent some pan-ethnic solidarity between extremely different people groups with little in common other than skin color. We might as well attempt to create a "pan-redhead consciousness" that celebrates redheadedness!

However, in an American context, "Black" can also refer to an ethnicity, a particular people group with a shared language, culture, and history—e.g., jazz music, soul food, Juneteenth, the Harlem Renaissance, etc. "Blacks" came to exist as a distinct ethnic group when Africans from various tribes and nations were brought to the Americas as slaves. Here, their very different ancestral origins merged and a new ethnic identity was forged, solidified by the fact that, until the Great Migration of the 1910s and 1920s, the vast majority of Black Americans were geographically concentrated in the Deep South. Thus, it does make biblical sense to celebrate Black ethnicity in various ways.

What many people fail to see is that the label "White American" can also refer to an ethnicity, a particular people with a shared language, culture, and history. Think about the Pilgrims, Conestoga wagons and the Oregon Trail, the Wild West, Ellis Island, country music, casseroles, etc. We fail to see these as elements of an ethnicity because we tend to see them simply as part of our shared American identity. But the two are conflated precisely because America was more than 80 percent White for most of its history!

Two possibilities seem feasible, one long-term and one short-term. Over the long term, White Americans and Black Americans and Hispanic Americans and Asian Americans should all recognize that "American" *is itself an ethnicity that can and should be celebrated.* For far too long, America segregated different ethnic groups such that White Americans and Black Americans and Hispanic Americans and Asian Americans came to develop different identities and sub-ethnicities. But we have always shared a language, a place, a culture, and a history together *as Americans*, and it is high time that we claimed it as ours.

In the short term, though, most of our culture has chosen to valorize the particular heritage and culture of Black Americans, and Hispanic Americans, and Asian Americans. This approach isn't necessarily wrong, but it does not seem workable to fracture the American identity into various subgroups whose ethnicities must be honored while simultaneously insisting that the remainder of Americans (Whites) have no ethnicity at all or only a shameful one that must be minimized or denigrated. Given the racial connotations of "White American," it may be more palatable to celebrate the heritage of "European Americans" or "Anglo Americans." But regardless of the words we use, forcing Whites alone to deny their ethnicity will make them more, not less, susceptible to the enticement of the far right.

With that said, we recognize that White identity discourse and movements are often imbued with racist and bigoted values that are pushing for a White ethnostate, perspectives that we categorically reject and repudiate. At times, certain uses of language become so toxic that one must run from any association with them. So we understand the rhetorical quandary that we're placed in. Yet we emphatically believe that our culture's attempt to solve this problem by ignoring or demonizing White Americans' ethnicity is backfiring, empowering the far right rather than weakening it.

Second, we should reject the idea—popular on both the far left and the far right—that ethnic groups are static and nonoverlapping and should be preserved in some imagined state of purity.

Think for a moment of what it means to be ethnically English. Prior to the Roman conquest in the first century AD, England was ethnically dominated by the Celts. After the fall of Rome, England was dominated by Germanic tribes, which is why English is classified as a Germanic language. Christianity was reintroduced to England in the late sixth century, eventually displacing traditional pagan and druid religions. The Norman Conquest of the eleventh century again dramatically changed the English language through the use of

French by the ruling aristocracy. The shift from monarchy to parliamentary democracy began slowly in 1215 with the signing of the Magna Carta and progressed over the following centuries through the Tudor era until it gradually took its present shape during the nineteenth century. Compared to the whole history of England, its most stereotypical cultural artifacts like tea and cricket (both introduced in the seventeenth century) are relatively modern.

We could perform the same exercise on other people groups and civilizations. How does Egyptian culture and language today compare to that of the ancient Egyptian Empire? Would modern Mexicans feel at home if they were transported to fourteenth-century Mayapan?

Oddly, both the far right and the far left are fixated on drawing hard lines between ethnicities. On the left, accusations of "cultural appropriation" are made whenever a "dominant" culture borrows from or even expresses appreciation for some aspect of a "marginalized" culture. On the right, kinists and ethnonationalists want people groups to remain sealed off from one another genetically, culturally, and geographically. Given the fluidity of peoples and cultures, this rigidity is a pipe dream. That isn't to say that there is no such thing as "the English people" or "the Egyptian people" or the "Mexican people." But, on a historical timeline, most people groups are constantly mixing and changing so that drawing sharp lines for the sake of purity makes little sense.

Finally, Americans in general and Christians in particular should focus on our commonalities more than our differences.

Recall that ethnic groups share a common language, culture, and history. We also saw that ethnic groups are not static but are generated over time through a process of migration, mixing, assimilation, and adaptation. If that's the case, then the label "American" can refer not only to legal citizenship, but also to the distinct ethnicity that has been forged within our borders.

From within the US, it's easy to focus on the distinctions between

"Black Americans" and "White Americans" and "Asian Americans" and "Mexican Americans." However, if you've lived internationally, you probably realize how much we actually have in common. Times of national tragedy (like 9/11) or triumph (like Olympic victories) also show how much we have grown into one people.

Furthermore, for Christians, the idea that we should center our commonalities, rooted in our identity in Christ and unity in the Spirit, over our differences is not merely a suggestion; it is an implication of a genuine embrace of the gospel. In the church, we are united in Christ (John 17:21; 1 Corinthians 12:12). We are commanded to keep the unity of the Spirit (Ephesians 4:3). We do not cease to have an ethnic identity (Revelation 5:9; 7:9), but it must always be radically subordinate to our identity in Christ (Galatians 2:20; 3:28; Philippians 3:4-10). The moment our ethnic identity becomes an obstacle to our friendship, fellowship, or solidarity with fellow Christians, it has become an idol.

HOW CAN WE PROMOTE RACIAL AND ETHNIC UNITY?

Many Christian books are rightly critical of CRT but say far less about how to pursue racial unity. Such a prescription is crucial for the health of the church and for the health of our nation. As Martin Luther King Jr. has reminded us, "We must all learn to live together as brothers [and sisters] or we will all perish together as fools."[29] In this section, we'll provide practical steps you can take to pursue racial unity within your church and your community.

While there is only one race, there are many ethnicities not only across the planet, but in the United States. Recent US Census data (2020) indicates there are nearly 1,500 distinct ethnic and tribal groups in the United States.[30] These groups will share aspects of culture with fellow Americans. But there will also be differences rooted in their particular ethnic (in some instances, tribal) distinctions. These differences, insofar as they are not unrighteous, should be tolerated and even celebrated by any who find them particularly compelling.

This perspective will foster cross-cultural community. In some cases, it will lead to notable enjoyment of things that are not part of one's ethnic background or home culture. For instance, Pat is not Asian (or specifically, Thai) or Indian, but he loves curry, particularly its Thai version. In fact, he is super based and very knowledgeable when it comes to curry and the best restaurants in his area that serve it, to the extent that Neil, who is half-Indian, is an amateur compared to Pat when it comes to curry. Pat's love of curry puts him in proximity to Asian people. His love of curry bleeds over into an appreciation for their culture and various sub-cultures. This has fostered cross-cultural and cross-ethnic community in his life with his next-door neighbors who are from Burma (Karen ethnicity). In a country as diverse as the US, these kinds of positive interactions are beneficial and should be encouraged.

As members of Christ's body, Christians should be at the forefront of racial/ethnic unity. While there has been exponentially more racism from Whites toward Blacks in US history than any other iteration of racism, it is incumbent of all Christians from every ethnicity to be vigilant in repudiating racism and pursuing racial/ethnic unity. Here are 12 action steps, best practices, you can take to increase racial/ethnic unity in the body of Christ and in your local community.

1. Pray. If you are engaging in or exercising racist attitudes, thoughts, or actions, you need to pray and repent. If you need to ask forgiveness from anyone, do it. Pray that God will calibrate your thoughts about race to exactly his thoughts about race. Pray for Christ to enable you to love across difference, to love those who are ethnically different from you. Pray to be salt and light (Matthew 5:13-16) in your community

for issues concerning racism and bigotry. Join or start an ethnically diverse prayer group. Among other things, pray for racial healing and unity in your church and community.

2. Challenge racism when you see it, at both the individual and societal levels. Keep in mind, "the fear of man lays a snare" (Proverbs 29:25), so pray regularly for courage.
3. When a genuinely racist action impacts those around you, be ready to "weep with those who weep" (Romans 12:15).
4. Seek those who are ethnically different from you and get coffee or a bite to eat. Get to know one another. Be intentional about asking questions like, "In your opinion, what are the things I need to be thinking about regarding racism?"
5. Develop ethnically diverse friendships. Do life together. Spend time in each other's homes. Be in it for the long haul.
6. If you attend a church that is largely homogenous with respect to ethnicity, periodically visit churches where the majority who attend are different from you. Stay after the service and converse.
7. Meet with community leaders in your area who have a strong understanding of the racial concerns that exist in your community. Such leaders include the police chief, local government officials, social service workers, homeless shelter and soup kitchen staff, clergy concerned about justice issues, social justice-minded educators, community organizers, various ministries concerned about the under-resourced, nonprofits with similar concerns, etc. Listen to understand.
8. Keeping your safety in mind, peacefully protest where there are clear instances of racism at the institutional level.

9. Visit the National Museum of African American History and Culture in Washington, DC. Be prepared to learn, weep, and pray.
10. Get an understanding of the racial history of your local city and state. Visit any museums, monuments, memorials, plaques commemorating what has happened. Get into edifying conversations.
11. There are certain institutions and social systems that have been racially problematized, such as the prison system and law enforcement. Gain an understanding of the facts, which often differ from what the media reports.
12. Think about your vocation, interests, and hobbies. Find someone with the same vocation, interests, and hobbies but who is of a different ethnicity and develop a connection. Your shared similarities will pave the way for appreciation of some of your differences.

While our list is by no means exhaustive, it is a good start toward dramatically increasing racial/ethnic unity in your church and local community. If this intentional approach is new to you, begin with what seems to be the most accessible. Over time, add more actions. Before long, fostering racial/ethnic connection and community will be a natural part of the rhythms of your life. You will be blessed because of it, and most importantly, God will be glorified.

RACIAL UNITY AND CHRISTIANITY

In this chapter, we've provided a framework for Christians to think about race and ethnicity. We've also explained exactly why the framework provided by CRT is fundamentally flawed. While our nation and the evangelical church have made significant steps toward racial unity, there is still work to be done, which is why CRT has found a foothold in both the culture and the church. When we don't address race adequately and from a biblical perspective, we leave a void that secular ideas rush to fill.

But Christians should care about race for reasons that go far beyond the culture war. One of the main themes of the New Testament is that, in Christ, God is reconciling all people to himself (2 Corinthians 5:19). The salvation that God brought to the nation of Israel has now been extended to people from every tribe, tongue, and nation (Revelation 7:9). Thus, the healing of ethnic enmity and the display of ethnic unity is a sign to the outside world of the power of the gospel (Romans 1:16).

Finally, we provided practical steps that you can take to promote ethnic unity within your community. Jesus' command to love our neighbors is not limited to those who share our ethnicity. Likewise, the church should be a place where we are pursuing unity across ethnic lines. But let's make sure we understand why we're doing so: not because we want virtue points from progressives, but because we love our neighbors and fellow believers and want to display God's glory to and in the nations.

7

GENDER

If critical theory entered the evangelical church through the front door of race, then it also entered the church through the side door of gender. Because feminism predates critical theory and has been part of our culture for almost two centuries, many people don't connect it to the excesses of the Great Awokening. However, as we'll see in this chapter, contemporary feminism is indeed a critical social theory like CRT or queer theory. And as a result, it will display the same incompatibility with Christianity as other critical social theories.

FEMINISM AND GENDER

The history of feminism is often divided into three successive waves.[1]

First-wave feminism began with the Seneca Falls convention of 1848. Led by figures like Susan B. Anthony and Elizabeth Cady Stanton, it focused on women's suffrage (voting rights), the abolition of slavery, and property rights. After the ratification of the Nineteenth Amendment in 1920, which gave women the right to vote, feminism entered a period of relative quiescence until it reemerged in the 1960s.

Second-wave feminism, promoted by philosophers like Simone

de Beauvoir and activists like Gloria Steinem, pushed for women's social and economic freedom. The legislative centerpiece of second-wave feminism was the Equal Rights Amendment, which passed Congress but failed ratification by the states.

Third-wave feminism began in the 1990s in response to allegations of sexual harassment from Anita Hill against future Supreme Court Justice Clarence Thomas at his confirmation hearing. Its central theme was the inclusion of non-White women's perspectives into the feminist movement.

Conventional wisdom among most conservative evangelicals today is that first-wave feminism was basically good and foundationally Christian, while second- and third-wave feminism were more secular and problematic. The actual history, however, is more complicated (and uncomfortable). For example, in 1895, first-wave pioneer Elizabeth Cady Stanton published *The Woman's Bible*, which, on its very first page, made statements like "instead of three male personages [within the Godhead], as generally represented, a Heavenly Father, Mother, and Son would seem more rational," and "The first step in the elevation of woman to her true position [is] the recognition by the rising generation of an ideal Heavenly Mother, to whom their prayers should be addressed, as well as to a Father."[2] Other prominent first-wave feminists embraced free love, female superiority, and various heterodox doctrinal positions.

We raise this issue not to poison the well against feminism, but to emphasize that Christians should be careful to distinguish between their support for particular goals within a movement and their support for the ideology or theology of said movement, a crucial point that we will return to later.

Like critical race theory and queer theory, modern feminism is a critical social theory and analyzes power and oppression along the axis of gender. Consider the four pillars of contemporary critical theory: the social binary, hegemonic power, lived experience, and social justice. We see these four ideas expressed clearly in feminist thought.

First, feminism has always understood women as a collectively subordinated group in need of liberation. Feminist scholar Deborah Cameron writes that despite the historical and geographical diversity of feminist movements, they all share two minimal feminist ideas: "1. That women occupy a subordinate position in society" and "2. That the subordination of women…can and should be changed through political action."[3]

Second, feminism in all its iterations has believed that female emancipation doesn't merely require legal equality, but also necessitates a change in social norms and commonly accepted views of gender. This emphasis grew in importance during feminism's second wave but, as we saw in the Stanton quotes above, was present even in first-wave feminism.

Third, consciousness-raising and the importance of "embodied knowledges" became increasingly central during second-wave feminism. Influenced by New Left thought, feminists turned to Marxist theories of "false consciousness" to explain the resistance they encountered not just from men, but from many women as well. They argued that men who rejected feminism were trying to protect their patriarchal power and privilege, while women who rejected feminism were suffering from internalized misogyny.

Finally, the importance of intersectionality to contemporary feminism cannot be overstated. In fact, feminist scholar Kathy Davis writes, "'intersectionality'—the interaction of multiple identities and experiences of exclusion and subordination—has been heralded as one of the most important contributions to feminist scholarship."[4] Intersectionality does not merely suggest but requires that feminists work for the liberation of all marginalized groups, whether people of color, or the poor, or the disabled, or the LGBTQ community. This insistence is part and parcel to feminist theory. As feminist bell hooks asserts, "eradicating the cultural basis of group oppression would mean that race and class oppression would be recognized as feminist issues with as much relevance as sexism."[5] Such solidarity is especially noticeable in feminist support for the demands of transgender women (i.e., biological men who identify as women) even when they conflict with women's interests (e.g., sex-segregated prisons or bathrooms or sports).

OBJECTIONS TO FEMINISM

Because feminism today is a critical social theory, our criticisms of contemporary critical theory as a whole from chapter 5 will also apply to feminism. However, here, we will also briefly mention some objections specific to feminism before explaining how Christians should think about gender from a biblical perspective.

First, contemporary feminism runs headlong into a biblical understanding of gender because it conceptualizes gender in the same way that critical race theorists conceptualize race. To feminists, gender is a social construct just like race is a social construct to critical race theorists. However, from a biblical perspective, this framework is fundamentally flawed: Race is a social construct, but gender is not. Race is indeed a category created by human beings. But gender is a category built into the fabric of God's good creation (Genesis 1:27). So any theory built on this fundamental misunderstanding of the nature of gender will necessarily be faulty.

Second, contemporary feminism accepts critical theory's incorrect conceptualization of oppression as ideological in character.

We should certainly recognize that in many societies and cultures, women are in fact oppressed and do experience systemic injustice. In some countries, women are denied education, face unimaginably high levels of domestic abuse, violence, and rape, and are sold into sex slavery at alarming rates. Perhaps one of the most glaring examples of the systemic oppression of women is found in sex-selective abortions, which have resulted globally in 200 million "missing" baby girls.[6] Christians should absolutely not reject the idea that the actual oppression of women can and does exist.

However, feminism as a critical social theory does not limit the nature of oppression to overt acts of cruelty and violence; it also sees oppression in norms and systems that value men over women. It is from these restrictive and confining norms that women need to be liberated. Again, we recognize women can face systemic injustice, even in the form of unjust norms and systems. We merely reject the idea that *all* norms are oppressive. Here, feminism comes into conflict with a biblical view of gender and gender roles, which we'll discuss later in the chapter.

Third, feminist theory—even more explicitly than critical race theory—rejects the idea that reason, logic, and objective evidence are the sole or even the primary ways we know truth and instead embraces "other ways of knowing" that are supposedly more aligned with female consciousness. This approach to knowledge has immediate implications for how we read Scripture. Feminist interpreters routinely challenge authorial intent and view attempts to determine the supposed objective meaning of a text as Western and male-centric. They instead commend more liberatory and embodied approaches to interpretation. Obviously, evangelicals should reject these perspectives.

Finally, contemporary feminism—like CRT—is deeply indebted to intersectionality, linking it inextricably to other critical social theories. An intersectional approach is being embraced not only by feminists but by evangelical egalitarians (i.e., evangelicals who deny that there are distinct roles for men or women within the church or within marriage). For example, the evangelical anthology *Discovering Biblical Equality* contains a chapter from Juliany Nieves entitled "When We Were Not Women." In her opening paragraph, she states that evangelical discussions of gender "are characterized by being White centered and male dominated, and often reflective of a privileged socioeconomic class" (p. 597).[7]

Throughout her essay, Nieves issues strident calls for "an intersectional approach," writing: "Unless there is an intersectional approach to decenter Whiteness and maleness from the theological discourse on womanhood and femininity, the conversations will continue to perpetuate the logic of true womanhood as Anglo and middle class" (p. 618); and "[t]he lens of gender is not enough to construct a true egalitarian position. Intersectionality is required" (p. 619).

As we pointed out in chapter 5, scholars can benefit from considering the perspectives of many different interpreters. But it is highly dubious to suggest that our theology will always be limited and blinkered by our privilege and that a "truly catholic approach" must somehow integrate all the (conflicting?) perspectives that emerge from dozens of intersectionally diverse interpreters. We would obviously never claim that White male mathematicians who are confident that 1 + 1 = 2 need to decenter their race and gender lest their equations perpetuate whiteness and patriarchy.

Of course, biblical interpretation is less straightforward than math. But the actual meaning of a text is no less objective than the truth of a math equation! We can remain self-critical and open to new interpretations without suggesting that our race, class, or gender blinds us to the true meaning of Scripture.

All that said, Christians can and should accept some ideas that feminists would also affirm. Human beings, male and female, are both made in God's image and therefore possess equal value and dignity. Some laws do, in fact, treat women unjustly and should be opposed. Men can and do sometimes misuse their power to disparage, make demands of, and abuse women. And cultural narratives can end up shaping our views on gender more than the Bible.

Having explained how contemporary feminism comes into conflict with Christianity, for the remainder of the chapter, we will focus on how Christians should think about gender from a biblical perspective.

WHAT IS GENDER?

Historically, the term *gender* was used to refer to a grammatical convention whereby nouns in some foreign languages—like French and German—were treated as masculine, feminine, or neuter. Because English is not a gendered language, the word *gender* was used as a synonym for *sex* until the mid-twentieth century, when feminists began distinguishing between the two. Sex, they argued, was a biological category, whereas gender was a social category. In other words, they used the word *sex* to refer to one's physical, biological classification as either male or female based on chromosomes, genitalia, and secondary sex characteristics. In contrast, they used the word *gender* to refer to the social categories of masculine and feminine, which dictate culturally acceptable roles, stereotypes, norms, and modes of expression.

By analogy, it is objectively true that some people have light skin and a predominantly European ancestry and that others have dark skin and a predominantly African ancestry. We could refer to these objective facts by speaking about people's ancestry as either European or African. On the other hand, society has simultaneously constructed the category of race, which classifies people as either White or Black. Yet the social construct of race includes various stereotypes, norms, cultural expectations, and acceptable modes of expression that don't follow from the objective fact of someone's ancestry. For example, the main character of the 1992 movie *White Men Can't Jump* is a White basketball hustler who takes advantage of racial stereotypes to scam his opponents. Feminists view gender in the same way: The social construct of gender does not follow from the objective facts of sex.

So how should Christians think about gender?

We can indeed acknowledge that some gender stereotypes or gender norms are socially constructed. For example, most men today would feel awkward expressing their love for poetry, despite the fact that the most well-known poets in history—including King David—were men. Similarly, what is considered masculine or feminine in styles of dress varies considerably across time and culture. An eighteenth-century French male aristocrat who wore bright colors, makeup, leggings, and a wig would not be flouting the gender norms of his culture, unlike a twenty-first-century American man who did the same. Similarly, the reality that men have XY chromosomes doesn't tell us what is considered a masculine hobby in a particular society.

Therefore, we can recognize that there is a difference between biological facts about our sex and the social expectations that supposedly follow from our sex.

However, we should recognize that gender as a social category is and ought to be rooted in sex. God created not only biological sex but ordained the social category of gender as well. The entire narrative of Genesis 1–2 shows that Adam and Eve were not merely different but were designed to be complementary. The two categories of male and female together bear God's image (Genesis 1:27) and are both necessary to perpetuate the human species. God created Eve to meet a need in Adam; he lacked "a helper fit for him" (Genesis 2:18). When he met her, he burst into poetry, declaring, "This at last is bone of my bones and flesh of my flesh; she shall be called Woman, because she was taken out of Man" (Genesis 2:19). The text then explains that this union was not just a one-off event, but a pattern for marriage: "Therefore a man shall leave his father and his mother and hold fast to his wife, and they shall become one flesh" (Genesis 2:24). When asked about divorce in Mark 10:2-9, Jesus himself quoted authoritatively from this narrative.

Again, pay close attention: In the first chapter of the Bible, God creates biological sex. But he also establishes social categories like husband and wife, mother and father, and marriage as the union of male and female. All of these categories are good, natural, and God-ordained.

Of course, human beings don't need the Bible to realize that male and female are different. Every human culture in history has created social categories rooted in biological sex. In the appendix of his book *The Blank Slate*, atheist Harvard psychologist Steven Pinker lists hundreds of "human universals" that are found in every known culture. They include items like "classification of sex," "division of labor by sex," "father and mother, separate kin terms for," and "sex (gender) terminology is fundamentally binary."[8] This universality is hardly surprising, since men and women need each other to have children. Even the handful of cultures that recognize the "third genders" frequently invoked by transgender activists are still not confused about where babies come from!

Of course, there do exist "intersex" individuals with rare biological conditions, including chromosomal abnormalities, that affect their sexual development. These conditions, which occur in roughly less than one-tenth of 1 percent of the population, [9] cause individuals to develop a mixture of male and female biological characteristics. However, intersex people do not represent a third gender, and do not challenge the gender binary. Accordingly, the Intersex Society of North America (ISNA) rejects the idea of a third gender.[10] Gender is a social category rooted in biological sex. Therefore, intersex individuals—whose biological sex is indeterminate—will belong to an indeterminate gender category. Like any person whose biology falls outside the norm, intersex people are made in God's image and possess all the value and dignity of anyone else, rich or old, young or poor, male or female.

In summary, Christians shouldn't merely affirm that God created biological sex, as if male and female were no more than trivial differences like eye color or height. Rather, God created two categories of human being who are joined in marriage to bring children into the world. The distinction between male and female is a basic, inescapable part of being human that every culture in history recognized until five minutes ago, relatively speaking.

Practically speaking, then, should Christians distinguish between biological sex and the social category of gender? Our suggestion is to use the terms *sex* and *gender* synonymously. However, if someone haughtily informs you that sex and gender are different, you don't need to argue the point. Rather, you can explain that it's possible to distinguish gender, the social expression of biological sex, from biological sex while still correctly maintaining that gender is rooted in biological sex.

In precisely the same way, we can acknowledge that the social categories of adult and child are expressed in different ways by various cultures. Moreover, the exact age at which a child becomes an adult is not determined by biology. Yet it doesn't follow that "child" and "adult" are completely arbitrary categories that can mean anything we want them to mean such that a 46-year-old man can decide to identify as a six-year-old.[11] Instead, these categories are rooted in age and development.

DOES THE BIBLE PRESCRIBE GENDER ROLES?

Evangelicals take two broad views on gender roles. All evangelicals believe that both men and women are made in God's image, equal in value and dignity, and coheirs of salvation. Beyond this important, fundamental agreement, there is disagreement over whether there are distinct roles for men and women.

Egalitarianism is the belief that there are no unique gender roles for men and women in the church or in the family. *Complementarianism* is the belief that there are unique gender roles for men and women in the church and family. First, complementarians believe that in marriage, husbands are called to exercise loving headship and wives are called to loving submission. Second, they believe that in the church, the office of elder (or pastor) is limited to qualified men.

There is a great deal of debate within the church over these two positions, particularly because the underlying assumptions of feminism have framed any role distinctions between men and women as oppressive and sexist. In what follows, we'll give a brief explanation of why complementarianism is correct and biblical and will then explain why this discussion matters in light of the growth of feminism.

Complementarians point to several passages of Scripture to support the view that men and women have different roles. The two most relevant are the following:

> Wives, submit to your own husbands, as to the Lord. For the husband is the head of the wife even as Christ is the head of the church, his body, and is himself its Savior. Now as the church submits to Christ, so also wives should submit in everything to their husbands.
>
> Husbands, love your wives, as Christ loved the church and gave himself up for her, that he might sanctify her, having cleansed her by the washing of water with the word, so that he might present the church to himself in splendor, without spot or wrinkle or any such thing, that she might be holy and without blemish. In the same way husbands should love their wives as their own bodies. He who loves his wife loves himself. For no one ever hated his own flesh, but nourishes and cherishes it, just as Christ does the church, because we are members of his body. "Therefore a man shall leave his father and mother and hold fast to his wife, and the two shall become one flesh." This mystery is profound, and I am saying that it refers to

> Christ and the church. However, let each one of you love his wife as himself, and let the wife see that she respects her husband (Ephesians 5:22-33).

> Let a woman learn quietly with all submissiveness. I do not permit a woman to teach or to exercise authority over a man; rather, she is to remain quiet. For Adam was formed first, then Eve; and Adam was not deceived, but the woman was deceived and became a transgressor. Yet she will be saved through childbearing—if they continue in faith and love and holiness, with self-control (1 Timothy 2:11-15).

Complementarians will also point to other passages like Genesis 2:16-18, Genesis 2:21-24, Genesis 3:1-13, 1 Corinthians 11:7-9, Colossians 3:18-19, Titus 2:3-5, and 1 Peter 3:1-7 to support their view.

The *locus classicus* for the egalitarian view is Galatians 3:25-29, particularly Galatians 3:28:

> Now that faith has come, we are no longer under a guardian, for in Christ Jesus you are all sons of God, through faith. For as many of you as were baptized into Christ have put on Christ. There is neither Jew nor Greek, there is neither slave nor free, there is no male and female, for you are all one in Christ Jesus. And if you are Christ's, then you are Abraham's offspring, heirs according to promise.

Egalitarians will also point to other passages (including some of the same ones as complementarians!) like 1 Corinthians 7:3-5, 1 Corinthians 12:7, Ephesians 5:21, 1 Peter 3:1-7, and 1 Peter 4:10-11 to support their view.

Obviously, we can't delve into the detailed arguments on both sides here, and we encourage readers to examine these passages for themselves.[12] However, there are three basic reasons to affirm the complementarian position.

First, the existence of prescriptive "egalitarian" passages is consistent with complementarianism because complementarians explicitly affirm that men and women are equal in value and dignity. In contrast, the existence of prescriptive "non-egalitarian" passages is inconsistent with egalitarianism because—on the egalitarian view—there are no distinct roles for men and women. To put it another way, complementarians don't have to explain away passages that affirm, for example, that men and women are both coheirs of salvation. But egalitarians do have to explain away passages that seem to affirm that only men can be elders.

Second, the contexts of passages invoked by both complementarians and egalitarians to support their views are important. If we read through all the passages listed, we'll find that the contexts of "egalitarian" passages are discussions about our spiritual standing before God or our duties of mutual love and obligation. In contrast, the contexts of "non-egalitarian" passages are discussions about the specific roles played by men and women in the church or family. In other words, equality is found precisely where complementarians believe it actually exists, and distinction is found precisely where complementarians believe it actually exists.

Finally, egalitarian arguments often prove too much. For example, egalitarians argue that the asymmetric commands in Ephesians 5:22-33 ("wives, submit to your own husbands…husbands, love your wives") must be understood in the context of the mutual submission commanded in Ephesians 5:21, "submitting to one another, out of reverence for Christ." Yet this same passage of Scripture commands children to "obey [their] parents in the Lord, for this is right." If Ephesians 5:21 overturns any unique obligation that a wife has to submit to her husband, then it also must overturn any unique obligation that children have to obey their parents. Few people would accept this reasoning.

While exegetical arguments that properly interpret the text of Scripture must remain preeminent in this discussion, a larger issue looms in the background. We often bring to the text our unspoken assumption that hierarchies are necessarily oppressive. In some sense, this view comes naturally to Americans, who have a cultural predisposition toward democracy, equality, and egalitarianism. But is this belief correct?

HOW SHOULD CHRISTIANS THINK ABOUT HIERARCHY AND AUTHORITY?

Despite twenty-first-century attitudes toward hierarchy and authority, both are an inescapable part of a biblical worldview.

To begin with, God is portrayed as the royal sovereign over all the universe from Genesis to Revelation. In the Old Testament, God is referred to as king (Psalm 29:10; 47:7; Isaiah 6:5; Malachi 1:14) and Lord (Genesis 15:2; Exodus 4:10; Deuteronomy 3:14; Judges 6:15; Psalm 86:5) hundreds of times.

To put it bluntly, the universe is not a democracy; it is an absolute monarchy. God is sovereign and does whatever he pleases (Psalm 115:3). Yes, God always does what is right and good (Psalm 145:9). Yes, he is the father to the fatherless and a defender of widows (Psalm 68:5). Yes, human beings have genuine authority under God and are called to have dominion over the earth (Genesis 1:26-28). But we are not autonomous and independent. Rather, we are God's creatures and his servants who were created to love and obey our Creator and to do his will (Deuteronomy 11:1; John 14:15; 1 John 5:3).

Not only does the Bible assume the absolute authority of God over man, it also assumes the legitimacy of earthly authority. Christians are commanded to submit to their elders. Wives are commanded to submit to their husbands. Citizens are commanded to submit to their rulers. Servants are commanded to submit to their masters. Children are commanded to submit to their parents.

Yes, submission is to be intelligent and qualified; we should never submit to commands to sin. Yes, any authority we possess is derivative and not absolute; none of us is to demand absolute allegiance from anyone else. But neither are any of the relationships we listed wholly symmetric. There is a genuine hierarchy of authority between God and humans, rulers and citizens, parents and children, husbands and wives. The Bible is radical not because it abolishes hierarchy, but because Jesus redefines leadership in terms of service. For example, Jesus told his disciples, "Whoever would be great among you must be your servant, and whoever would be first among you must be slave of all" (Mark 10:43-44). Here, Jesus did not reject the idea that the church would include roles of leadership, but insisted that the greatest leaders should be the greatest servants.

Ironically, both the far left and the far right view hierarchy as the wholesale subjugation of the individual. The far left thinks wholesale subjection is a bad thing and therefore wants to destroy hierarchy. The far right thinks wholesale subjection is a good thing and therefore wants complete obedience to the fascist state. In contrast, Jesus saw hierarchy as a means by which legitimate authority is exercised for the good of those under that authority. Jesus himself is the perfect model of biblical leadership. He is the King of kings and the Lord of lords (Revelation 17:14), yet he came not to be served but to serve and to give his life as a ransom for many (Matthew 20:28).

The underlying assumptions of feminism have made the idea of submission particularly distasteful to women. Human sinfulness has also given women many legitimate reasons to fear the domination of men. Indeed, part of the curse of Genesis 3:16 was that marriage would turn into a power struggle: Wives would desire to rule over their husbands, and husbands would, in turn, rule harshly over their wives. But, in Christ, the curse can be reversed as both husband and wife submit to God's authority and his design for marriage.

One way for Christians to rediscover the goodness of authority and submission within marriage is to recognize our acceptance of it elsewhere. For example, many men and women who are uncomfortable with submission within marriage nonetheless submit to their managers at work. Similarly, men and women with managerial roles who would view authority within marriage as inherently abusive have no problem giving instructions to their employees.

If we so casually accept authority and submission at work, even when our managers and employees dislike us, why would authority and submission be anathema within marriage, a relationship in which our spouse loves us and is committed to us? Wives, you'll meekly submit to the capricious whims of your boss, but bristle at the idea that you'd submit to your husband who pours out his life to serve his family? Husbands, you'll use your authority at work to provide direction to your team, but shudder at the idea of leading your wife and children spiritually? Why is our thinking so clouded on this issue?

A final, and increasingly prominent, area in which Christians fail to have a biblical view of authority and hierarchy is with regard to the role of parents in the lives of their children. One reason for this failure is the secular culture's view of children.

Parental Authority

In 2013, MSNBC analyst and political scientist Melissa Harris-Perry said, "We have to break through our kind of private idea that kids belong to their parents, or kids belong to their families, and recognize that kids belong to whole communities."[13]

Harris-Perry's statement received national attention and a degree of pushback. Her willingness to declare such a perspective publicly and forthrightly signaled a growing ideological trend, a trend that challenged conventional thinking that children belong to their parents and are therefore first and foremost subject to their parents' authority and direction.

The critical tradition sees the world through the lens of power along the vector of an oppressor/oppressed binary in which children are positioned as oppressed by their oppressor parents. This discourse is designed to influence society to view and treat children as adults in the name of agency and respect for children. Such efforts are also a dominant theme in queer theory, a prominent critical social theory committed to the deconstruction of norms (sexual and otherwise) and the destabilization of social, cultural, and political institutions, structures, traditions, and systems that establish and reinforce what is considered to be normal and normative.[14,15]

In contrast to the narrative promoted by critical theory, Christians should insist that parents have not only the right, but the authority and the duty to care for, instruct, guide, and discipline their children. The critical tradition attempts to eliminate hierarchies and frame adults and children in an oppressor/oppressed binary in which children should be given emancipation and agency from parental authority and societal constraints. E. Kay M. Tisdall argues that "childism," which "recognizes that embedded power relations [in society] privilege adult norms," may be tied to "systematic discrimination against or disadvantages for children that bring age into assessments of *intersectional* oppression [her emphasis]." Childism is defined as "societal prejudice against children, akin to racism, sexism, and anti-Semitism."[16] Via this reasoning, Tisdall and Kristina Konstantoni argue that "the physical punishment of children by their parents/caregivers" is one of many "important children's rights issues."[17]

Queer theory's pervasive deconstruction project also includes efforts to "eroticise children in an ethical way."[18] The combined goals of both movements ultimately put pressure on society to dismantle age-appropriate laws, paving the way for the decriminalization and normalization of pedophilia. This reality alone, along with many other reasons, underscores that Christians must be unequivocal and undaunted in asserting their authority over the direction and control of their children.

The case for parental authority is rooted in revelation, natural law, and social science.

First, the Bible insists that parents have *authority* over their children by its repeated injunctions that children are to obey their parents. Colossians 3:20 states, "Children, obey your parents in everything, for this pleases the Lord" (cf. Ephesians 6:1). The Bible emphasizes that parents have *direction* over their children by exhorting children to listen to their parents' instruction and follow their teaching. Proverbs 1:8-9 states, "Hear, my son, your father's instruction, and forsake not your mother's teaching." The Bible demonstrates that parents have *control* over their children by its charge to parents to discipline their children when they disobey. Proverbs 22:15 states, "Folly is bound up in the heart of a child, but the rod of discipline drives it far from him."

In regard to parents' jurisdiction over their children, pastor Paul David Tripp asserts,

> God does call you to exercise daily control over your children...you must give them God's law and the household rules that apply those laws to daily living. You must constantly teach them what is right and how to live right. You must step in again and again and protect your kids from themselves...You must structure their days and teach them how to invest in their future. You must impart wisdom to them and teach them what it looks like to live it out. You must confront them when they do what is wrong. You must discipline them in the face of their rebellion. To do these things you must be in control and you must exercise faithful control over your children.[19]

Many parents today, even evangelical parents, have bought into the lie that discipline is contrary to love. The Bible says exactly the opposite. The author of the book of Hebrews reminds Christians that "the Lord disciplines the one he loves, and chastises every son whom he receives" (Hebrews 12:6). Discipline demonstrates the presence, not the absence, of fatherly love. Children crave boundaries, structure, and rules. To provide them is to promote their welfare and flourishing.

What's more, distraction or diversion from bad behavior should never replace loving but candid rebuke. Children (and adults) need to be taught that we live in a moral universe with categories of right and wrong, where actions have consequences. The gospel is not that God ignores our sin, but that God loves us in spite of our sin and sent Jesus to die for us. The primary goal of discipline is not retribution, but training. We want our children to grow in self-control, patience, virtue, and dependence on God. That will never happen if we refuse to confront their sinful hearts and their sinful actions.

Similarly, children need to be taught that they are not the ultimate authority in their lives. Their relationship to their parents (and especially to their father) will inevitably shape their picture of God. If they are led to believe that they are in charge and that the universe revolves around them, they will bristle at or reject the idea that God is actually in charge and that the universe revolves around him. They must come to see that their earthly father, like their heavenly Father, is just and good, firm and loving, authoritative and kind. How great is the task of fatherhood! Christian adults obviously ought to embrace these same truths!

Of course, discipline and the exercise of authority are only part of parenting. In chapter 9, we will say much more about the importance of prayer, encouragement, praise, and communication. But we cannot abdicate our genuine God-given roles as our children's primary authorities, guides, and teachers.

Second, natural law indicates that children belong to their parents and are to be subject to their authority. What is natural law? Theologian and ethicist Andrew Walker offers a helpful definition that is both thorough and succinct. He states:

> Natural law is the God ordained, God upheld system of moral order engraved upon an image bearer's conscience that enables them to rationally perceive moral goods and moral wrongs by interacting with their world through sapiential [i.e., rational] investigation. The natural law directs rational creatures to know what actions to do and what goods to fulfill consistent with their natural and supernatural ends, and correspondingly, what actions to avoid and vices to shun. The principles of natural law morality are principles that have no prior proof of their intelligibility apart from obedience to these norms and the experiences of these goods as goods and ends pursued for their own sake.[20]

Since the world began to this very moment, billions and billions of parents have known, without having to be told or taught, that the responsibility to take care of their children is theirs and theirs alone. That at the end of the day, they are ultimately responsible for the safety and well-being of their children. The parent knows this in his or her conscience. This is the natural law at work.

To unpack natural law a bit further and to drive the point home that (under God) parents have preeminent authority over their children and not the state, societal stakeholders, or other human beings, especially strangers, we must understand there is a profound ontological relationship between *special obligations*, *authority*, and *rights*. Melissa Moschella, philosophy professor at The Catholic University of America, states:

> There are three highly interconnected elements within natural law theory that are particularly important for my understanding of parental rights: the notion of obligation, the notion of rights, and the notion of authority...parental

> rights...are coextensive with parental authority which is coextensive with the special obligations the parents have to foster the overall well-being of their children.[21]

And crucially, what is the special obligation that parents have towards their children rooted in? The "biological bond between parent and child."[22]

This relationship between rights, authority, and obligation establishes that children—whether biological or adopted—belong to their parents and are under their primary direction. No other entity—not the state, not other people—has a natural right to disrupt this reality. May we fight to keep this perspective a cultural good in our society.

Finally, we should take up this fight not only because it is true and right but also because social science "research clearly demonstrates that family structure matters for children, and the family structure that helps children the most is a family headed by two biological parents in a low-conflict marriage."[23] If we love our neighbor, we will use the relational, social, and political means at our disposal to protect, promote, and strengthen the optimal environment for children's growth and development: the nuclear family.

HOW SHOULD CHRISTIANS THINK ABOUT #METOO?

In chapter 2, we discussed some of the valid concerns of the #MeToo movement. Namely, that sexual abuse is a grievous and widespread sin, that allegations of abuse are often mishandled, and that power dynamics are a real phenomenon. However, many people aligned with the #MeToo movement also made serious mistakes that Christians should not repeat. In what follows, we will offer some important correctives to these aspects of the #MeToo movement.

First, the slogans #BelieveWomen and #BelieveAllWomen should not be used to place women's testimony beyond the reach of scrutiny.

Yes, we do generally believe people's testimonies. If an acquaintance tells us that a reckless driver hit his car, we don't immediately doubt him. This trust is even more justified if the testimony is offered by someone whom we know to be trustworthy. Moreover, activists will point out that victims of abuse face tremendous social and psychological barriers to coming forward, which means that we ought to give their testimony even more credence than we accord to other claims. In the same way, if we know that a whistleblower will likely be fired for his accusations, it makes his testimony that much more credible.

On the other hand, the credence we give toward a testimony should not prevent us from seeking confirmation, objective evidence, or counter-testimony. This is especially true if legal redress is being requested. All things being equal, we tend to believe the man who says that his car was totaled by a reckless driver. But if he then tells us that the reckless driver is our employee and demands that we fire her, we would first want to hear her side of the story and examine the available evidence.

Second, feminist and activist literature often reduces sexual ethics to consent; any sexual behavior of any kind between consenting adults is viewed as morally acceptable. However, this view is incorrect. There are many consensual sexual practices that the Bible condemns, such as premarital sex, adultery, polygamy, and homosexuality. Thus, while non-consensual sex is obviously sinful, consensual sex is also sinful if it occurs outside the confines of marriage.

Third, power dynamics are real, but they do not render one party completely free from moral obligations. This discussion is connected to feminist understandings of consent. An important example is how some feminists understand sex between an employer and an employee. If a male boss has sex with his female employee, many feminists will insist that the sex was, by definition, non-consensual because of power imbalances between men and women and between employers and employees. Thus, the man raped the woman even if she gave what we would otherwise interpret as consent (e.g., verbal permission, affirmation, and even encouragement).

In contrast, Christians should parse this situation differently. Yes, the boss abused his power. Yes, the woman may have felt pressure to comply. Yes, refusing his advances might have cost her job. But no, power imbalances do not render her incapable of consent. And to the extent that she willingly participated, she is not free from sin, even if his sin was substantially greater.

Here, it helps to recognize that coercion and culpability come in degrees. A woman who is merely propositioned to have sex without any coercion is fully culpable if she participates. A woman who is violently assaulted has no culpability whatsoever. But what about a woman who is told that she will be promoted if she agrees to sex? What if she feels pressured, but neither her job nor her safety is ever threatened? Or what if the genders are reversed and a married male employee is propositioned by his unmarried female employer? Is he automatically guiltless for whatever happens?

In her book *#ChurchToo*, Emily Allison writes about a girl named Shauna who had sex with her boyfriend Bryan because he said he would break up with her if she didn't, and "the fear of losing [him] overcame her." Allison writes: "*Bryan is actually a rapist*...If someone doesn't want to have sex with you but you convince them to have sex with you anyway using threats and fear, that is rape."[24] In light of the fact that Shauna consented, this is incorrect. While Bryan's behavior was immoral, it was not rape. And while he bears the primary moral responsibility for the couple's sin, Shauna also bears some moral responsibility.

Finally, someone may legitimately ask, "Why all this nit-picking over culpability and agency and standards of evidence? The horror of sexual abuse is so great and the church has so mishandled it that we should only be talking about how we can be better allies."

We understand this objection but believe it is misplaced.

First, truth matters. Like critical race theory, a great deal of feminist discourse within #MeToo encourages a posture that treats women as infallible and perpetually victimized. Therefore, women who have experienced legitimate harassment and abuse can be sucked into an echo chamber in which their every emotion, every fear, and every suspicion is only ever affirmed and validated. Moreover, #MeToo activism is suffused with the faulty ideological assumptions of critical theory. For example, the National Sexual Violence Resource Center's page on rape prevention states:

> Primary prevention [of sexual violence] requires that we make the connection between all forms of oppression (including racism, sexism, homophobia, ableism, adultism, ageism, and others) and how these create a culture in which inequality thrives and violence is seen as normal. Effective prevention efforts utilize prevention theories to change communities, shift social norms, end oppression, and promote norms of equity, consent, and safety for all.[25]

The #MeToo movement's official webpage offers resources like "Healing Justice Practice Spaces: A How-To Guide," which aims to create "an all-gender, all-bodied, inclusive and accessible space" by "centering black and brown/disabled and chronically ill/queer and trans voices." Their "healing justice practice spaces" offer "first aid, counseling and crisis support, mediation services, massage therapy, acupuncture, energy work, herbal therapy, divination, art therapy, nutritional counseling, and yoga."[26]

This subject is extremely sensitive, because victims of abuse should be treated with kindness, gentleness, and sensitivity. But at some point, they also need to be warned to exercise discernment and to seek counsel from godly Christian leaders who will support them while also shepherding them wisely.

Second, teaching children, especially girls, that they have moral agency is a source of empowerment. Constantly harping on "gendered power imbalances" subtly teaches girls and women that they are perennially powerless victims. It's important to teach them the counternarrative that they are daughters of the King of kings. They have value. They can say no. They can push back. They can choose to do what is right, no matter what pressure is applied to them.

Finally, both women and men need to take ownership of their own sin. If they do not, there will be spiritual and temporal consequences. For example, a woman who repeatedly gets drunk and has sex with strangers is not only sinning but is putting herself in dangerous situations. It absolutely does not follow that if she is raped, she is to be blamed for the rape. We repeat: She is absolutely not to be blamed for the rape. But it does follow that if we truly love her, we will call her to repentance for her own actions, even though she is in no way responsible for the actions of others. Feeding her the lie that—as a woman—she has only ever been a victim and that anyone who tells her to repent is merely trying to control her body is likely to harden her toward her own sin and self-destructive behavior.

CONTEMPORARY FEMINISM AND CHRISTIANITY

Contemporary feminism is deeply indebted to the fundamentally false assumptions of critical theory. Its understanding of gender set the stage for the eruption of queer theory, which has convinced vast swaths of women that it is somehow empowering for them to be bulldozed on a rugby field by a 6'1" biological male. Legitimate fear of controlling, abusive husbands has made both men and women flee from God's design for authority and submission within marriage. The idea that hierarchy is inherently oppressive has led parents to abandon their rightful and crucial role in teaching, disciplining, and guiding their children, to the great detriment of the children themselves. The horrors of sexual assault and the abuse of power exposed by #MeToo have led many to abandon procedural justice, evidentiary standards, and female moral agency.

In all these areas, what is needed is not a return to "traditional values" per se but a return to the Bible. The Bible, not feminism, is what teaches us that men and women are equal in value and dignity, coheirs of salvation, and gifted for service in the body of Christ. The Bible, not patriarchy, is what teaches us that men and women are called to different roles in marriage and in the family, that authority is not inherently oppressive, and that leadership is to be exercised not to dominate but to serve. May both men and women embrace their genders as a gift from God and embrace his design as wise, good, and life-giving.

8

SEXUALITY

If the sexual revolution began with the widespread introduction of hormonal birth control in the 1960s, then a second sexual revolution may have begun with the Supreme Court's *Obergefell* decision in 2015, which legalized same-sex marriage throughout the United States. Today, modes of sexual and gender expression that were viewed as immoral and even unthinkable a few decades ago are increasingly accepted publicly. Pride Month, which celebrates LGBTQ+ identities every June, is turning into a secular holiday that receives substantially more media coverage and corporate attention than some federal holidays. When was the last time Target dramatically changed its social media profile and in-store merchandise for Washington's Birthday or Veterans Day?

We will spare readers the graphic details, but Pride events are becoming more and more open about promoting behavior that even many gays and lesbians find abhorrent. In 2021, *The Washington Post* published an op-ed piece entitled "Yes, kink belongs at Pride. And I want my kids to see it."[1] Nudity and even public sex acts have taken place during Pride parades in multiple cities.[2] Viral videos of "family friendly" drag shows reveal transgender strippers dancing in front of toddlers.

To understand this sudden, dramatic shift in accepted standards of public sexual morality, we have to understand queer theory, the academic discipline undergirding these phenomena.

QUEER THEORY AND SEXUALITY

Queer theory is far more deeply indebted to postmodern philosophy than many other critical social theories. Postmodern philosophers like Michel Foucault did not merely attempt to discover how particular truth claims served to advance the power of the ruling class, but suggested that truth itself was merely a manifestation of power. Queer theory embraces this claim, particularly as it pertains to sexuality and gender.

In the previous chapter, we saw how second-wave feminists divorced the biological category of sex from the social category of gender. Queer theorists take this split several steps further, insisting that sex and gender are merely two of many independent categories, that all such categories are unstable and fluid, and that all norms must be deconstructed and dismantled.

Queer theory does not only divorce sex from gender, but also fractures gender into multiple other categories, like gender expression (how you socially express your gender), gender identity (how you conceive of your own gender), and sexual orientation (which gender you're attracted to). This understanding of gender and sexuality is demonstrated by popular teaching infographics like the Genderbread Person[3] or the Gender Unicorn,[4] which bifurcate the sex binary into multiple independent spectra.

Even these new categories are incredibly unstable and fluid. The rapid evolution of the infographics mentioned above is a good illustration of this phenomenon and is worth considering in more detail.

Cartoonist Sam Killerman originally created the Genderbread Person in January 2012. The infographic showed a yellow cartoon gingerbread person with icons identifying four categories: gender identity, gender expression, biological sex, and sexual orientation. Each category was represented by a single double-headed arrow—e.g., gender identity ran from "woman" on the left to "genderqueer" in the middle to "man" on the right. Two months later, Killerman released Genderbread Person 2.1. Now the four categories were each represented by two separate single-headed arrows that began on the left and pointed right—e.g., gender identity started on the left with "Nongendered" and then ran along an arrow toward "Woman-ness" or along a separate, parallel arrow toward "Man-ness." Genderbread Person 3.3 was posted in 2015 with several updates, including the bifurcation of the single "sexual orientation" category into two new categories: "sexually attracted to" and "romantically attracted to." The most recent edition, version 4.0, was created in 2018 and includes a sixth category, a set of checkboxes labelled "Sex assigned at birth" (see Figure 5).

A rival infographic, the Gender Unicorn, was created in 2015 in order to "recognize genders outside of the western gender binary, which the Genderbread Person does not" and to correct "several other issues with this graphic such as the use of the inaccurate term 'biological sex.'"[5]

While it might be tempting to dismiss these infographic cartoons as esoteric internet artifacts with little real-world impact, that would be a mistake. These concepts are indeed shaping the way that young people think about gender and sexuality, with concrete consequences.

For example, queer theorists debate whether sexual orientation should by defined in terms of sex or gender (i.e., should a lesbian be defined as a woman who is attracted to biological women, or as a woman who is attracted to anyone with a female gender identity?). In 2021, the BBC ran an article entitled "The lesbians who feel pressured to have sex and relationships with trans women."[6] The subtitle of the article summarizes its content: "Is a lesbian transphobic if she

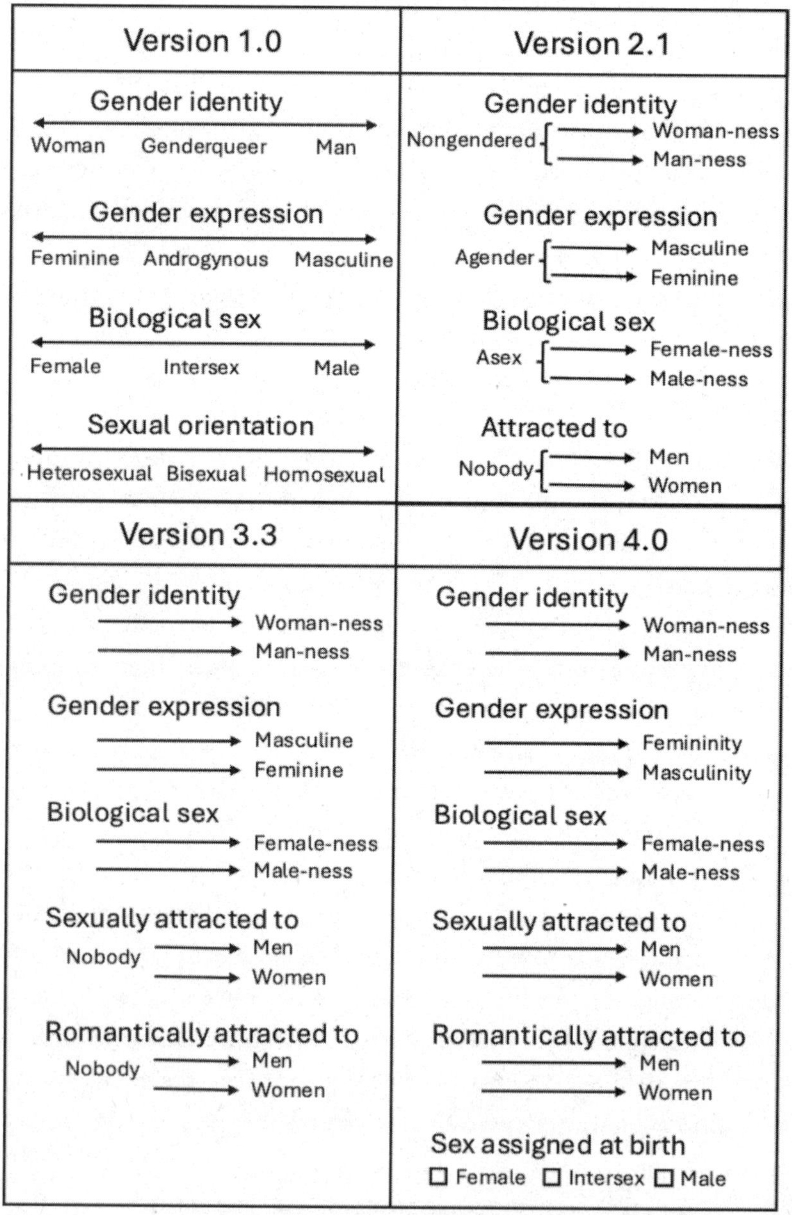

Version 1.0

Gender identity
Woman ⟷ Genderqueer ⟷ Man

Gender expression
Feminine ⟷ Androgynous ⟷ Masculine

Biological sex
Female ⟷ Intersex ⟷ Male

Sexual orientation
Heterosexual ⟷ Bisexual ⟷ Homosexual

Version 2.1

Gender identity
Nongendered → Woman-ness
Nongendered → Man-ness

Gender expression
Agender → Masculine
Agender → Feminine

Biological sex
Asex → Female-ness
Asex → Male-ness

Attracted to
Nobody → Men
Nobody → Women

Version 3.3

Gender identity
→ Woman-ness
→ Man-ness

Gender expression
→ Masculine
→ Feminine

Biological sex
→ Female-ness
→ Male-ness

Sexually attracted to
Nobody → Men
→ Women

Romantically attracted to
Nobody → Men
→ Women

Version 4.0

Gender identity
→ Woman-ness
→ Man-ness

Gender expression
→ Femininity
→ Masculinity

Biological sex
→ Female-ness
→ Male-ness

Sexually attracted to
→ Men
→ Women

Romantically attracted to
→ Men
→ Women

Sex assigned at birth
☐ Female ☐ Intersex ☐ Male

Figure 5–The evolution of the Genderbread Person

does not want to have sex with trans women? Some lesbians say they are increasingly being pressured and coerced into accepting trans women as partners—then shunned and even threatened for speaking out." This real-world phenomenon follows directly from queer theory's reasoning about sex, gender, and sexuality.

However, queer theory is not content to only problematize the categories of sex and gender (and gender expression and sexual orientation). It is also committed to a much larger project of destabilizing all norms. As queer scholar Sara Ahmed asserts, "For some queer theorists, this is what makes 'the perverse' a useful starting point for thinking about the 'disorientations' of queer, and how it can contest not only heteronormative assumptions, but also social conventions and orthodoxies in general."[7] Consequently, queer theory sees all binaries, including the gender binary, as restrictive and arbitrary social constructs that must be dismantled.

The most troubling consequence of this unbridled deconstructive impulse relates to queer theory's ambivalent attitude toward pedophilia. Queer theorist Annamarie Jagose writes:

> Variously referred to as intergenerational sex, child abuse, man-boy love and paedophilia, even the semantic continuum of terms used to describe the concept evokes a variety of positions in a debate structured overwhelmingly by such issues as consent, power and the legal definition of childhood...the issue of intergenerational sex continues to be debated vigorously in many gay and lesbian communities. The protection of children is deemed by some to be ethically crucial to the development of gay identity, but is dismissed by others as "erotic hysteria" (Rubin, 1993:6). What is the status of different, and arbitrary, age-of-consent laws? Do children have a sexuality and a right to sexual agency? Why is age—unlike, say, race or class—understood as a

> sexualized power-differential protected by law? Is it possible to eroticise children in an ethical way? These are questions commonly raised—and by no means yet resolved—in the controversy over intergenerational sex.[8]

When it comes to the acceptance of pedophilia, queer theorists' reasoning—though horrific—is logical. If we agree that all binaries are arbitrary social constructs that need to be dismantled, why not dismantle the adult-child binary? In the same way that women were once deprived of sexual agency and freedom by labelling them as "weak" or "pure" or "vulnerable," aren't we depriving children of sexual agency and freedom by labelling them as "weak" or "pure" or "vulnerable"? If we can't—as a society—distinguish between the culturally universal categories of male and female, how can we distinguish between the much more culturally variable categories of adult and child?

Most Christians realize in a general way that queer theory is incompatible with Christianity, but they don't always realize the extent of the incompatibility.

WHAT IS THE BIBLICAL SEXUAL ETHIC?

In a culture that has come completely unmoored from traditional understandings of gender and sexuality, it's sometimes intimidating to advance a biblical sexual ethic. Two points should give us confidence.

First, we should recognize that the biblical sexual ethic has *always* been countercultural and revolutionary. In the ancient world, religious prostitution was common. Male and female gods had sex with one another and with humans. Kings acquired large harems and concubines. The practices of homosexuality, incest, and even bestiality were widespread. In contrast, Mosaic law forbade and condemned these behaviors. While Israel's patriarchs and many of her kings practiced polygamy, these unions were always portrayed as ending in disaster.

By the time of Jesus' ministry, polygamy had virtually disappeared from Israel. However, there was an ongoing debate over divorce within Judaism, with some rabbis granting wide latitude for husbands to divorce their wives for virtually any reason. Homosexuality, prostitution, and pederasty (sexual abuse of children by adults) were still widespread in the Greco-Roman world. In this context, Jesus insisted on complete abstinence outside of marriage and complete monogamy within the lifelong marriage covenant. Once again, the Bible's sexual ethic was intensely countercultural.

In other words, we are not facing new resistance, but merely the resurgence of resistance that has always existed.

Second, we can appeal to Jesus himself in defense of a biblical sexual ethic. Despite rejecting Christianity, non-Christians often have a fairly positive view of Jesus (in theory) and are hesitant to denounce his teachings. Yet when asked about the permissibility of divorce, Jesus appeals to the Genesis account to argue that marriage is a lifelong union between a man and a woman (Matthew 19:1-11; Mark 10:1-12) that can only be dissolved in response to adultery. He warns that not only is adultery a sin, but that looking lustfully at a woman is a sin (Matthew 5:27-30). And in Mark 7:21, he names *porneia* (a catch-all Greek term for sexual immorality) alongside theft and murder as a sin for which we need forgiveness.

Although Christians should recognize that all Scripture is inspired by God (2 Timothy 3:16), it can help to show non-Christians that our views on sex and gender do not only and ultimately come from Paul or Peter, but from Jesus. With that said, we of course recognize that the words of Paul and Peter and every biblical author are all divinely inspired and can all be equally trusted (2 Timothy 3:16). We are merely pointing to a tactic that may help you with non-Christians who have a distinct affinity for what they feel Jesus directly said over and above other biblical writers.

Over the next few pages, we want to offer you an introduction to the biblical sexual ethic. Over the last 25 years, Pat has at times been asked to counsel professing evangelical Christians who attended conservative evangelical or fundamentalist churches yet were engaging in various forms of sexual sin, including pornography, premarital sex, and adultery with little to no compunction. This reality signals that many evangelicals and fundamentalists do not have God's perspective on the seriousness of sexual sin. Moreover, while sexual sin is sometimes contextualized from the pulpit as a male problem, this is a serious error. Both men and women face and succumb to sexual temptation.

At the outset of our review of a biblical sexual ethic, we want to immediately disabuse our readers of the spurious notion that the Christian faith is prudish about sex. In fact, the opposite is the case. Sex rightly understood and rightly experienced is righteous, beautiful, and full of intense, overwhelming pleasure. This cannot be overstated. The Song of Solomon is unadulterated and unapologetic in this regard. It does not blush in its description of erotic pleasure given and received by the husband and wife.

The book begins with a woman saying of her beloved, "Let him kiss me with the kisses of his mouth! For your love is better than wine; your anointing oils are fragrant; your name is oil poured out; therefore virgins love you. Draw me after you; let us run. The king has brought me into his chambers" (Song of Solomon 1:2-4). She goes on, "As an apple tree among the trees of the forest, so is my beloved among the young men. With great delight I sat in his shadow, and his fruit was sweet to my taste" (Song of Solomon 2:3).

The man responds with similar language: "Your two breasts are like two fawns, twins of a gazelle, that graze among the lilies" (Song of Solomon 4:5), and "Your lips drip nectar, my bride; honey and milk are under your tongue; the fragrance of your garments is like the fragrance of Lebanon" (Song of Solomon 4:11). "Your rounded thighs are like jewels, the work of a master hand. Your navel is a rounded bowl that never lacks mixed wine" (Song of Solomon 7:1-2).

We see similar language in the book of Proverbs. "Let your fountain be blessed, and rejoice in the wife of your youth, a lovely deer, a graceful doe. Let her breasts fill you at all times with delight; be intoxicated always in her love" (Proverbs 5:15-19).

From such passages and many others, Christians should understand that marital sex is not to be a stilted or perfunctory exercise. Rather, it is to be free, uninhibited, and frequent, as the bodies of the husband and wife are not their own but are under the loving authority of the other in the context of sexual desire and satisfaction (1 Corinthians 7:3-5). As Tim and Kathy Keller underscore in their excellent work on marriage, *The Meaning of Marriage*, "Since the Bible confines sex to marriage, we should not be surprised to find that various passages instruct married couples to enjoy sex and do so frequently."[9]

Of course, some women and men are in such genuinely abusive marriages (emotional and even physical) that sexual desire has been severely diminished. This is a legitimate reason for decreased sexual intimacy. While not everything that is labeled "abuse" is actual abuse, if you are in a truly abusive marriage, we encourage you to get help immediately. Talk to people you trust, including your church leaders and elders. Talk to the police if physical abuse is involved. While the typical Christian marriage will not involve abuse, if you are in an abusive marriage, take the steps necessary to protect yourself (and your children) with an ultimate goal of healing your marriage, if at all possible.

With this necessary caveat, the importance of sex within marriage reminds us that sexless marriages are not God's design. Bearing in mind the realities of old age, outside of an extreme, extenuating providence, sexless marriages betray pronounced, sinful dysfunction. Again, barring an unusual providence, a general lack of both sex and sexual desire by either the husband or the wife is directly counter to God's view of sex and marriage (Proverbs 5:18-19; Song of Solomon 4:16; 1 Corinthians 7:1-5). Christians must understand the devil's schemes.

He has come to steal, kill, and destroy (John 10:10). Consequently, he is constantly pushing for rampant sex outside of marriage and he is constantly pushing to reduce and eliminate sex inside of marriage.

It is often said, "If you want things to go well in the bedroom, they need to go well in the living room." This can be true, at least to an extent, but it is also true that if you want things to go well in the living room, they need to go well in the bedroom. As Tim and Kathy Keller underscore, "Kathy and I often liken sex in a marriage to oil in an engine—without it, the friction between all the moving parts will burn out the motor. Without joyful, loving sex, the friction in a marriage will bring about anger, resentment, hardness, and disappointment."[10] If a Christian man or woman believes that their lack of sexual interest in their spouse is normal or even spiritual, they are mistaken and this attitude can wreak havoc on a marriage. Therefore, Christian couples should be active and diligent in praying for God to increase their emotional, spiritual, and sexual love for one another. Don't merely count on the initial attraction and sexual interest that led to the marriage in the first place. Inertia is no safe harbor. Be intentional.

Sexual union in a marriage is both the establishment and the ongoing reinforcement of the couple's *oneness* (Genesis 2:24; Matthew 19:6; Mark 10:8; Ephesians 5:31). As Tim and Kathy Keller assert, "sex is a method that God invented to do 'whole life entrustment' and self-giving."[11] A healthy, vibrant sex life (consistent with age and taking into account unusual providences) is important to a thriving emotional and spiritual connection between the couple. Sex nourishes the emotional and spiritual dynamics of the relationship. Without it, deficits will be felt in these areas that will lead to significant harm to the overall relationship.

Another characteristic of the biblical sexual ethic is the fact that sex and all sexual activity is reserved only for marriage. Adultery is roundly condemned in the Scriptures (Exodus 20:14; Leviticus 20:10;

Proverbs 6:32; 1 Corinthians 6:9-10; Hebrews 13:4), underscoring that sex is for those who are married to each other and not for any other context. An ongoing lifestyle marked by physical adultery is indicative of a person who does not know God, who is an unbeliever, and who will not inherit the kingdom of God (1 Corinthians 6:9-10; Galatians 5:19-21), no matter how much they may protest to the contrary.

The Scriptures also emphatically assert that both marriage and sex are to be between a man and a woman, not between two men or two women. God created humanity as male and female (Genesis 1:27). When asked about the permissibility of divorce, Jesus restated this truth (Genesis 2:24; Matthew 19:4-5) and Paul also repeated it (Ephesians 5:31): "Therefore a man shall leave his father and mother and hold fast to his wife, and the two shall become one flesh." The Scriptures expressly condemn same-sex sex (Leviticus 18:22; Romans 1:24-27) explicitly stating that those who "practice homosexuality" will not "inherit the kingdom of God" (1 Corinthians 6:9-10).

An immediate, obvious deduction of what we just reviewed is that there is no such thing as "gay marriage," just as there is also no such thing as a square circle. It is a nonreality from God's standpoint. He created marriage and defines it in terms of the lifelong union of a man and a woman. Therefore, human beings can no more redefine marriage than we can redefine a circle. Christians must take this tack and approach in their efforts to influence culture.

This brings up another central aspect of the sexual union within marriage: children. There is a direct connection between the gift of sex in marriage and the reproduction of life. Children are a blessing and heritage from God (Psalm 127:3). Yet homosexual sex does not produce children and does not propagate the species. Therefore, at a certain threshold, widespread and pervasive homosexuality becomes an existential threat to the continuance of humanity. This reality alone should influence one's ultimate position regarding homosexuality.

While organizations like the Reformation Project and Revoice and movements like Spiritual Friendship have caused significant confusion among professing evangelicals, it should be clear for the reasons listed above that "gay Christianity" is just as much a contradiction in terms as "racist Christianity" or "idolatrous Christianity." Not only is homosexual sex in thought and behavior condemned in the Scriptures, but the notion of a positive or neutral homosexual identity is rejected as well. Consequently, in the words of the Nashville Statement, "adopting a homosexual or transgender self-conception is [not] consistent with God's holy purposes in creation and redemption."[12] Or, as Rosaria Butterfield rightly observes, "Once born again, I can never see homosexuality as part of my essence or nature, because I am a new creation by God's regeneration. While homosexuality arises out of my sin nature, once redeemed, I am no longer in Adam but in Christ. When I sin or desire to sin, as a new creation in Christ I am now acting against my new nature."[13]

Thus far, we have spoken primarily of behavior, but sexual purity relates not just to our actions but to our thoughts as well. God is not only concerned with physical acts that compromise our sexual purity, but also with how the thoughts we indulge in transgress his moral standards. For example, Jesus said that "everyone who looks at a woman with lustful intent has already committed adultery with her in his heart" (Matthew 5:28). His statement is directly relevant to the sin of pornography.

Pornography is soul-destroying and rampant, not only among men but increasingly among women. It proves the proverb: the eyes of man are never full (Proverbs 27:20). Although the vast majority of men are tempted by lust and by pornography, that is no excuse to give up and surrender to it. We are not strangers to the temptation of pornography and wrestling against it.

Nevertheless, we are shocked at the number of professing Christians who are owned by it. We encourage you strongly to go to war against this sin as if your life and marriage depend on it. Be honest with friends and pastors who will hold you accountable in this area. Use technological help, like porn filters and blockers. Get rid of your smartphone, if necessary. If pornography is an issue for you, and you are married, you need to tell your spouse, unless you think your spouse is going to commit self-harm or physically hurt you. Talk with your elders or a trusted friend about the best way to move forward. Pornography is not a biblical justification for divorce, but it is a high evil that will greatly hurt your marriage and your soul. Flee from it (1 Corinthians 6:18).

We realize that some readers may be surprised at our stance regarding sexual purity. One might remark, "It seems like you are saying that those who are not married cannot have any sexual activity whatsoever, that God is against any and all sexual activity by those who are not married, even, for instance, a couple that are 32 and 30 years old, engaged, and getting married in two months. Is that what you are saying?"

Yes, that's exactly what we are saying. While we would counsel that an engaged couple can show one another physical affection by holding hands or a lingering hug, or even a kiss, each of those things should stay in the lane of only affection and not sexual arousal. After all, hugging your best friend or kissing your grandson is not a sexual act! But when it comes to romantic relationships, as sexual arousal begins, stop and desist. It should also go without saying that one's clothes need to stay on and there should be no touching of areas of the body that are sexually centric.

Yet rather than merely compiling a list of dos and don'ts when it comes to sexual purity, we should seek to understand the reasoning behind them. Because lust is a sin, we should avoid actions or situations that we know will provoke lust. In other words, lust should be treated like any other sin. If a man found himself fantasizing about murdering his neighbor, we would be horrified to discover that he'd purchased a gun and had started taking practice shots at his neighbor's property. The fact that he had not yet technically murdered his neighbor would not exonerate him. In the same way, if we treat both lustful thoughts and lustful actions as seriously as Jesus did (Matthew 5:27-28; 18:7-9), we will take the necessary steps to avoid temptation.

We recognize that what we've said about the biblical sexual ethic may have made for heavy reading, and we'll say more at the end of the chapter about how the nature and danger of sexual sin should drive us to the cross of Christ. With that in mind, we'd like to close by listing several errors that Christians can fall into with regard to God's commands surrounding sex.

The first error is the idea that God's moral law is so strict that we should not even try to keep it. This is false. No, the law cannot save us. Not even a little. Yet our obedience to God's law is how we demonstrate our love for God. As Jesus said, "If you love me, you will keep my commandments" (John 14:15). We should strive to obey God not to merit his love for us, but to express our love to him.

The second error is the idea that through law-keeping, we can be pure in God's sight. This idea is also false. There are certainly relative degrees of purity; a pornographer is far less pure than a faithful, loving husband. But in God's eyes, even momentary lusts are still lusts and are unacceptable to him. This recognition should humble us. While it shouldn't quench our desire for holiness, it should make us gentle toward fellow sinners, since we are also sexually impure people in need of grace.

Finally, we must reject the lie that sexual purity is something we can achieve on our own. Even at a human level, we are surrounded by fellow believers who should be committed to helping us live lives of virtue, kindness, and faithfulness. More importantly, God has sent his Holy Spirit to live in our hearts, to console us, to comfort us, and to empower us. This is not a fight we can win on our own. But this is a fight we can win through God's power (Philippians 4:13). We both can attest that growth in sexual virtue is a reality. Even if slow, over time, it will happen because of God's sanctifying power at work in his people (1 Peter 1:2). So trust in God's strength and keep fighting, knowing that your pursuit of holiness is not in vain (Hebrews 12:14).

HOW SHOULD CHRISTIANS THINK ABOUT TRANSGENDERISM?

Transgenderism is the idea that a person's biological sex can differ from their gender identity. To even understand this idea, we have to adopt both the feminist distinction between sex and gender and queer theory's belief that we can determine our gender identity based on our experience. Queer theory dictates that a trans woman (i.e., a biological man who identifies as a woman) is in fact a woman, while a trans man (i.e., a biological woman who identifies as a man) is in fact a man. As we've seen, this belief is connected to the idea that we can bifurcate the discrete gender binary into multiple, completely independent spectra of biological sex, gender identity, gender expression, and sexual orientation.

In contrast, the Christian view is that there is a single gender binary that divides humanity into two halves: male and female (see Figure 6). Social categories, gender expression, and sexual ethics are all rooted in these biological categories. Biological men should be socially recognized as male, should express themselves as male, should identify as male, and should either marry women or remain single. Biological women should be socially recognized as female, should express themselves as female, should identify as female, and should either marry men or remain single. Yes, cultures have developed different ways of expressing masculinity and femininity that are not universal or God-ordained—e.g., pink is not an inherently feminine color. But Christians should embrace the various social expressions of biological sex that are prevalent in their culture in order to communicate the fact that they accept and delight in their God-given sex.

Christians should also firmly deny that a person can declare that they belong to a particular gender based on their "gender identity." Indeed, upon reflection, it is nonsensical to think that "gender identity" actually determines gender, an idea that is expressed in the oft-repeated phrase "trans women are women." Even on a feminist understanding, gender is a social category, not an objective attribute that characterizes an individual. Therefore, when a man says, "I identify as a woman," what he is actually saying is, "I view myself as belonging to the female social category," or "I want people to treat me as if I belong to the female social category." What he cannot be saying is, "I have an objective attribute called 'gender,' which is female."

A request that people use preferred pronouns is an expression of the same impulse, but it can extend much further, to the point that

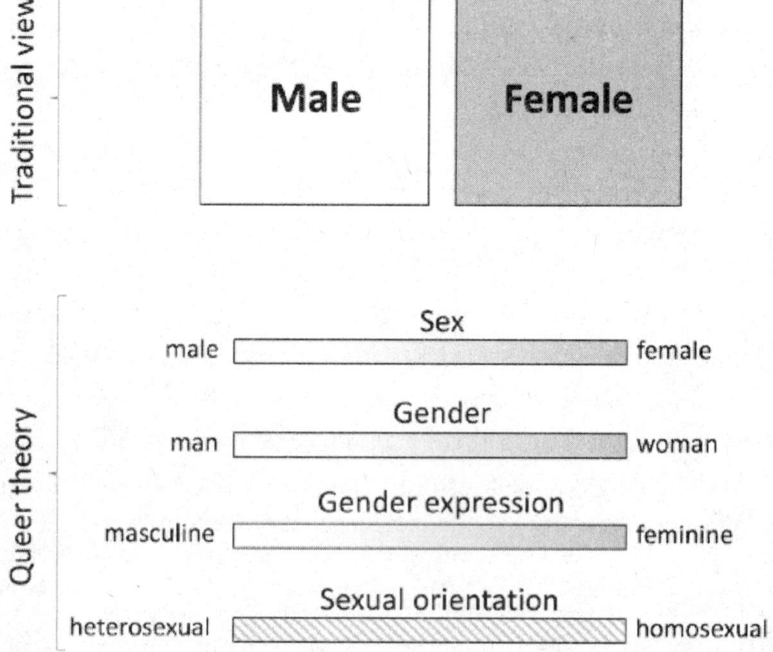

Figure 6—The traditional view of sex/gender versus queer theory

many trans activists will claim that it is transphobic for straight men to refuse to date trans women.[14] When a biological man insists that you address him with female pronouns or demands to use a women's locker room and play women's sports, he is saying that you must act as if he is actually a woman, when he is not.

Christians today are under tremendous cultural pressure to accommodate queer theory's claims. However, reflection on the two greatest commandments should strengthen our opposition to LGBTQ+ practice and identity.

The greatest commandment is to love God with all our heart, mind, soul, and strength (Mark 12:28-30). Loving God entails honoring the good categories that he created, including male and female, even when we will be deemed unloving and bigoted for doing so. To claim that a man is a woman is a lie, and even to refer to a man with female pronouns is to communicate that their preferred gender identity takes precedence over their God-given sex. When speaking about them to a third party, we recommend either using the gender-neutral pronoun *they* or using their name in place of pronouns. If you're asked why, you can say, "I respect their right to their beliefs, which means that I will not force them to say what they don't believe. But I would also like them to respect my beliefs, which means not being forced to say what I don't believe."

The second greatest commandment is to love our neighbor as ourselves (Mark 12:31). But love must be grounded in truth. Even from a purely secular perspective, it is not at all clear that affirming people's chosen genders leads to their happiness. For example, many European countries, like England and Norway, are pulling back and urging caution regarding gender transition in teens, partially in response to an explosion of teenage girls suddenly identifying as boys and seeking life-changing medical and surgical interventions.[15,16,17] Even these very progressive nations are realizing that they were far too quick to recommend experimental medication and life-altering surgeries to children with little to no empirical evidence that it would promote their long-term happiness.

Similarly, rising numbers of detransitioners (men and women who transitioned to the opposite gender and then detransitioned back to their birth gender) are speaking out about their regret and the poor-to-nonexistent screening process that shunted them into the gender medicine pipeline. We will say more below, but these realities should make us hesitant to equate loving your neighbor with affirming their gender identity.

ARE PEOPLE "BORN THIS WAY"?

Over the last few decades, various LGBTQ+ organizations have won massive victories both in the courts and in the court of public opinion, often through drawing a parallel between their mission and the mission of the Civil Rights Movement. This strategy was, at times, very explicit and is detailed in Kirk and Madsen's 1989 book *After the Ball*.[18] One of the key components of tying gay rights to civil rights is the idea that homosexuality is an innate, immutable characteristic like skin color. LGBTQ+ people were "born this way." Therefore, the argument went, discriminating against someone because of their sexual orientation or gender identity, which they were born with and cannot change, is as immoral as discriminating against someone because of the color of their skin.

Given the proper aversion Christians feel toward racism, we're often cowed by the "born this way" slogan. But is it a good argument? No, it's not, for several reasons.

Even if we were to grant for the sake of argument that same-sex attraction were innate, it would not follow that gay rights are analogous to civil rights because *behavior* is not analogous to *skin color*. We may not always be able to choose our desires, but we can choose whether we act on them. For example, we might strongly desire to seek vengeance against our enemies. We may have even been born with strongly vindictive personalities. But we can choose to not act on that desire. In contrast, we cannot choose to not have a particular melanin count. Consequently, it is not true that homosexuality is analogous to skin color.

Additionally, sexuality is a moral category regulated by the Bible whereas ethnicity is not. The Bible calls us to repent of our sexual immorality, our pride, and our greed, but never our ethnicity. Indeed, the Bible explicitly states that people from every tribe, nation, and tongue will be welcomed into God's kingdom (Revelation 7:9). Yet it also explicitly states that the sexually immoral, idolaters, and liars will not (Revelation 21:8). Therefore, it's invalid to compare morally neutral categories like ethnicity or height or age to moral categories like sexuality, greed, or honesty.

In a similar way, the category of "LGBTQ+ rights" includes many elements that are not natural rights at all. For instance, same-sex marriage is often viewed as a right when it is actually a contradiction. Marriage is, by definition, a lifelong union between a man and a woman. Therefore, as we mentioned earlier, we can no more have a right to marry someone of the same sex than we can have a right to draw a circle with four sides. In the same way, male and female are categories rooted in biology. Therefore, men cannot become women even if the Supreme Court declares that men have the right to become women.

Again, there is a major contrast here between the Civil Rights Movement and the LGBTQ+ movement. The former wanted to overturn laws that were inconsistent with biblical moral standards, while the latter wants to overturn laws that are consistent with biblical moral standards.

Finally, we come to the question, Are gay or transgender people really "born this way"? As we've shown above, the answer to this question doesn't affect the morality of homosexuality or transgenderism. Regardless of whether the answer is yes or no, we should still deny that the LGBTQ+ movement is analogous to the Civil Rights Movement or that homosexuality or transgenderism are morally neutral. That said, the answer to the question seems to be no.

In 2019, *Science* magazine published a study of more than 450,000 individuals from the US and the UK. Researchers attempted to discover which genes, if any, were responsible for same-sex attraction and sexual behavior. They concluded that "all tested genetic variants accounted for 8 to 25 percent of variation in same-sex sexual behavior, only partially overlapped between males and females, and do not allow meaningful prediction of an individual's sexual behavior."[19]

Another way to probe the connection between genetics (and shared prenatal environment) and sexuality is through twin studies. Briefly, identical twins have an identical genetic makeup and also shared a womb before birth. In contrast, fraternal twins are biological siblings who shared a womb but who do not have an identical genetic makeup. Thus, twin studies can determine the extent to which some trait is determined by genetics and prenatal environment or other factors.

Yet twin studies have also found limited correlation between genetics, shared prenatal environment, and sexuality. A 2010 Swedish study of more than 11,000 men and more than 14,000 women found that genetics or prenatal environment contributed to 34 percent to 39 percent of the variation in male sexuality and 34 percent to 36 percent of female sexuality.[20]

To put these numbers in some context, it is well established among scientists that if one of your parents is an alcoholic, then you are more likely to become an alcoholic as well. For decades, researchers have attempted to disentangle the relative contributions of genes and prenatal environment from other factors. A 2013 article in *Current Psychiatry Reports* stated: "It has now been firmly established, largely through numerous studies in thousands of twin pairs and some adoption studies, that the heritability (the genetic component of the variance)...of alcoholism is around 50%."[21]

In other words, the best scientific data currently supports the idea that alcoholism is more influenced by genetics than homosexuality. Therefore, if we have reason to reject the idea that an alcoholic was "born this way," we have even more reason to reject the idea that homosexual people were "born this way."

Research on the origins of gender dysphoria, the experience of profound discomfort with one's biological sex, is even murkier than research on the origins of homosexual desire. Every few years, headlines claim that some new study has proven that transgender people have brains that align with their gender identity, but—so far—the actual science does not support these grandiose claims. Mount Sinai Hospital's information page summarizes the issue succinctly when it states: "No one knows exactly what causes gender dysphoria."[22]

Furthermore, we can grant that some small number of people do experience real, severe mental discomfort with their biological sex. But why should the solution be to mutilate a healthy body rather than to help the person accept and delight in their body? Our culture has taken completely opposite and irreconcilable approaches to different types of body dysphoria. When a young girl says that she feels fat, we (rightly) criticize the constant hyper-sexualization of women in our culture and encourage her to love her body as it is. Yet when a young girl says that she feels like a boy, we tell her that she is a boy and encourage her to cut off her body parts? This is wildly inconsistent.

From a Christian perspective, we should emphasize that biology isn't destiny. It's possible to grant that some people may be predisposed, even genetically predisposed, to certain sins. We may have been born with a nasty temper, a strong inclination to gluttony, or a tendency toward laziness and procrastination. But it doesn't follow that these inborn, unchosen traits are good. Nor does it follow that we bear no moral responsibility for our actions.

The Bible insists that mankind is fallen, that we have inherited a sinful nature from Adam, and that we are sinful from our mother's womb: "Behold, I was brought forth in iniquity, and in sin did my mother conceive me" (Psalm 51:5). Our latent, disordered desires emerge as soon as we can communicate them. Therefore, it doesn't follow that just because we were "born this way," the way we were born is good.

Imagine someone saying, "For as long as I can remember, I have wanted to steal things that weren't mine. Sharing didn't come naturally. I constantly fought the urge to be selfish and cruel. I felt the strong desire to mock others, to live for my own pleasure, and to disobey my parents." For many of us, this description is barely a hypothetical! Yet would any of us conclude that the presence of these unchosen desires makes them legitimate? Or would we argue that acting on these sinful desires is morally neutral? In the same way, we should reject the idea that innate, unchosen sexual desires we have experienced since early childhood are necessarily good.

When it comes to sinful desires, affections, and tendencies, all of us are "born this way." The Bible doesn't excuse us, but rather, insists that our inborn corruption is exactly the reason that we all need to be born again.

Jesus offers us forgiveness and healing for our corruption. We don't need to hide it or excuse it or downplay it. If we come to him, he will freely forgive and freely save.

DOES LOVE REQUIRE AFFIRMATION?

One of our culture's mantras, which is endlessly repeated on bumper stickers and yard signs, is "love is love." This slogan is meant to express support for same-sex marriage on the grounds that love between two people of the same sex should be regarded as no different than love between two people of opposite sexes. "Marriage equality" is another phrase used to defend same-sex marriage, again on the grounds that marriage between individuals of the same sex ought to be legally and socially equal to marriage between two individuals of opposite sexes. Opposition to same-sex marriage or a belief in the sinfulness of homosexuality can then be cast as anti-love and anti-equality.

Similarly, support for transgenderism is often framed in terms of compassion. We're told that transgender people are suffering terribly and will commit suicide unless their gender identity is affirmed. Doctors often ask parents of transgender teens, "Would you rather have a dead daughter or a live son?"[23] To oppose transgenderism is then to be anti-compassion and even pro-suicide.

Christians feel the weight of these slogans because the Bible commands us to love our neighbor, to show compassion, and to treat others the way we want to be treated. However, the LGBTQ-affirming arguments and slogans listed above rely on sloppy reasoning that is not only incompatible with the Bible but with the beliefs of the vast majority of non-Christians.

For example, take the slogan "love is love." As stated, it could be merely a tautology, a trivially true statement like "4 = 4" or "A cat is a cat." However, most people intend it to mean something like "all sexual love is equally good and ought to be celebrated." But few people believe this! The vast majority of people who loudly proclaim that "love is love" will utterly (and rightly) condemn sexual love between adults and children or between two siblings. We can make this judgment only by tacitly admitting that not all sexual love is good and worth celebrating.

Similarly, we can have compassion on those who experience discomfort with their biological sex without affirming that they can choose their own gender identity. In other situations, we make this distinction between compassion and affirmation constantly. For example, if a young anorexic girl thinks she's fat when she is actually starving to death, we can have compassion on her without in any way affirming her delusion. If a depressed friend thinks his life is meaningless, we can comfort him without agreeing with him. In both cases, our compassion is and must be rooted in the truth. Telling people lies that will ultimately harm them is not compassion, but cruelty.

This consideration is especially true from an eternal perspective. Think of sin as a cancer that is slowly killing all of us. What people most need is to recognize the seriousness of their situation and to put themselves under the care of Jesus, the Great Physician. Telling someone that their sin is not sin is like telling a cancer patient that the dull ache in his head is nothing to worry about. It is singing a lullaby to a person who is asleep at the wheel as their car hurtles down the interstate. To the extent that we actually love our neighbors, we will risk offending them by telling them the truth.

SEXUALITY AND CHRISTIANITY

Queer theory is false and spiritually deadly. The Bible has a high and rapturous view of sex within marriage but also requires complete sexual abstinence outside of it. Pornography is an affront to God. Lustful thoughts are sin. Divorce outside of strict, biblically specified grounds is hated by God (Malachi 2:16). Homosexual actions and desires are both sinful because they are oriented toward what is inherently sinful. Transgenderism is a repudiation of God's good created order that must therefore be rejected.

If the demands of God's law feel crushing to you, they should! We have all transgressed God's good and righteous standard of sexual purity hundreds, thousands of times. God's law is not meant to comfort us; it is meant to drive us to the love of Jesus, who alone can rescue us from the wrath we deserve. No matter how sexually pure you look on the outside, God knows the truth.

And no matter how filthy you are, God can forgive you and cleanse you. He can renew you, restore you, and heal you. He can make all things new and beautiful. He can fill you with his Spirit and empower you to live a life of joy, holiness, and purity.

Our message to sexual sinners should be the same message we preach to all sinners and the same message we preach to ourselves on a daily basis: Jesus saves.

9

REACHING OUT

Up to this point, we have explained the ideas at the heart of wokeness, have shown why they're incompatible with Christianity, and have offered a biblical framework for thinking about race, gender, and sexuality. Now we're ready to get practical about what we've discussed: How can we communicate these truths to our children, our neighbors, or our pastors?

Keep in mind what we said in chapter 2 about the factors that incline people to embrace contemporary critical theory as a worldview. We're not dealing with a mere error of judgment, as if people simply made a mistake on an addition problem and can be put right by showing them where they forgot to carry the one. Rather, we're asking people to reject their way of thinking about identity, morality, and truth. We're potentially pulling them out of an activist community where they feel at home. From their perspective, we're asking them to turn their back on the "right side of history" and start walking toward the Dark Ages. This is not a minor decision!

Therefore, we need to make sure that we're not calling them out of a worldview into a vacuum. It's not enough to show, for example, that not all racial disparities are caused by discrimination, or that gender is binary. If we stop there, people are likely to favor a flawed but familiar worldview over a nonexistent one. Making a purely negative case against critical theory is like telling a starving man all the reasons he shouldn't eat moldy bread without offering him any other food. Consequently, we need to present people with an alternative.

For this reason, your conversations should have the gospel at least in the background. Obviously, when you're approaching your human resources director about your objections to the company's new Diversity, Equity, and Inclusion training, you don't have to lead with an explanation of the doctrine of justification by faith. In fact, we'll argue below that in secular settings, it will often be more fruitful to offer arguments grounded in values like freedom of speech, freedom of conscience, and diversity of thought, which your employer already ostensibly supports. However, when you're talking to your children, your friends, and certainly with fellow Christians, you need to show that contemporary critical theory functions as a religion and that Christianity is the alternative.

So, for example, when speaking to a zealous, non-Christian fan of Ibram X. Kendi, you can say, "I think Kendi's theories are empirically false, but—like him—I'm opposed to racism. However, I'm opposed to racism because God created all human beings in his image. If you think you can rid the world of racism merely by changing laws, you'll always be disappointed because racism, like all sin, springs from our sinful hearts. And only in Christ can our hearts be cleansed."

At a deep level, everyone is seeking to be declared righteous. We all want to feel like we're a good person. This impulse is deeply human; it is not the domain of Christians alone. Buddhism, Islam, and contemporary critical theory all claim to offer us a way to scratch that itch, to wash out that stain, to silence the nagging voice of conscience that tells us we're moral failures. But Christianity is unique in saying you can't cleanse yourself. You are hopeless and lost. Only Jesus can forgive you and heal you. This is the central message of Christianity, and until people embrace it, they will always be drawn to other messages that promise to fill the void in their souls.

Given the magnitude of the issues involved and people's emotional and spiritual investment in them, conversations about race, gender, and sexuality will be hard. In the next section, we offer suggested best practices that will help you to better navigate uncomfortable conversations.

HOW TO HAVE HARD CONVERSATIONS

Wouldn't it be great if there were a magic pill you could take right before a hard conversation that would ensure complete success? Imagine a discussion in which every one of your responses was perfect and every answer profound and praiseworthy. In which not only the content of your speech was exactly what was needed, but also your paralanguage (rate, tone, pitch, etc.) and body language. Where you would never have to think again, *I wish I hadn't said that*, or *I wish I could go back and say XYZ.*

While there is no such magic pill, there are best practices that you can use to greatly increase your chance of dialogic success. As those who routinely get into difficult conversations, we offer 15 such practices that have proven to be effective in producing better conversations with our interlocutors.

1. PRAY. PRAY. PRAY. Pray in advance of the conversation, pray during the conversation (in your mind, not out loud, unless you want to make the situation really awkward), and pray after the conversation. Prayer cannot be overemphasized.

Even before a specific conversation is planned or scheduled, make it a habit to regularly pray for God to lead you into uncomfortable conversations for his glory. Pray to know and sense his presence with you. Pray that he will give you the words to say that will be the most effective and edifying.

If you think the person is not a Christian, first and foremost be praying that your connection with them will point the way to Christ and to salvation. Be praying for truth to prevail, and for God to change their minds and to change your mind if it needs to be changed, so that you both will be in line with exactly how God thinks about the subject.

2. Equip yourself by becoming informed about critical social theory. Do some significant study. The endnotes in this book will point you to important primary sources. And if you'd like an even more thorough analysis and critique from a Christian perspective, our previous book *Critical Dilemma* includes lengthy direct quotes from source scholarship to give you an accurate understanding of what critical theorists actually believe and teach, in their own words.

3. Know your Bible. We cannot state this strongly enough. Study to get a good grasp of systematic theology and the Scripture passages that support each topic. If a systematic doctrinal study of the Bible is brand new to you, start with the 107 questions of the Westminster Shorter Catechism. Introduce yourself to the best confessions in church history. As a young Christian in his early twenties, Pat got a copy of the London Baptist Confession of Faith of 1689 and went through it cover to cover. It was invaluable to him and set him on a pathway of doctrinal integrity and understanding.

4. Remember that you are not so much trying to win an argument as you are trying to win the person. This posture will feel (and will be) more collaborative than competitive. More conciliatory than adversarial. More proactive than reactive.

Out of a range of conflict strategies and styles that are studied in the scholarly literature in the communication field (such as avoidance, compromise, accommodation, competition, collaboration, etc.), collaboration consistently possesses a win-win dynamic and yields a win-win outcome. While the biblical position will ultimately "win," this result is not at the expense or deficit of the person (like a competing strategy would produce). The person will also win by seeing for themselves and believing the truth of what you are saying and contending. They will genuinely benefit from the truth you share. A collaborative posture and atmosphere is most ideal in handling difficult and awkward conversations of this type.

5. Commit in your heart, mind, and behavior that you are going to be a genuine friend to the person regardless of how the conversation goes. This will necessitate that you get to know the person and begin to share some life outside of your discussions.

6. Play the long game. Try to start an ongoing dialogue, not just a one-shot conversation. This approach will give you time to build a friendship and establish trust. Over time, you will be able to make stronger, more gospel-centric and biblically centric affirmations that will likely land more effectively because of the love and care that has developed between you. If you are limited to only a one-off conversation, then you will need to present biblical truth at the outset, trusting God to lead and give his benediction to your interaction.

7. Start with a softball question just to get the conversation going. This will help you assess your conversation partner's beliefs. You could ask something like, "DEI is being eliminated in some institutions but still going strong in others. How are things at your workplace?" And then, no matter what is said, ask, "Do you appreciate the direction your employer has taken?" Or you could ask, "It seems that trans perspectives are growing in our society. Do you view that as a good thing, or does it concern you in any way?" There are many easy, disarming questions that will spark a conversation. In advance, take some time to think about specific questions you would be comfortable asking.

8. Try to contextualize and verbalize your thoughts as gently as possible while, at the same time, saying hard truths. Say something like, "I know this may strike you as offensive, and trust me, I'm in as much need of grace as you, but, as a friend, I need to tell you…"

9. When you are dealing with an objection to your viewpoint

that is defensive or adversarial or outright hostile, remember that a soft answer turns away wrath (Proverbs 15:1). Make this text a core value for how you communicate.

10. Along these lines, we must remember that all our speech must be governed by the totality of God's Word. We must keep in mind the fruits of the Spirit in Galatians 5:22-23, which apply to both men and women. We must remember the following texts:

- The man of God is not quarrelsome (2 Timothy 2:24).
- We are to speak the truth in love (Ephesians 4:15).
- No unwholesome talk should come out of our mouths (Ephesians 4:29).
- All our words should be full of grace, seasoned with salt (Colossians 4:6).
- As much it depends on us, we should be at peace with all men (Romans 12:18).
- We should generally have a good reputation among outsiders (1 Timothy 3:7).
- No man can tame the tongue in his own strength, so we must have God directing our words (James 3:8).
- Out of the overflow of the heart the mouth speaks (Luke 6:45), so guard your heart against hate, spite, and malice.
- We will be held accountable for every idle and careless word spoken. By our words we will be justified, and by our words we will be condemned (Matthew 12:36-37).

There are people in hell who knew a lot of sound doctrine but did not take Christ's directives and commands regarding speech seriously. Look at X (formerly Twitter) and other social-mediated environments.

Look at the vitriol, condescension, hubris, invective, insults, taunting, trolling, slander, and hate spewed out by professing Christians against professing Christians. God hates this. Many will go to hell condemned by their own words—words that were the fruit of an unregenerate heart.

11. A relatively easy way to enter into difficult conversations is to read a book together. Have your interlocutor pick out the first book. Take a chapter at a time and discuss. Then you pick out the second book and discuss.

12. Try to find something you can genuinely affirm about the person's ideas or the way they carry themselves. Because of what Christ has done for you, make this a life verse: "Encourage one another and build one another up, just as you are doing" (1 Thessalonians 5:11). In Pat's graduate programs where critical social theory was dominant, Pat regularly encouraged his classmates and faculty. This prepared the soil for them to better receive his challenges and critiques.

13. Toward the end of each conversation, be sure to ask a question like this and sincerely mean it: "What is the one thing that you really think I need to know or understand about what we have discussed today? I genuinely want to consider what is important to you and contemplate what you think I should be thinking about." Listen well to what they say, and follow through.

14. Get some receipts in your pushback against racism and all forms of bigotry. Protest and openly challenge racism or any actual bigotry, including against the gay and trans communities, recognizing that many things labeled as homophobic are not actually homophobic. When real bigotry happens, and it does, stand against it overtly and publicly as you have opportunity in your providence. This opposition will strengthen your credibility when you offer challenges and critiques.

15. Finally, be front and center in your local community in building up and strengthening racial connection, racial healing, and racial

unity. These actions will help you in manifold ways. They will aid your confidence; they will aid you in knowing what to say and how to say it; and they will aid in the respect your dialogic partner will have for you as you critique the narratives of critical social theory.

Yes, we must challenge our culture, push back, critique, and repudiate. However, we must not merely tear down. We must also build up, offering and exemplifying a positive vision for loving across difference. Our lives should be an ongoing testimony to the world of the power of Christ, the love we have for one another as brothers and sisters in Christ, and the love we have for our fellow human beings.

As we close out this section, we want to give a word of encouragement and exhortation. If you are born again and reading this text, then you, like us, are a child of the one, true, and living God. Do you understand how glorious this is?! God is our Father. Christ is our Savior and Lord. The Holy Spirit is our comforter and power. We are part of the church, God's gathered people. We are ambassadors for Christ (2 Corinthians 5:20), and we go into the world under his power and charge.

We are salt and light (Matthew 5:13-14), and in Christ's power we, the church, the people of God, can be and *must be* the pacesetters for society regarding racial reconciliation, racial connection, racial healing, and racial unity. Remember, God is love (1 John 4:16), and he is in us. The world will know us by our love for one another (John 13:35). Church, we and we alone are in the vanguard of hope, redemption, and renewal for the planet—so let's be who we are and be in the forefront of loving well across racial difference.

REACHING YOUR CHILDREN

No matter how much we feel that we're surrounded by wokeness, our kids have it worse. Recall the data we presented in chapter 1. When it comes to attitudes toward LGBTQ+ identities or an oppressor/oppressed social framework, there is a tremendous generational divide. In chapter 7, we discussed the importance of parents exercising loving authority. In this section, we'd like to offer some best practices for parents that will protect your kids not merely against the malign influences of critical social theory, but against all kinds of other errors and temptations.

Proverbs 22:6 tells us that parents should "train up a child in the way he should go; even when he is old he will not depart from it." While the proverbs are not meant to be absolute guarantees, they do represent what typically occurs, and this verse is no exception. So be encouraged!

In this section, we want to give you some perspectives and best practices for protecting your kids from falling for the deleterious perspectives and implications of woke ideology. Whether the issue is race, class, sexuality, gender, nationality, etc., following these directives will go a long way in protecting your children from the seduction of woke thinking.

Prayer

As you commit to bringing up your children in the fear and admonition of the Lord (Ephesians 6:4), first and foremost, *pray*. As stated earlier, prayer cannot be overemphasized. Without God's blessing and benediction, all our efforts will be futile. Consequently, become a prayer warrior.

Pray for God to protect your children from the false and destructive ideas of critical social theory and its attendant woke ideas. Pray for wisdom (James 1:5) in how to lead your children away from woke perspectives and into biblical truth. Pray individually, as couples (if you are married), and with your children. In our experience, most professing Christians have a low view of prayer and therefore do not pray nearly enough. The church tends to talk about prayer more than it actually prays. Consequently, we have not because we ask not (James 4:2). How desperately do you want to see your children saved and thinking rightly about the plethora of issues plaguing our society? Then you need to be praying fervently, multiple times a day, remembering that we "ought always to pray and not lose heart" (Luke 18:1) and that God "[withholds] no good thing...from those who walk uprightly" (Psalm 84:11).

In our praying, we need to be like Jacob, who wrestled with God and determined that he would not let God go until he had the blessing (Genesis 32:26). Remember that the "kingdom of heaven has suffered violence, and the violent take it by force" (Matthew 11:12). God wants our extreme aggressiveness when it comes to seeking him and his kingdom. He wants us to cast our cares upon him because he cares for us (1 Peter 5:7).

Do you fear what will become of your children if they embrace ideas about race, gender, and sexuality that are firmly planted in critical social theory? Psalm 34:4 states, "I sought the Lord, and he answered me and delivered me from all my fears." What troubles you the most as a parent? Is it not the safety of your children's souls? Psalm 34:6 states, "This poor man cried, and the Lord heard him and saved him out of all his troubles."

When it comes to our children, we must be supremely earnest in seeking after God and crying out to him for the safety of their souls. The Hebrew word for "cried" in Psalm 34:6 carries the freight of "to cry out," "to implore," "to call aloud." Have you ever been on your knees prostrate, *crying, imploring, calling aloud* after God to save your children and to keep them from false and spurious ideas that would harm their souls? Saints, this *must* be part of our prayer life and approach to God on behalf of our children. If you know nothing of this, start immediately. Now.

Encouragement, Praise, and Discipline

From the moment your children come out of the womb, make encouragement and praise a regular part of your interaction with them. Similar to prayer, we cannot overstate how important this is in fortifying your children's hearts and minds against embracing anti-biblical thinking as they grow older. All your children are a gift from God (Psalm 127:3). They are fearfully and wonderfully made (Psalm 139:14). It is a joy that they have been born and brought into the world (John 16:21). So praise them! Encourage them! Every day, tell them you love them, multiple times a day! If you don't feel this way about your children, repent, and beg God to change you.

Direct your body language to communicate your love for your children. Smile at them often. Show them affection. Make them *feel* that they are an overwhelming joy to you. Cheer for them. Literally. At ball games, recitals, whatever they are doing, show up and show out.

If you are a Christian reading this book, you have every reason to be optimistic that God's covenant promises will extend to your children. Just as the church is commanded to "encourage one another and build one another up" (1 Thessalonians 5:11), covenant families should be marked by this posture and practice. Given that our children are born totally depraved and come forth from the womb speaking lies (Psalm 58:3), there will be plenty to critique and correct, so get started immediately looking for ways that you can encourage and praise your children.

Along these lines, be sure to never provoke your children to wrath. Fathers should especially be mindful of this admonition (Ephesians 6:4). While there *is* a time for parents and particularly fathers to get righteously angry with their children, this should be rare. Our encourage/praise to critique/correct ratio should be, at minimum, 5:1. Remember that "a soft answer turns away wrath" (Proverbs 15:1). Make this a family verse that all are striving to live by.

When it comes to discipline, children should not be disciplined in anger and exasperation, but calmly and methodically. While corporal punishment should be employed in your overall plan of discipline for your children (Proverbs 13:24; 23:13-14) up to a certain age, it should never be done in a way that is out of control, unmeasured, injurious, or erodes the dignity of your children. It should include an explanation of the violation. After you discipline, you should pray together (both of you when your child is able), show affection, and verbally remind your child how much you love them. Afterward, if they disobey again, repeat the cycle. Parenting is not for the faint of heart.

At times, go through the first few steps but then withhold discipline. Show *mercy*. Talk to them about the gospel and how God, in Christ, shows us mercy and *withholds from us the punishment we deserve*. Remember, you want your son or daughter to have not only a healthy respect for you but also a genuine love for you. At times, go even further and immediately do something fun for your child, like getting ice cream. Explain to them that you are showing *grace*, just as Christ does with his children, *blessing us with what we don't deserve*.

The overriding posture of the father to his children should be modeled after God's posture to his people, his children. God is our *Abba* Father (Romans 8:15; Galatians 4:6). Biblically speaking, *Abba* is a rich Aramaic term of endearment, tenderness, and intimacy between father and son, like a young child calling his father Daddy. It is the term Christ used of the Father in the garden of Gethsemane while he was in anguish as he was about to be crucified (Mark 14:36).

Compassion is a mark of true fatherhood (Psalm 103:13). Godly fathers and mothers are to exemplify the fruit of the Spirit as they lead and nurture their children: "love, joy, peace, patience, kindness, goodness, faithfulness, gentleness, self-control" (Galatians 5:22-23). Spirit-empowered consistency here will go a long way in winning the hearts, not just the behavior, of your children, which will significantly fortify them against embracing woke ideology.

Offense and Defense

What follows are offensive and defensive efforts, some being both, to strengthen your children from embracing woke ideas. Saturate your children in the truth. Just like bank tellers spotting counterfeit bills, the more you know the truth, the easier it is to spot a counterfeit. Catechize your children from an early age. Have regular family devotions. Be in a solid, doctrinally sound church that prioritizes the Word of God and discipleship. Dads should take the lead in the instruction, but moms should be involved as well. We say this recognizing that there will be certain providential situations where mom will lead the instruction. Consider doing extra theological and apologetics teaching. Pat had the "Boom Daddy School of Theology" on Saturday mornings for his kids starting around age three. Neil, who led his family's homeschooling efforts, added various apologetics instructions throughout. Neil's book *Why Believe?* is an excellent apologetics text for high schoolers and college students.[1]

Get acquainted with, study, and understand the prevailing issues of the day that are attacking the church and pressing against the Christian position on various issues. Make 2 Corinthians 10:5 a family verse and live it out ("We destroy arguments and every lofty opinion raised against the knowledge of God, and take every thought captive to obey Christ"). Find the best material to combat the ideas attempting to undermine truth in both the church and the public square. Study and learn the issues and teach your children.

Above all, mom and dad…love each other deeply. Let your kids see your love for one another. Demonstrate and model a gospel-centric marriage before your kids. This will do wonders in protecting them from the forces vying for their souls.

Conversely, parents who are hypocrites, who act like a model couple and family at church and in public but at home are vindictive, passive-aggressive, ill-tempered, unforgiving, or harsh with one another and/or their children will all but ensure their children will grow up to hate the God they claim to worship. Children brought up in these kinds of homes tend to view the Christian faith as a joke and want nothing to do with it. Who could blame them? Parents, if this is you, we implore you to repent, to seek Christ (possibly for the very first time), and to call a family meeting where you plead with your children to forgive you. You must change, or you will likely lose your children, if not your own souls.

If you have a vision for homeschooling and the competency to do it, do it. Neil's kids have been homeschooled from K-12. Pat's kids were homeschooled through elementary and some middle school years, then went to public school. If you can afford a solid Christian school and one is nearby, do it. If you must send your kids to public school, be courteous but aggressive in knowing what is taught. Counter and supplement where needed. At times, a combination of educational approaches may make the most sense for families. Pat's kids had a 150-volume supplementary reading list put together by him and his wife that was digested from sixth through twelfth grades throughout the year with concentrated reading during the summers. While its level of completion varied among his kids—some texts not started or not finished, others read several times—it set the tone that their family and his kids' minds would not merely be acted upon by the world, but would act upon it.

Be intentional and restrictive about who your kids' friends are and who they spend time with. Heavily regulate screen time and ensure it is more than 90 percent instruction-oriented versus entertainment. Do not give your toddler a screen. We will say it again: Do not give your toddler a screen. See to it that your kids are playing outside much more than they are in front of a screen. Make sure you know *everything* your kids (from elementary age to teenagers) are looking at on the internet. This will mean you will have to greatly restrict their access to keep up. Use all software technology protections.

Reject the lie that your kids must have a smartphone. Pat's kids did not get smartphones until their late teens and early 20s. And they wouldn't have been given smartphones then if he hadn't been confident that they could handle them based on their demonstrable godly attitudes and obedient behavior. They were not allowed to have their phones alone with them in their rooms or anywhere in private. They were not allowed to sit around and scroll. At times, Pat required them to have sabbaticals from their phones. He required obedience, his kids survived (easily), and they are infinitely better for it today. Smartphones are destroying young people (and many older people). Get serious about being countercultural when it comes to smartphones. If your school system requires a smartphone, restrict its usage to schoolwork. See Jonathan Haidt's excellent book *The Anxious Generation* for relevant research and more suggestions.[2]

Discussion

Watch the news together as a family and discuss current events. Pat's kids relate that this practice put them ahead of their peers regarding what was happening in the world, which led to confidence in dealing with various forms of peer pressure when it arose. Discuss the prevailing ideas of the day. Talk about pop culture and entertainment. Address concerns and issues you see in society and apply God's Word to them. When you ask your kids a question, let them talk. Create an environment that is generally noncritical. When they give a good answer, applaud it. When they say something wrong or incorrect, point them to God's Word. When you have to critique and correct, do it gently and affirm what you can, then correct. Your goal is to create an environment in which they *want* to discuss things with you. If their response is sinful, then correct and rebuke with the appropriate strength. At times, keep the conversation light and fun.

Have no fear in asking any question you want to ask your children. Your children, including your teenagers, are not their own. They are under *your* authority. Don't be intimidated. God expects them to honor you (Exodus 20:12). They are to obey you in every righteous directive (Ephesians 6:1; Colossians 3:20). So ask questions. God is a pursuing God (Matthew 18:12). Imitate God. Pursue their hearts.

Ask about their interests, hurts, fears, worries, and joys. Listen. Truly listen. Be fully present. Empathize. Rejoice. Hug. Pray. Whenever you can, and this will be often, push their responses toward God and the gospel. Let your kids see that you are desperately earnest about their soul's salvation and continued safety.

The more parents ask questions and get directly involved with their kids' interests, hurts, fears, worries, and joys, the more they become the primary "ear" and "voice" in their kids' lives. This will go a long way toward creating a family environment in which the parents are *both* the authority *and* the friends (even best friends for critical seasons of time) of their kids. Related to this, when your son or daughter shows an interest in something that is new to you, join them in it. Have them pull you along and get involved with them. Share in their interest. Have them show you, teach you, and lead you in it. This will strengthen your friendship while you remain their authority. These dynamics will reduce any harmful voices pulling at them and will amplify yours.

While more could be said about reaching your children, we are confident these practices will go far in enabling you to reach and keep their hearts, protecting them from jumping ship to ideas inimical to the best interests of their souls. Woke ideology is pernicious. Applying what we have said in this section will not only inoculate your children from detrimental and destructive ideas, but will also help you lay out a salutary mission and vision for your family.

REACHING YOUR NEIGHBORS

Woke ideology is not just a problem for Christians; it's also a problem for society. To the extent that contemporary critical theory is embraced by institutions, those institutions will make policy based on false premises. The same is true of any fundamentally false ideology. For example, a company that embraces the idea that success is measured solely by profit will have no qualms about selling harmful products. A criminal justice system that denies the reality of male and female will place male sex offenders in women's prisons. A government that doesn't value human rights will trample on them.

For this reason, Christians need to be active in, or at least should not avoid, speaking to their neighbors about uncomfortable issues.

Consider this scenario:

> David has noticed that his neighbor's 13-year-old daughter Tara has suddenly begun cutting her hair short and dressing like a boy. At a neighborhood event, the neighbor addresses her as Tom and says that she is using he/him pronouns. David feels uncomfortable, but doesn't know what to do. His neighbor isn't a Christian, and they aren't well-acquainted.

Situations like this will become increasingly common as the second sexual revolution progresses.

What are some principles we should follow?

First, Christians need to have existing relationships with their neighbors. Sadly, people today are so isolated that our neighbors are often no more than strangers who happen to live on our street. Take proactive steps to change that. When new people move in, greet them immediately and ask if you can help them unpack. Bake them Christmas cookies. Offer to watch their pets while they're on vacation. Shovel their driveway when it snows.

Second, you should work to establish trust with your neighbors. You should be known for your honesty, integrity, kindness, and genuine concern for them. Invite them into your home. Get to know them. Find out who they are and what they care about.

Third, let topics like race, gender, and sexuality arise naturally. As Christians, the message we most want to share with the world is the gospel, not a political or cultural program. That said, the culture war matters because people matter. As John Stonestreet says, "Ideas have consequences; bad ideas have victims."[3] When we see people being harmed by bad ideas, it is loving and compassionate to counter those ideas.

Finally, be prepared with secular as well as Christian arguments against woke ideas. We'll explore this issue further in the section on reaching your workplace, but your non-Christian neighbors will not share your Christian presuppositions and may reject them outright. That doesn't mean the discussion needs to end. You should also be prepared to make arguments based on objective evidence and values that they themselves affirm. Remember, the Bible does not *accidentally* provide the correct perspective on race, gender, and sexuality. Rather, its perspective is true because its picture of reality is true. The same God who created the world inspired the Bible.

REACHING YOUR SCHOOLS

Students will be exposed to the slow drip of critical theory even in their earliest years of education. But that slow drip will become a torrent once they enter high school, college, and graduate school. Science, math, and engineering majors should not assume that they will be immune. While STEM fields are naturally resistant to postmodernism, even the most hard-nosed academic scientist or corporate researcher is overseen by HR departments, administrators, and grant agencies whose ideologies will have been deeply influenced by critical social theory. How, then, should students in every field respond to woke ideas, regardless of where they encounter them?

First, be humble. If you are a student, recognize that your primary role is to learn. Your teachers have spent tens of thousands of hours mastering the material they are presenting. No matter how absurd the ideas of critical theory sound to you, it would be both disrespectful and unwise to interrupt your professors' lectures with angry diatribes about the follies of intersectional feminism. There is absolutely a place for disagreement. But that disagreement should come after, not before, a full and careful engagement with the course material.

Second, work hard. As the only openly evangelical student in his graduate programs, Pat was surrounded by very progressive classmates and professors, many of whom were less than thrilled by his social and political views. However, his academic performance helped insulate him from criticism and softened the ground for any discussions where he had to disagree. Yes, it is quite possible that you will receive a low grade merely because you refused to toe the line on issues like abortion or transgender. But you should not receive a low grade because you didn't do the reading and put insufficient effort into the class!

Finally, be a witness not an antagonist. The likelihood that your brilliant arguments during an hour-long seminar on eighteenth-century French poetry will overthrow the entire field of postmodern literary criticism are slim to none. Indeed, a protracted verbal dispute with your teacher will strike many as arrogant and may even harden them to your claims. Rather, you should aim to gently and respectfully offer an alternative perspective supported by evidence and reason. Many people have doubts about woke ideology that they are afraid to voice. By quietly showing that you share their concerns, you will give them mental permission to dissent.

REACHING YOUR WORKPLACE

Resisting wokeness in the workplace presents unique challenges. The vast majority of businesses are secular and will have no commitment to biblical authority. Employees will come from a variety of religious backgrounds and company policy will often be designed to, at least in principle, accommodate a variety of beliefs and practices.

However, despite their alleged neutrality, many major companies have in fact pushed hard in the direction of wokeness through both official policies and unofficial workplace culture.

While our section above on "How to Have Hard Conversations" provides helpful counsel for all our "Reaching" sections, it is particularly applicable to this section. We encourage you to review that material as you prepare for edifying and productive conversations with your co-workers.

In this section we will give some brief direction on two matters that have come to plague our work environments: DEI and pronoun hospitality.

Diversity, Equity, and Inclusion

DEI, short for Diversity, Equity, and Inclusion, has taken institutions by storm. While there has been some backlash against DEI, we expect a resurgence. DEI is both an *ideology* and a *practice* that—in its best iteration—companies and organizations use for training to promote equal treatment and full participation of all people with a concerted effort to ensure the involvement of historically marginalized groups. Too often, however, DEI is simply the practical application of contemporary critical theory (or, as author Robin DiAngelo calls it, critical social justice) to an organization or institution. Within a critical social justice framework, DEI aims to displace individuals whose leadership and voice are associated with so-called oppressor groups and replace them with individuals whose leadership and voice are associated with so-called oppressed groups. Under this rubric, genuine diversity of viewpoint is anathema. What is required is a uniform commitment to progressive cultural positions and politics, particularly along the vector of justice issues, animated by critical social justice.

What should you do if you are required to attend DEI training? We recommend initially attending without any outward resistance or consternation so that you signal you are a team player. It's possible the training will be relatively benign, perhaps even beneficial, and require little of you. However, it is very possible, and even likely, that the training will be driven by an unequivocal allegiance to critical social justice ideology, suffused with antiracism and intersectionality, and will require an official (and heavy-handed) agreement and commitment from you that your conscience will not permit.

Therefore, before you attend, you need to get a lay of the land as to what type of DEI content you will likely be receiving. Here, it can be helpful to ask which scholars, academics, and writers the content is drawn from. If your investigation uncovers that you will be receiving illiberal instruction rooted in critical social justice, we suggest you take the following seven steps in order to have the greatest impact in voicing your concerns and effecting change in your organization's DEI program. This list is taken from the work of secular author Helen Pluckrose, who has written extensively on critical theory and social justice.[4]

Step 1: Understand Critical Social Justice terminology and concepts.

Step 2: Understand your own principled objections to Critical Social Justice.

Step 3: Understand and keep records of the communications and/or policies and programs being proposed.

Step 4: Network with others in your organization.

Step 5: Determine a strategic response that will be the most effective and least risky.

Step 6: Be part of ongoing change and build a community.

Step 7: Seek immediate support from relevant organizations and groups.

We highly recommend consulting Pluckrose's *Counterweight Handbook* for practical, secular approaches to countering wokeness in secular workplaces.

Pronoun Hospitality

Next, we want to consider pronoun hospitality. We are often asked whether we should honor someone's pronouns when they differ from their biological sex. In other words, if a biological male asks you to refer to him as she or her, should you assent? The short answer is no. With that said, there is no need to be rude or demeaning. Just don't use the person's preferred pronouns. It is easy to verbally navigate around such usage.

For example, when speaking directly to someone who identifies as transgender, pronouns are unnecessary. Use the person's name or the pronoun *you*. When you are speaking about them, use their first or last name. The word *they* has also been used colloquially as a genderless singular pronoun for centuries (e.g., "I talked to the bank teller, and they told me to come back next week").

If your company or organization wants you to verbally state your pronouns at the start of a meeting or in your signature line on your email, you should respectfully decline. You should not aid and abet an ideology premised on lies about human biology and human nature. In the context of your work environment, under Title VII of the Civil Rights Act of 1964, you have a right and a degree of legal protection surrounding your "sincerely held beliefs." Get acquainted with what protections you have.

Refusing pronoun hospitality is your way of recognizing that pronouns have been weaponized by the transgender movement in order to conscript people to its cause. Transgenderism is a lie. Consequently, as theologian and ethicist Andrew Walker has stated,

> In the transgender debate, Christians must be vigilant to avoid using language that serves falsehood. We should

> not allow our language to be drafted into a cause that is fundamentally false on the one hand, and positively harmful on the other. Not yielding on this point might be cumbersome at times, but one must really understand the insidious subterranean elements at work in something as putatively routine as pronouns.[5]

Regardless of how the ideas of critical social theory are manifested in the workplace, Christians should consider framing their critiques in terms of values that their company already espouses. For example, if your company's DEI training casts opposition to same-sex marriage as bigotry, you could appeal to the Bible. However, your company's HR department likely feels no compulsion to embrace biblical values. In contrast, if they are committed to values like inclusion or freedom of conscience, you could say something like this: "Many religious people—including Jews, Muslims, Hindus, and Buddhists—are opposed to same-sex marriage for reasons that have nothing to do with hatred. Your training material misrepresents them and will likely make them feel unwelcome and marginalized. I know our company is committed to respecting people's freedom of conscience. I share this commitment. So I will respect others' right to disagree with me and want them to respect my right to disagree with them." Such an approach, which is outlined in *The Counterweight Handbook*,[6] will often be more fruitful than an appeal to Scripture because you are calling the company to reaffirm values they already claim to hold rather than asking them to alter their values.

REACHING OTHER CHRISTIANS

Over the years, we've met many Christians who are either skeptical or outright hostile to the idea that contemporary critical theory is a problem. Resistance comes in several forms.

Some Christians insist that any critique of wokeness is merely an excuse to promote conservative politics. This is incorrect. While people *can* conceal political motives underneath the cloak of anti-woke analysis, we've shown throughout the book that our primary concerns are theological in nature. First and foremost, contemporary critical theory is incompatible with Christianity. Political implications come later.

Other Christians may argue that criticism of wokeness is just an excuse to shut down biblical discussions about race and justice. Again, while this *can* be the case, it need not be. Our consistent message has been that we should reject racism and critical race theory because both are incompatible with Christianity.

It's also worth pointing out that both of these criticisms amount to Bulverism (see chapter 4). Even if it were the case that criticism of wokeness came only from political operatives who were wholly indifferent to biblical justice, it wouldn't follow that those criticisms were false.

Finally, Christians may argue that we should take an "eat the meat and spit out the bones" posture toward contemporary critical theory, the same posture that we take toward Platonic concepts like forms or Freudian concepts like the ego. However, as we've shown, the errors of contemporary critical theory are located in its most central concepts. In the same way that we'd never recommend "eating the meat and spitting out the bones" of Satanism or Nazism, we should not recommend "eating the meat and spitting out the bones" of queer theory. This is especially true when many Christians are mistaking bones for meat and are choking to death.

Having considered these common objections, two approaches are helpful for reaching fellow believers.

First, being able to point people toward primary literature is immensely important. Unfortunately, few Christians have actually read critical race theorists or queer theorists for themselves and may accept a simplistic and often inaccurate summary from a pundit who shares their own views. The direct quotes and references in this book (and the far more comprehensive catalog in *Critical Dilemma*) let critical theorists explain what they believe in their own words. More often than not, Christians will see the contradictions between what they say and what the Bible teaches.

Second, the concept of a "woke breaking point" is important. Even if someone agrees in principle that contemporary critical theory is unbiblical, they may be skeptical that these ideas are influencing conservative Christians. If so, ask them what would convince them. What if authors from major evangelical outlets embraced liberal theology or apostatized altogether? What if major evangelical publishers were printing defenses of critical race theory? What if major evangelical organizations were platforming woke speakers? All of these are happening or have happened. Our goal is to have them identify concrete scenarios that would prompt them to reevaluate their position. Then show them the receipts. For instance, you could point them to books like *God Is a Black Woman* by Dr. Christena Cleveland[7] or *Can "White" People Be Saved?* from Love Sechrest et al.[8] to demonstrate the trajectory that some evangelicals are on.

Patience is especially important when it comes to fellow Christians. Of course, some professing Christians may not be genuine believers at all; their lack of saving faith could be the main reason they cannot see these issues clearly. However, some true believers genuinely don't see the danger of these ideas and will be uninterested in abstract arguments. In such cases, it may take a concrete, personal encounter with woke ideology to shake them out of their complacency. Your job is to give them a framework for understanding what they're seeing and why it's part of a larger, unbiblical worldview.

REACHING CHRISTIAN LEADERS

Both of us have received numerous emails, some of them frantic, asking for help with churches or Christians organizations that are perceived to have "gone woke." Alternatively, a church or an organization may simply be staying silent on certain issues, feeling that topics like race or transgenderism are too political to address in any official capacity. So how should concerned Christians speak to Christian leaders?

More than anything, apply the principle of charity. Treat others as you want to be treated. Don't assume that your pastor has become a cultural Marxist because he used the phrase *social justice* or because he preached a sermon about racism. Assume good intentions. Meet in person. Ask questions. Seek clarification.

Once you are clear on their views, provide specifics about your own concerns. Don't say something vague like "I think you're promoting critical theory." Instead, cite explicit statements from sermons or Sunday school lessons. Point to specific authors. Explain your objections, and then listen to the response.

Throughout conversations like these, you should continually refer back to the Bible. Don't say, "I reject the concept of 'white privilege.'" Instead, point out that Peggy McIntosh's conception of white privilege relies on her embrace of collective guilt. In contrast, the Bible insists that we are individually morally culpable and does not hold us accountable for the guilt of our ancestors (Deuteronomy 24:16; Jeremiah 31:27-30; Ezekiel 18:14-20).

Finally, make it clear that your ultimate concerns are theological, not political. Obviously, a consistent rejection of woke ideology has political implications, which we'll discuss in the next chapter. But the primary mission of the church is spiritual, and spiritual concerns need to be foregrounded in discussions with Christian leaders. To the extent that Christians embrace critical theory, they will abandon biblical views on gender, sexuality, identity, morality, and truth. These conflicts go far beyond the culture war and are matters that must be addressed by church leadership if they want to be faithful to God's command to shepherd the flock under their care (1 Peter 5:2-3).

REACHING THE DISSIDENT RIGHT

While Christians are quite rightly concerned about the tremendous inroads that critical theory has made within the culture and within the church, we can't overlook a backlash against wokeness that often takes the form of White identitarianism and antisemitism.

Those of us who are over 40 can remember the Before Times. In other words, to us, the Great Awokening is an aberration that we're seeking to correct. In contrast, to anyone under the age of 20, the insanity of the Great Awokening may be the only world they can remember. They grew up being taught about their white privilege in public schools where classmates came back from summer vacation with a new gender. They've spent thousands of hours scrolling through TikTok and reading edgelord bait posts on 4chan. Consequently, they tend to go in one of two directions: a zealous embrace of wokeness (which we've already discussed) or an equally zealous repudiation of anything that even reminds them of wokeness. The latter group may be safe from the insanity of the progressive left, but they are in danger of embracing other unbiblical, reactionary ideas.

For example, within contemporary critical theory, straight White men are classified as a canonical oppressor group. They are told that whiteness is inherently oppressive and simultaneously that they must identify as White, not as Irish-American or Italian-American.[9] They are positioned as patriarchal imperialists who live on stolen land and whose cultural heritage is nothing more than an uninterrupted history of enslavement, rape, and violence. Is it any wonder that some are turning to the far right, whom they see as the only group that won't mock them for their inborn characteristics?

Therefore, the nonnegotiable first step in reaching the dissident right is to actively oppose contemporary critical theory. A person who embraces racism because they hate CRT has no excuse. They will give an account to God for their sin. Full stop. But if a pastor has been soft-pedaling CRT, then he will also give an account to God for his failure in leadership. In God's eyes, anti-White racism is neither more nor less sinful than anti-Black racism. Even making this basic biblical point can pull some people off the pathway to radicalization.

Discipleship is another important component. Young people are attracted to ideas that are edgy, transgressive, and defiant. They don't need condescension, but they do need mature Christians who will listen to their concerns and model love, joy, peace, patience, kindness, gentleness, goodness, faithfulness, and self-control. This is especially true given how much online content is consumed by the younger generation. Their minds and hearts are being formed by online communities. Provide them with a real community that will support and shape them.

Finally, keep the focus on theology, not on politics. Some younger evangelicals are turning to Magisterial Reformers like Luther and Calvin and are discovering that they had very different views than typical American evangelicals on the relationship between church and state, the best form of government, and the role of the civil magistrate. It would therefore be unwise to attack someone for holding political perspectives that were common among conservative Protestants for centuries. A young person who romanticizes monarchy is different from a young person who believes that Whites are superior to non-Whites. Be careful not to confuse unconventional political opinions (the former) with sin (the latter).

TURNING THEORY INTO PRACTICE

Theoretical knowledge of contemporary critical theory is necessary but not sufficient to protect society and safeguard the church. We also have to reach people who are being influenced by its ideas. In this chapter, we've outlined strategies for speaking boldly, graciously, and truthfully to your children, your neighbors, your schools, your co-workers, your Christians friends, your pastors, and others. We'd like to close with two final admonitions: be prayerful and be patient.

The conflict between Christianity and contemporary critical theory is a clash between two worldviews, two religions, two sources of meaning, purpose, and value. In its most extreme forms, wokeness is a spiritual stronghold against which all our philosophical, rhetorical, and political weapons are powerless. The pink-haired, gender-fluid, radical anarchist Antifa otherkin shouting "Death to Israel" needs more than just an ideological adjustment. He needs the gospel. So pray that God would use you to bring the gospel of grace and truth to your neighbors and to your culture.

We also need patience. When you make a well-reasoned, biblical case for your beliefs and are rebuffed, don't become cynical or angry. Don't abandon God-honoring conduct or biblical principles for the sake of "winning." Jesus regularly compared working in the kingdom of God to farming. Hard ground needs to be broken up, seeds need to be planted, weeds need to be pulled, sprouts need to be watered. Growth takes time. Obey God and leave the results to him.

10

WHAT NOW?

We began this book by comparing the Great Awokening to a religious revival. After nine chapters, that analogy hopefully makes more sense. Wokeness is the contemporary cultural expression of critical theory, a set of academic ideas that has come to function as a comprehensive worldview. It offers a vision of social reality, knowledge, identity, morality, and justice. It is driven by utopian dreams and longings. It catechizes young people into its central precepts via social media and gender studies classes. And then it sends them out to be its witnesses in Hollywood, and in all California and America, and to the ends of the earth.

We've also shown that this new religion is fundamentally incompatible with Christianity. Its basic assumptions will constantly run up against core biblical truths about God, man, revelation, truth, sin, redemption, authority, hierarchy, gender, and sexuality. These are serious problems that Christians cannot overlook. Yes, we need to think carefully. But we also need to take action.

Therefore, we'd like to close our book by offering two admonitions and an encouragement when it comes to opposing woke ideology. First, we need to speak out against critical theory in the public square. Second, we need to keep critical theory out of the church. And finally, we need to trust in God's sovereignty, love, and power.

INFLUENCING SOCIETY

One of our goals as Christians should be to influence society for good. In this book, we've spent almost all of our time arguing that critical theory is theologically incompatible with Christianity. That is and will always be our primary concern in relation to this topic. However, because Christianity is true, the incompatibility of contemporary critical theory and Christianity puts contemporary critical theory at odds with reality itself, inevitably leading to bad policy prescriptions.

For example, contemporary critical theory views all disparities as evidence of systemic oppression and sees unequal treatment as the remedy to be applied as needed until outcomes are equal. This approach guarantees injustice, partiality, and strife all in the name of social justice. Similarly, contemporary critical theory views all expressions of gender and sexuality as equally valid, views gender roles as inherently oppressive, and believes in questioning all moral norms. This attitude has accelerated the breakdown of the family, producing neglected children, generational poverty, and existential emptiness.

Consequently, we as Christians should be public in our criticism of critical theory and our promotion of a Christian worldview.

A City on a Hill

One major obstacle to some Christians' engagement with critical theory is their innate aversion to what is called the culture war—the endless, internecine battle between conservatives and progressives over their vision of public morality, justice, government, and the common good. Some evangelicals view this debate as a distraction from the primary spiritual work of Christians: to preach the gospel. However, this aversion is a mistake.

Jesus expects us to not merely believe the gospel but to live out and act on our beliefs in a way that will positively affect the culture around us. He calls us to be "the light of the world," "a city on a hill," and a "light...on a stand...that gives light to all in the house" so that people "may see [our] good works and give glory to [our] Father who is in heaven" (Matthew 5:14-16). In the same way, Peter writes: "Keep your conduct among the Gentiles honorable, so that when they speak against you as evildoers, they may see your good deeds and glorify God on the day of visitation" (1 Peter 2:12). Our good works are meant to be seen and recognized by non-Christians who, even if they reject Christianity and revile us, will be shown what is good and right by our actions.

Christians should do good not merely in the cultural sphere, but in the political sphere. Throughout the Bible, God commands earthly rulers to wield their power justly and to do good to those under their authority (Leviticus 19:15; Proverbs 29:4; Romans 13:4-5). Therefore, Christians with any kind of authority ought to strive to do what is right and just in their public office. Yet even Christians without public offices cannot withdraw from working for the common good. In a representative democracy, Christians should try to elect leaders who will do what is right and just. Laws and public policies affect our neighbor in a myriad of ways. They will affect his education, his access to health care, his living conditions, his safety, and his income. Therefore, Christians should use their vote to elect officials they believe are most likely to enact good laws that will honor God and bless their neighbor.

Here, we should start small. Too many of us ignore local politics and pay attention only to national or statewide elections where, ironically, our votes are the least impactful. So don't confine "political activity" to pulling a lever once a year. Write a letter to your school superintendent. Speak up at a city council meeting. Send an email to your state representative.

Despite these arguments, some Christians will still reject any kind of cultural and political involvement as worldly. However, they are rarely consistent. Normally, they will still look back on the abolition of slavery in the UK and in the US as a great act of justice and righteousness. But in both cases, Christians were deeply politically involved and invested in dismantling the unjust laws that permitted those systems. Just laws do not change human hearts and cannot save anyone. But they can genuinely improve the lives of both Christians and non-Christians alike. As Dr. Martin Luther King Jr. said, "It may be true that the law cannot make a man love me...but it can restrain him from lynching me."[1]

Here, it is helpful to distinguish the mission of the church from the work of individual Christians. We agree that the church, as the church, should not be deeply invested in politics. Its primary duty is to preach the gospel to a lost world, administer the ordinances of baptism and the Lord's supper, call believers together for corporate prayer and worship, and disciple Christians. However, individual Christians have callings that go beyond the primary mission of the institutional church. The church is not called to be a doctor or a lawyer or an engineer or a mechanic or a teacher or a janitor. But an individual Christian may be called to any of these vocations. While the church should never turn into a political action committee, it should teach Christians how to steward all of their resources and abilities, including their right to vote, for the glory of God and the good of their neighbor.

Finally, Christians do not need to choose between promoting Christian values in our culture and preaching the gospel. Mere "cultural Christianity" does not save anyone. A person can imbibe and even promote biblical values and still be dead in their sin. But why should we welcome the disappearance of cultural Christianity if it is preserving Christian norms and restraining evil? A non-Christian husband may remain faithful to his wife only in response to social pressure and out of fear for his reputation. But his children will nonetheless reap the benefits of growing up in an intact family. A rich man may give to the poor only to burnish his public image and not out of love for God. But the hungry will still be fed and the homeless will still be housed. If we love our neighbor, we will want them to live in a society where Christian values are widespread even if the people embracing them are not Christians.

What does it look like for Christians to oppose contemporary critical theory in the public square?

Individually, it means one-on-one conversations that don't avoid hot-button issues like race, class, gender, and sexuality. Of course, the gospel should always be central. But we can't always avoid all other topics to avoid giving offense. Remember, bad ideas hurt people.

An example from Neil's life is illustrative. After George Floyd's death, social media was flooded with claims that Black Americans were under constant threat from police and had to live in fear of being killed. With some hesitation, Neil wrote an article summarizing the actual data on police shootings.[2] He was careful and sympathetic, but pointed out that an unarmed Black man has roughly the same chance of being killed by police as he has of being struck by lightning. Neil was too nervous to share the article publicly, but sent it to a few friends. One of his friends had a Black roommate who had been so terrified by popular narratives about law-enforcement officers hunting Black men that he didn't want to leave his house. After reading Neil's article, he realized that the narrative that had been peddled to him was false. He stopped worrying and went out for pizza.

What was more compassionate in this case? Allowing someone to live in terror? Or telling them the truth in love? How many of our neighbors can be freed from faulty narratives, bad ideas, false identities, and the burden of shame or enmity or resentment with simple, gentle correction? Your neighbors with a transgender-identified daughter may be desperate for someone to offer them a perspective that differs from the 3,000-member Facebook Moms group urging them to start puberty blockers. Your co-worker may need marriage advice that doesn't come from *The View.* You can be gentle and kind and confident and forthright all at the same time.

Culturally, opposing critical theory means opposing it not just in private conversations, but in public spaces where the risk is often greater. In interpersonal contexts, you can establish some level of trust with your interlocutor. When speaking out in the presence of strangers, that trust will not necessarily exist. You may be called racist for criticizing critical race theory. You may be called a bigot for opposing transgenderism. You may be called lots of names. You cannot let that silence you. By all means, interrogate your own heart. Test your motives. Be honest with God about your own sin. Take the log out of your own eye. But then be willing to tell the truth.

Here's another real-world example: In September 2020, the North Carolina School Board proposed "A Resolution to Support Equity and Excellence in North Carolina Public Education."[3] Parts of the proposal defined equity as "equality of opportunity," which Christians should support. But elsewhere in the proposal, it stated that "historical and current systems of inequitable and inadequate resource allocation, disproportionate suspensions and expulsions, lack of access to and supports for teachers of color, unequal access to educational opportunities and supports, implicit and explicit biases, and segregation perpetuate inequity *in the outcomes of students*" (emphasis added). Note the sleight of hand here. The motte of "equality of opportunity" quietly transformed into the bailey of "equality of outcome" for more than a million students in the North Carolina public school system.

Worse yet, the same policy stated that the State Board of Education would henceforth "[embrace] equity as a framework" and would "review and appropriately revise its policies through an equity lens and commit to...create and maintain an equity officer to ensure consistency and continuity with this essential guiding principle." In other words, the entire educational framework for all public schools in North Carolina was shifted to "equity," which would be used as the singular lens to evaluate all policies, and the power to enforce this expansive vision would be placed into the hands of a single person.

Recognizing the dangers of this resolution, Neil published an article in *The Federalist* critiquing it and talked at length to school board members about its flaws. Unfortunately, the resolution was still adopted.[4] But Neil's advocacy helped raise state officials' awareness of the dangers of social justice ideology.

One objection that Christians may have to this kind of public activism is that it will alienate non-Christians. They might say, "It's inevitable that non-Christians will be offended by the gospel. But shouldn't that be the only offense? Why create stumbling blocks that will keep people from Jesus?" This worry is understandable, but fundamentally mistaken.

God's law is not an obstacle to the gospel. Indeed, it is a prerequisite to the gospel. If we do not know that God's moral law exists and that we have broken it, we will not seek salvation. Thus, it makes little sense to say that we should avoid any discussion of what God requires of us in his law.

There is also a problem of consistency for many who raise this objection. For example, they will speak out loudly (and rightfully) against certain evils like racism or greed with little concern that they might offend racists or greedy people! The only way for us to truly avoid the possibility of offending anyone is to never make any public moral judgments about anything. But do we really believe that Christians should never publicly condemn greed or murder or adultery or cruelty?

Taking a public stand against critical theory doesn't mean that we should only be known for this opposition. We can put most of our energy into sharing the gospel, showing hospitality, defending the truth of Christianity, visiting prisoners, or caring for the poor. What we must not do is to refuse to take a stand on issues of great significance merely because they are controversial.

What are some of the practical areas in which the ideological underpinnings of critical theory must be exposed and challenged?

Abortion

First, Christians should vehemently resist abortion. We should note that professing Christians who are pro-abortion are calling into question the veracity of their faith. If this is you, you need to look into the issue further, because the Bible repeatedly affirms the value and personhood of the unborn (Psalm 139:13-14; Jeremiah 1:5; Luke 1:41-44) and God's hatred of murder (Exodus 20:13; Proverbs 6:16-19; Isaiah 59:7).

Despite the *Dobbs* Supreme Court decision that overturned *Roe v. Wade*, approximately one million babies are still killed in the womb every year, and only a small minority of Americans think abortion should be illegal in all circumstances.[5] The Democratic National Committee's platform has shifted from wanting abortion to be "safe, legal, and rare" to vowing to "repeal the Hyde Amendment [that bans federal funding of abortion], and protect and codify the right to reproductive freedom [i.e., abortion]."[6] Grievously, in 2024, the Republican Party removed language from its platform asserting "the sanctity of human life" and that "the unborn child has a fundamental right to life."[7] Therefore, at the time of this book's writing, neither party's platform demonstrates God's love for the unborn and his hatred of abortion.

Critical theory props up abortion by insisting that it is an entailment of social justice. Prominent Black feminist and critical pedagogue bell hooks makes this connection crystal clear in her book *Feminism Is for Everybody*:

> If feminism is a movement to end sexist oppression, and depriving females of reproductive rights is a form of sexist

> oppression, then one cannot be anti-choice and be feminist. A woman...cannot be anti-abortion and an advocate of feminism...there [can be] no genuine sexual liberation for women and men without better, safer contraceptives—without the right to a safe, legal abortion.[8]

Popular pro-choice groups routinely apply the same intersectional feminist logic. For instance, on the Planned Parenthood website, an article entitled "Feminism—A Process" insists:

> As with others who have been targets of bigotry, including people of color, the LGBTQ community, the physically or mentally disabled, immigrants, and so many others who are objects of blame and projection, women can and must claim the dignity that humanizes our society. Control over our sexuality is but one area in which we must demand our rights.[9]

Thus, Christians must oppose not only abortion but the ideological justifications offered in defense of it.

Sexuality

Second, Christians should resist the normalization of LGBTQ+. The ideas of queer theory are coming to dominate our discussions of sexuality and gender identity but are fundamentally opposed to biblical sexual ethics and, as a result, are fundamentally opposed to human flourishing.

Christians must be willing to publicly and unashamedly affirm that marriage is, by definition, the union of one man and one woman, and that the gender binary is rooted in biology. We should also be willing to protect the sexual innocence of children, shield them from gender ideology, and defend the rights of parents. We encourage you to check out the work of Katy Faust on this front, along with her organization Them Before Us.[10]

An example of steadfast Christian engagement with culture comes from Rosaria Butterfield, a former lesbian professor of gender studies at Syracuse who became a Christian through her friendship with a local Presbyterian pastor and his wife. In 2023, she attended a Durham Public School Board meeting to support parental rights bill SB49, which prevented schools from concealing students' professed gender identity from their parents. Amidst a crowd of people who opposed the new state legislation, Butterfield voiced her support for the bill, speaking about her former life as an LGBTQ+ activist, the importance of parental rights, and scientific evidence against child transition.[11] Butterfield's three-minute speech is an excellent example of making a public case in the public square for values and policies grounded in God's reality.

Merit

Third, Christians should resist the erosion of meritocracy. It is wholly legitimate to ask whether or to what extent we actually live in a meritocracy in which ability and hard work trump wealth and personal connections. This question even has biblical origins. The author of Ecclesiastes lamented the lack of fairness and justice in the world and wrote, "There is a vanity that takes place on earth, that there are righteous people to whom it happens according to the deeds of the wicked, and there are wicked people to whom it happens according to the deeds of the righteous" (Ecclesiastes 8:14). Yet, as we noted in chapter 6, critical race theory attacks not only the inaccurate assessment of merit but the concept of merit itself. This cynicism will lead to social dysfunction and injustice.

A recent example of how the push for equity can be used to justify injustice is found in the Supreme Court's 6-3 decision in *Students for Fair Admissions, Inc. v. President and Fellows of Harvard College.*

The case was brought on behalf of Asian students who charged that Harvard and the University of North Carolina were discriminating against them in the admissions process. During the discovery process of the lawsuit, Harvard was forced to release admissions data that revealed shocking evidence of discrimination against Asians.

For example, when Harvard applicants were sorted into deciles by academic achievement (grade-point averages and standardized test scores), the top 10 percent of applicants were disproportionately Asian. Yet only 13 percent of Asian students and 15 percent of White students in this highest-performing tier were admitted to Harvard. In contrast, 31 percent of Hispanic students and 56 percent of Black students in the same tier received admission. Similarly, in the fifth decile by academic performance (between the fortieth and fiftieth percentiles, which corresponds roughly to the median applicant), 3 percent of Whites and 2 percent of Asians were admitted compared to 9 percent of Hispanics and 22 percent of Blacks. In other words, in this group of students with roughly equal academic scores, a Black student was more than ten times more likely to receive admission to Harvard than an Asian student.[12]

It could be argued that Harvard does not admit students solely on the basis of academics, but includes other factors like extracurricular activities. But here, the data are even more disturbing. Evangelical lawyer Hohn Cho summarizes the findings: "over a six-year period, as a group average, Asian applicants had the highest academic ratings (including GPA, test scores, AP exams taken, AP exam scores), highest extra-curricular ratings, highest alumni interview overall scores, and either highest or second-highest scores on letters of reference from counselors and teachers."[13] Asians were rated significantly below every other group of applicants only on their "personal ratings." Cho concludes "either the bulk of the Asian cohort year-after-year was made up of misanthropic miscreants in comparison to their fellow white, Hispanic, and African American applicants, or the Harvard admissions staff—who again, had never even met the applicants in the vast majority of cases—had their fists on the scale when it came to the highly subjective personal ratings."

In this case, the label of "institutional racism" does seem appropriate. The evidence shows strongly that college applicants were not being impartially admitted based on their merit, and the Supreme Court rightly found that "admissions programs at Harvard College and the University of North Carolina violate the equal protection clause of the 14th Amendment."[14]

This willingness to jettison impartiality in the pursuit of desired social outcomes is becoming increasingly widespread. For instance, in 2022, the website Resume Builder commissioned a survey of 1,000 hiring managers to find out how Diversity, Equity, and Inclusion initiatives were perceived to be affecting actual hiring practices. Despite their insistence that DEI programs "create more positive workplaces and offer great [returns on investment]," their findings were alarming. Of the hiring managers surveyed:

- "52% believe their company practices 'reverse discrimination' [against white men] in hiring"
- "1 in 6 have been asked to deprioritize hiring white men"
- "48% have been asked to prioritize diversity over qualifications" and
- "53% believe their job will be in danger if they don't hire enough diverse employees"[15]

As Christians, we should oppose discrimination in all its forms, whether it is directed against Blacks or Asians or Whites or women or men. It is certainly legitimate to ask whether supposedly meritocratic systems are indeed based on merit. It is also legitimate to ask whether there are barriers to access that unintentionally act as obstacles to certain groups. Or to ask whether managers are objectively assessing candidates' merit rather than being influenced by personal prejudices. Nevertheless, we must press this question: Does objective merit exist, and are we committed to evaluating people based on their merit rather than on their gender or skin color? The solution to injustice isn't more injustice, and the solution to discrimination isn't more discrimination.

Parental Rights

Finally, Christians should stand up for parental rights, which, as we alluded to in chapter 7, are being eroded by the idea that children belong to the community or to the state rather than to their parents. This tepid view of parental rights has played out in recent court cases and in comments by school boards and educators.

For example, in 2018, a judge in Ohio removed a transgender teen from the home of Christian parents because the judge deemed the parents to be unfit for the sole reason that they would not allow their child to undergo hormone treatment in an attempt to transition.[16]

In May of 2021, Jeremy and Mary Cox lost custody of their child when the Indiana Department of Child Services (DCS) received two complaints that they were being abusive because they disagreed with and obstructed their son's attempt to transition.[17] Despite a DCS investigation finding no abuse or wrongdoing by the Coxes, DCS was able and willing to use the state's CHINS (Children in Need of Services) procedures to prevent the Coxes from getting their son back.[18] In March of 2024, the Supreme Court officially declined to hear the Coxes' petition contending that the state of Indiana had violated their parental rights, putting an exclamation mark on a three-year horror story and nightmare for the Coxes.

In 2023, the Montgomery County Board of Education in Maryland ruled that parents could not opt out of their elementary school-age children's instruction regarding sexuality and gender transitioning. The board argued and the district court agreed "that once parents drop their children off at school, they have no right to know what is taught inside."[19]

In 2020, Harvard Law School professor Elizabeth Bartholet recommended a "presumptive ban" on homeschooling.[20] She argued that "some parents can't be trusted to not abuse and neglect their children…kids are going to be way better off if both parent and state are involved."[21] Bartholet believes it is crucial that "the state have some say in protecting children and in trying to raise them."

We, of course, recognize that there is a point when parental neglect or abuse requires the removal of children from a home via state power. Yet a major problem that plagues the issue of parental rights is the determination of what constitutes *actual* neglect and *actual* abuse. In the cases above, the state wielded or was being urged to wield its power unjustly, suppressing the good, just, and reasonable concerns of parents.

Cultural assaults on the unborn, the family, meritocracy, and parental rights are not the only issues that Christians should care about. But they are threats to the common good because they undermine Christian values. As we said earlier, the Bible does not just *accidentally* provide the correct perspective on these topics. Because it is God's Word, its prescriptions will always promote human flourishing at both the spiritual and material levels.

PROTECTING THE CHURCH

Though Christians should push back against critical theory in the culture, it is even more imperative that we remove it, root and branch, from the church. If the church itself is captive to unbiblical thinking, it will be much harder for us to reach the world.

Worldview

The gospel runs counter to contemporary critical theory for innumerable reasons. The gospel is the good news that Jesus the Son of

God and the Jewish Messiah came to live a sinless life, die a substitutionary death on the cross in our place, and rise from the dead to save us from God's just wrath. We receive the benefits of Christ's sacrifice not by going to church or by doing good works but trusting in him, resting in his mercy, grace, and forgiveness.

To critical theorists, this narrative is intensely problematic. It assumes a hierarchy of power; God is our Creator and our judge who has the authority to rightly condemn us to hell. It assumes the existence of objective moral values and duties that transcend culture and that all human beings are obligated to obey. It claims to be the one true story of religion such that all competing religious traditions are false. It is positioned as patriarchal, Western, and imperialist, driving out indigenous religions. It is contained within a divinely inspired book that was written almost entirely by Jews and entirely by men, thereby excluding female and non-Jewish voices. God himself is portrayed as Father rather than Mother, and King rather than Queen. And Jesus is presented as the Son of God, not the Daughter of God, thereby giving a divine stamp of approval on patriarchy. This is a stark reminder that professing Christians who are constantly lamenting and deriding patriarchy wholesale are grossly out of step with the God they claim to know.

Most problematic of all, the gospel is primarily a message of spiritual salvation, not temporal social transformation. Its primary aim is not improved conditions on Earth, and it urges Christians to set their ultimate hope on eternity. It sees sin, not oppression, as the ultimate evil, and the eschatological restoration of the universe, not social justice, as the ultimate goal. Therefore, from the perspective of critical theorists, it is a mechanism by which Christian clerics shore up their own power by blunting demands for revolution in the present.

In the face of these objections, Christians must reject critical theorists' framing wholesale. The gospel is not Western; it is universal, like math or logic. It did not come from White males, but from God.

Middle-Eastern Jews, not Europeans, were chosen to be God's people, and through them, the Messiah of all humanity came to redeem all humanity. It does indeed exclude other religions—not because it is bigoted but because it is true, and truth necessarily excludes error. Finally, the life to come does matter more than the few short decades of our earthly existence, and Jesus is right to insist that we should prioritize the former over the latter.

Obviously, we can raise specific objections to how contemporary critical theory conceptualizes identity, oppression, justice, and truth. But Christians must grow accustomed to simply refusing to enter the conceptual universe that critical theory inhabits. In the same way, when we engage atheists or adherents of New Age religion, we should recognize at the outset that we have extremely different ideas about human nature, the universe's origin, and the meaning of life. When a progressive insists that Christianity is a Eurocentric religion that justifies hierarchical oppression, before we address the veracity of this (objectively false) claim, we should say (or at least think!) something like this: "I reject the idea that religions can be known to be true or false by their geographical origin. I reject the idea that hierarchy is bad. I understand where you're coming from, but I am a Christian, so I think about truth, morality, and power differently than you."

Hermeneutics

Contemporary critical theory also threatens an evangelical approach to hermeneutics, the practice of properly interpreting the Bible. Protestants and evangelicals traditionally have interpreted the Bible by using historical-grammatical exegesis—that is, by parsing the grammar and syntax of the original writings and placing them in their historical context to understand the author's intent. The goal of exegesis is to discern the objective meaning of the text.

Unfortunately, contemporary critical theory undermines this approach. Contemporary critical theory constantly attempts to see through supposedly objective interpretations of texts to show how they really function to prop up the power and privilege of the interpreter. Relatedly, contemporary critical theory insists that the social location of straight, White, Western, male interpreters will undermine their attempts at objectivity such that non-straight, non-White, non-Western, non-male interpreters are necessary to truly understand the meaning of Scripture. The postmodern assumptions of many critical theorists will call into question whether texts even have objective meanings. Not only do our race, class, and gender make it difficult for us to interpret the text, but perhaps the text doesn't even have an objective meaning in the first place.

Again, in addition to arguing that historical Protestant theology is not exclusively White or Western or male, evangelicals need to cut to the heart of the matter and point out that the interpreter's social location does not determine whether their interpretation is true or false. When someone accuses us of offering a White, Eurocentric, male interpretation of Scripture, we should respond, "Interpretations of Scripture don't have genders or ethnicities. I reject the idea that good theology is Asian or African or European, just like I reject the idea that good mathematics or science is Asian or African or European. There is ultimately only true theology and false theology, biblical theology and unbiblical theology."

From that starting point, we can certainly go on to ask whether our particular experiences and social context have led us to misinterpret Scripture. But the central question must always be, What does the text actually say?

Unity

Even apart from these abstract problems, contemporary critical theory will create very concrete ones by shattering the unity of the church. Put bluntly, Whites and men will be forced into a posture of perpetual contrition and apology, while people of color and women will be expected to express perpetual grievance. If Whites or men object to this framework, they will be dismissed as fragile or bigoted. If people of color or women object, they will be dismissed as victims of internalized oppression.

This dynamic will be particularly destructive to discipleship, correction, and church discipline. If a straight White male pastor declares that—as an oppressor—his only role in discussions of race or gender or sexuality is that of a listener, what will he do when a member of his congregation begins to make dubious or even outright false claims about these topics? He will either have to retract his former statement and exercise his God-ordained duty to shepherd his flock, or he will have to bite his tongue, say nothing, and let the error spread. His mistake was submitting to the role of "oppressor" in the first place.

Of course, pastors should be humble, open to correction, slow to speak, and quick to listen. All Christians should display these qualities. But he and his fellow elders cannot abdicate their responsibility to wield genuine authority for the good of their fellow congregants.

Sexual Ethics

Another major practical concern is that contemporary critical theory's understanding of gender identity and sexuality is fundamentally unbiblical. Sexuality is not analogous to race or ethnicity. LGBTQ+ people are not oppressed by the gender binary or by biblical sexual ethics. Christians should not embrace sexual sin (either heterosexual sin or homosexual sin) as an identity. Both acts of sin and the desire to sin are sinful and should be resisted. In this way, Christians ought to treat sexual sin like we treat other sins.

Yes, we as Christians should be open about our own sinfulness, gentle toward sinners of all kinds, and ready to accept all who trust in Christ. But we can and must do this while holding fast to the Bible's repudiation of homosexuality and transgenderism. We must also do this by resisting the practice all too prevalent in the church, even the evangelical church, of casting the sinner as principally a victim. In every case when we commit a sin, we should be principally understood as a perpetrator versus a victim.

The Dissident Right

Finally, in the face of widespread wokeness, Christians still need to beware the unbiblical counterreaction arising from the far right. In his brilliant book the *Screwtape Letters*, Christian apologist C.S. Lewis warned readers that the devil's strategy is to convince people to

> direct the fashionable outcry of each generation against those vices of which it is least in danger and fix its approval on the virtue nearest to that vice which we are trying to make endemic. The game is to have them all running about with fire extinguishers whenever there is a flood, and all crowding to that side of the boat which is already nearly gunwale under.[22]

Oddly, this passage is sometimes used to downplay any threat that might emerge from anti-woke reactionaries on the right. If we're screaming and shouting about actual racism or antisemitism, aren't we merely running around with fire extinguishers in the midst of a flood? Isn't the real, imminent threat coming from the cancerous woke ideas that have infected our culture at the highest levels?

But here, it's important to recognize that Lewis was speaking in general terms. Yes, each age and culture may have certain characteristic errors. But elsewhere, in the very same book, he talks about how each individual can be inclined toward different sins and temptations. The same is true of churches. Regardless of the overall bent of each historical epoch, the greatest threat to individual people or to individual churches is always contextual.

A 30-year-old barista living in Manhattan probably doesn't need to be warned about the dangers of sexism. But a 17-year-old redditor with a bedroom covered in Donald Trump memorabilia probably doesn't need to be warned about the dangers of wokeness. The average church in a deep-blue urban county will not face the same threats as the average church in a deep-red rural county. In a polarized age, we will be pulled toward one of two extremes and will always be tempted to hyperfocus on the sins to which we are least susceptible. Therefore, no church should ever be dismissive of some particular type of sin on the grounds that the opposite sin is more prevalent. We don't cease to preach against sloth because some people make an idol of their work. We don't cease to preach about legalism because some people are antinomians.

Warning people about the dangers on both sides can help deradicalize them. We've often been told that critical race theory would be far less appealing to people if Christians had sufficiently repudiated racism during the Jim Crow era. We tend to agree. But, for exactly the same reason, the racism and antisemitism of the far right will be less appealing to people if Christians sufficiently repudiate the Great Awokening. Articulating a biblical vision of race, gender, sexuality, morality, and justice does not guarantee that people will reject sinful ideas. But it may convince those who are teetering on the edge that the Bible really does have better answers than those offered by the world.

Finally, many staunch anti-woke figures, including author James Lindsay[23] and podcaster Konstantin Kisin,[24] have warned about the rise of the dissident right, a group whose ideology is eerily reminiscent of the woke left. Those on the dissident right are also obsessed with racial categories, victimhood, hegemonic power, and radical social transformation, but their goal is an authoritarian state ruled by a Christian (or neo-pagan) Prince rather than a communist utopia.[25] Most ironic of all, at least some prominent members of the radical right are quite open about their appreciation for and reliance on the ideas of neo-Marxist Antonio Gramsci, the critical theorists of the Frankfurt School, and postmodern philosophers like Michel Foucault![26] While the dissident right is still small and relatively powerless, they are growing. And insofar as they adopt the same false, unbiblical ideas as the woke left, they should be opposed by Christians for the very same reasons.

ENCOURAGEMENT

We want to end our book with a note of encouragement. Despite what the media says, we are not living through unprecedented times. The United States was birthed out of the Revolutionary War, which witnessed a scrappy band of colonists defeat a global superpower. During the War of 1812, our nation's capital was captured, the White House was burned, and the president and his wife had to flee the city. More than 600,000 men died during the Civil War, and the president was assassinated less than a week after General Robert E. Lee surrendered at Appomattox Courthouse. The deadly Spanish Flu swept the globe during the height of World War I, killing approximately 50 million people on top of the 20 million who had died in the conflict. Another 75 million would die in World War II, not including the roughly six million Jews and millions of others who were victims of the Holocaust. The war ended when the US unleashed nuclear weapons on Japan, killing 350,000 with just two bombs. The Cuban Missile Crisis of October 1962 brought the world to the brink of nuclear war. Millions of people watched in horror as Muslim terrorists crashed planes into the Twin Towers and the Pentagon on September 11, 2001. And, of course, by mid-2024, the global COVID pandemic had killed just over seven million people, as estimated by the World Health Organization.[27]

These events should temper our attitude toward the cultural upheaval brought about by the Great Awokening. For all we know, we are on the cusp of some even greater historical turning point that will relegate Black Lives Matter and the second sexual revolution to a few brief paragraphs in future US history texts.

However, as Christians, our concerns are not and should not primarily be political, but spiritual. As C.S. Lewis reminds us, "Nations, cultures, arts, civilizations—these are mortal, and their life is to ours as the life of a gnat. But it is immortals whom we joke with, work with, marry, snub and exploit—immortal horrors or everlasting splendors."[28] One day, the United States of America will be a distant memory. It is no more invincible than the Hittite Empire, the Roman Empire, or the Ottoman Empire—which is to say that it is vulnerable, fragile, and transitory. But human beings will live eternally.

The primacy of the human soul should deeply encourage us as Christians. Yes, go vote. But your vote will be swallowed up in millions of others. And voting is always a choice between two or more sinners who may or may not deliver on their campaign promises, who may ignore their party's official platform, and who will likely make decisions that have unforeseen and unforeseeable negative consequences.

In contrast, we can be completely confident that the gospel answers every human's deepest need. It has no downsides. It has no unforeseen negative consequences. And it is not subject to chance or change.

In the same way, cultural change can be slow, erratic, and unpredictable. Again, speak up in your local school board meeting, at work, and in the public square. But don't neglect the far more sure and certain power you have to influence the individuals you know. Invest most deeply in the people around you: your children, your friends, your neighbors, your church family.

Remember, contemporary critical theory functions as a worldview. As a result, it will act as a barrier to Christianity. In challenging its presuppositions, assumptions, and precommitments, you are tilling the soil so that people can hear and respond to the gospel. In equipping Christians to recognize and reject contemporary critical theory, you are helping them to resist the cultural pressure to compromise, soften, or reject what the Bible teaches. You're fighting a spiritual battle, but not a new one. It's one that every generation of Christians has had to fight, a battle for people's minds and hearts. "For we do not wrestle against flesh and blood, but against the rulers, against the authorities, against the cosmic powers over this present darkness, against the spiritual forces of evil in the heavenly places" (Ephesians 6:12).

The hour is late. Let's get started.

GENERAL INDEX

SCRIPTURE INDEX

MALACHI

MATTHEW

MARK

LUKE

JOHN

ACTS

ROMANS

1 PETER

1 JOHN

REVELATION

NOTES

CHAPTER 1—THE GREAT AWOKENING

1. Amanda Hess, "'In This House' Yard Signs, and Their Curious Power," *The New York Times*, October 29, 2021, https://www.nytimes.com/2021/10/29/arts/in-this-house-yard-signs.html.

2. James Lindsay and Mike Nayna, "Postmodern Religion and the Faith of Social Justice," *Areo*, December 18, 2018, https://areomagazine.com/2018/12/18/postmodern-religion-and-the-faith-of-social-justice/.

3. Marina Watts, "In Smithsonian Race Guidelines, Rational Thinking and Hard Work Are White Values," *Newsweek*, July 17, 2020, https://www.newsweek.com/smithsonian-race-guidelines-rational-thinking-hard-work-are-white-values-1518333.

4. "Whiteness," National Museum of African American History and Culture, archived at https://web.archive.org/web/20230410021527/https://nmaahc.si.edu/learn/talking-about-race/topics/whiteness.

5. Zach Goldberg, "How the Media Led the Great Racial Awakening," *Tablet*, August 4, 2020, https://www.tabletmag.com/sections/news/articles/media-great-racial-awakening.

6. Damon Young, "Straight Black Men Are the White People of Black People," *The Root*, September 19, 2017, https://www.theroot.com/straight-black-men-are-the-white-people-of-black-people-1814157214.

7. Ekow Yankah, "Can My Children Be Friends With White People?," *The New York Times*, November 11, 2017, sec. Opinion, https://www.nytimes.com/2017/11/11/opinion/sunday/interracial-friendship-donald-trump.html.

8. Suzanna Walters, "Why Can't We Hate Men," *The Washington Post*, June 8, 2018, https://www.washingtonpost.com/opinions/why-cant-we-hate-men/2018/06/08/f1a3a8e0-6451-11e8-a69c-b944de66d9e7_story.html.

9. James Barnes, "I'm a Trans Man. I Didn't Realize How Broken Men Are," *Newsweek*, August 6, 2023, https://www.newsweek.com/trans-man-broken-men-1817169.

10. Ruby Hamad, "How White Women Use Strategic Tears to Silence Women of Colour," *The Guardian*, May 7, 2018, https://www.theguardian.com/commentisfree/2018/may/08/how-white-women-use-strategic-tears-to-avoid-accountability.

11. Paul Waldman, "The Most Dangerous Threat to America? White Male Entitlement," *The Washington Post*, July 22, 2022, https://www.washingtonpost.com/opinions/2022/07/22/white-male-entitlement-threat-to-america/.

12. Simon Hattenstone, "The Dad Who Gave Birth: 'Being Pregnant Doesn't Change Me Being a Trans Man,'" *The Guardian*, April 20, 2019, https://www.theguardian.com/society/2019/apr/20/the-dad-who-gave-birth-pregnant-trans-freddy-mcconnell.

13. Charles M. Blow, "How White Women Use Themselves as Instruments of Terror," *The New York Times*, May 27, 2020, https://www.nytimes.com/2020/05/27/opinion/racism-white-women.html.

14. "What We Believe," *Black Lives Matter*, archived July 1, 2020, accessed December 7, 2022, https://web.archive.org/web/20200901000000*/https://blacklivesmatter.com/what-we-believe/.

15. Jenna Scherer, "Inside the Groundbreaking Queer Reboot of 'She-Ra,'" *Rolling Stone*, June 12, 2020, https://www.rollingstone.com/tv-movies/tv-movie-features/she-ra-reboot-netflix-queer-creator-interview-1013623/.

16. J.K. Rowling, Twitter Post, Dec. 19, 2019, https://x.com/jk_rowling/status/1207646162813100033?lang=en.

17. Abby Gardner, "A Complete Breakdown of the J.K. Rowling Transgender-Comments Controversy," *Glamour*, April 11, 2024, https://www.glamour.com/story/a-complete-breakdown-of-the-jk-rowling-transgender-comments-controversy.

18. J.K. Rowling, "J.K. Rowling Writes about Her Reasons for Speaking out on Sex and Gender Issues," jkrowling.com, June 10, 2020, https://www.jkrowling.com/opinions/j-k-rowling-writes-about-her-reasons-for-speaking-out-on-sex-and-gender-issues/.

19. "Prison Bosses Defend Sending Rapist Isla Bryson to Women's Jail," *BBC*, February 22, 2023, https://www.bbc.com/news/uk-scotland-scotland-politics-64729029.

20. "Black Lives Matter Grassroots Statement in Solidarity With the Palestinian People," October 10, 2023, https://blmgrassroots.org/black-lives-matter-grassroots-statement-in-solidarity-with-the-palestinian-people/.

21. David Propper and Alex Oliveira, "BLM Chicago under Fire for Pro-Palestinian Post Featuring Paragliding Terrorist: 'Disgusting and Disgraceful,'" *The New York Post*, October 10, 2023, https://nypost.com/2023/10/10/blm-chicago-under-fire-for-pro-palestine-post-featuring-paragliding-terrorist/.

22. Neil Shenvi and Pat Sawyer, "What Are We To Make of 'Queers for Palestine'?" *Substack*, February 12, 2024, https://www.realityslaststand.com/p/what-are-we-to-make-of-queers-for.

23. Harvard CAPS/Harris Poll, December 13-14, 2023, https://harvardharrispoll.com/wp-content/uploads/2023/12/HHP_Dec23_KeyResults.pdf.

24. TheDemocrats, Twitter Post, December 6, 2023, https://x.com/TheDemocrats/status/1732585789744120131.

25. Netflix Jr., "Family Time Fun! CoComelon Lane Singalong for Kids | Netflix Jr," YouTube video, December 11, 2023, https://www.youtube.com/watch?v=dmNwKPRzyfM&t=289s.

26. Jones, Jeffrey M., "LGBTQ+ Identification in U.S. Now at 7.6%," *Gallup*, March 13, 2024, https://news.gallup.com/poll/611864/lgbtq-identification.aspx.

27. John Bitzan, "2023 American College Student Freedom, Progress and Flourishing Survey,"

NDSU, 2023, 18-19, https://www.ndsu.edu/fileadmin/challeyinstitute/Research_Briefs/American_College_Student_Freedom_Progress_and_Flourishing_Survey_2023.pdf.

28. "Protecting Children from Chemical and Surgical Mutilation," *Federal Register,* January 28, 2025, https://www.federalregister.gov/documents/2025/02/03/2025-02194/protecting-children-from-chemical-and-surgical-mutilation.

29. "Additional Measures to Combat Anti-Semitism." *Federal Register,* January 29, 2025, https://www.federalregister.gov/documents/2025/02/03/2025-02230/additional-measures-to-combat-anti-semitism.

30. "Ending Radical Indoctrination in K-12 Schooling," *Federal Register,* January 29, 2024, https://www.federalregister.gov/documents/2025/02/03/2025-02232/ending-radical-indoctrination-in-k-12-schooling.

31. "Keeping Men Out of Women's Sports," *Federal Register,* February 5, 2025, https://www.federalregister.gov/documents/2025/02/11/2025-02513/keeping-men-out-of-womens-sports.

32. Kwame Anthony Appiah, "As a White Man, Can I Date Women of Color to Advance My Antiracism?," *The New York Times*, February 24, 2025, https://www.nytimes.com/2025/02/14/magazine/interracial-dating-antiracism-ethics.html.

33. Heather Hahn, "LGBTQ advocates aim to build on 2024 gains," *UM News*, February 26, 2025, https://www.umnews.org/en/news/lgbtq-advocates-aim-to-build-on-2024-gains

34. Nancy Armour, "Simone Biles shows her greatness again in standing up for transgender community," *USA Today,* June 7, 2025, https://www.usatoday.com/story/sports/columnist/nancy-armour/2025/06/06/simone-biles-stands-up/84080176007/.

35. The *Overton window* is the range of political and cultural opinions considered to be mainstream and socially acceptable.

36. Neil Shenvi and Pat Sawyer, *Critical Dilemma* (Eugene: Harvest House, 2023).

CHAPTER 2—HOW WE GOT HERE

1. Proposition 8, *Legislative Analyst's Office*, July 17, 2008, https://lao.ca.gov/ballot/2008/8_11_2008.aspx.

2. Jonathan Weisman, "A demand to define 'woman' injects gender politics into Jackson's confirmation hearings," *The New York Times*, March 23, 2022, https://www.nytimes.com/2022/03/23/us/politics/ketanji-brown-jackson-woman-definition.html.

3. Thomas Kidd, "'John Brown Is Immortal': Charles Spurgeon, the American Press, and Slavery," *MBTS*, July 2024, https://www.mbts.edu/2024/07/john-brown-is-immortal-charles-spurgeon-the-american-press-and-slavery/.

4. While slaves actually arrived in South Carolina in 1526, we are working from the widely referenced date of 1619 as the beginning of documented enslaved Africans arriving in what would later become the United States.

5. Henry Louis Gates Jr., "How Many Slaves Landed in the U.S.?," *PBS*, https://www.pbs.org/wnet/african-americans-many-rivers-to-cross/history/how-many-slaves-landed-in-the-us/).

6. See Olaudah Equiano and Shelly Eversley, *The Interesting Narrative of the Life of Olaudah Equiano: or, Gustavus Vassa, the African* (New York: Modern Library, 2004).

7. Alexander Falconbridge, *An Account of the Slave Trade on the Coast of Africa* (London: J. Phillips: 1788), 25, https://www.gutenberg.org/cache/epub/69178/pg69178-images.html.

8. Gates Jr., "How Many Slaves Landed in the U.S.?," *PBS.*

9. "The Middle Passage, 1749," *The Gilder Lehrman Institute of American History*, https://www.gilderlehrman.org/history-resources/spotlight-primary-source/middle-passage-1749.

10. Theodore D. Weld, *American Slavery as It Is: Testimony of a Thousand Witnesses* (New York: American Anti-Slavery Society, 1839), 9. Available online at https://docsouth.unc.edu/neh/weld/weld.html.

11. "Mississippi Black Codes (1865)," *Facing History and Ourselves*, May 12, 2020, https://www.facinghistory.org/resource-library/mississippi-black-codes-1865.

12. "What Was Jim Crow?," *Jim Crow Museum*, January 6, 1998, https://jimcrowmuseum.ferris.edu/what.htm.

13. Neil Shenvi and Pat Sawyer, *Critical Dilemma* (Eugene: Harvest House, 2023), 53.

14. Arthur F. Raper, *The Tragedy of Lynching* (Chapel Hill: UNC Press, 2013), 1.

15. *Shelley v. Kraemer*, 334 U.S. 1, 1948, https://www.loc.gov/item/usrep334001/.

16. *Brown v. Board of Education*, 347 U.S. 483, 1954, https://www.archives.gov/milestone-documents/brown-v-board-of-education.

17. *Loving v. Virginia*, 388 U.S. 1, 1967, https://supreme.justia.com/cases/federal/us/388/1/#annotation.

18. Justin McCarthy, "U.S. Approval of Interracial Marriage at New High of 94%," *Gallup*, September 10, 2021, https://news.gallup.com/poll/354638/approval-interracial-marriage-new-high.aspx.

19. Devah Pager, "The Mark of a Criminal Record," *American Journal of Sociology* 108, no. 5 (March 2003): 937–75, https://doi.org/10.1086/374403.

20. Marianne Bertrand and Sendhil Mullainathan, "Are Emily and Greg More Employable Than Lakisha and Jamal? A Field Experiment on Labor Market Discrimination," *American Economic Review* 94, no. 4 (September 1, 2004): 991–1013, https://doi.org/10.1257/0002828042002561.

21. Bradley Wright, *Christians Are Hate-Filled Hypocrites—and Other Lies You've Been Told: A Sociologist Shatters Myths from the Secular and Christian Media* (Minneapolis: Bethany House, 2010), 168.

22. Ryan Burge, Twitter post, December 17, 2021, https://twitter.com/ryanburge/status/1471966136950534149.

23. Ellora Derenoncourt et al., "Wealth of Two Nations: The U.S. Racial Wealth Gap, 1860–2020," *The Quarterly Journal of Economics* 139, no. 2 (March 30, 2024): 693–750, https://doi.org/10.1093/qje/qjad044.

24. E. Ann Carson, "Prisoners in 2020 – Statistical Tables," *Bureau of Justice Statistics*, December 2021, https://bjs.ojp.gov/content/pub/pdf/p20st.pdf.

25. "Public high school 4-year adjusted cohort graduation rate (ACGR)," *National Center for Educational Statistics*, 2018, https://nces.ed.gov/ccd/tables/ACGR_RE_and_characteristics_2017-18.asp.

26. Dante Chinni, "Supreme Court decision highlights racial disparities in higher education," *NBC News*, July 9, 2023, https://www.nbcnews.com/meet-the-press/data-download/supreme-court-decision-highlights-racial-disparities-higher-education-rcna93271.

27. Nambi Ndugga, Latoya Hill, and Samantha Artiga, "Key Data on Health and Health Care by Race and Ethnicity," *KFF Health News*, June 11, 2024, https://www.kff.org/key-data-on-health-and-health-care-by-race-and-ethnicity/?entry=executive-summary-introduction.

28. Nadia Khomani, "#MeToo: how a hashtag became a rallying cry against sexual harassment," *The Guardian*, October 20, 2017, https://www.theguardian.com/world/2017/oct/20/women-worldwide-use-hashtag-metoo-against-sexual-harassment.

29. Audrey Carlsen, Maya Salam, Claire Cain Miller, Denise Lu, Ash Ngu, Jugal K. Patel, and Zach Wichter, "#MeToo Brought Down 201 Powerful Men. Nearly Half of Their Replacements Are Women," *The New York Times*, October 29, 2018, https://www.nytimes.com/interactive/2018/10/23 us/metoo-replacements.html.

30. Jodi Kantor and Megan Twohey, "Harvey Weinstein Paid Off Sexual Accusers for Decades," *The New York Times,* Oct. 5, 2017, https://www.nytimes.com/2017/10/05/us/harvey-weinstein-harassment-allegations.html.

31. Carlsen et al., "#MeToo Brought Down 201 Powerful Men," *The New York Times*, Oct. 29, 2018.

32. "Harvey Weinstein timeline: How the scandal has unfolded," *BBC*, February 24, 2023, https://www.bbc.com/news/entertainment-arts-41594672.

33. Becca Andrews, "As a Teen, Emily Joy Was Abused by a Church Youth Leader. Now She's Leading a Movement to Change Evangelical America," *Mother Jones,* May 25, 2018, https://www.motherjones.com/criminal-justice/2018/05/evangelical-church-metoo-movement-abuse/.

34. Emily Joy Allison, *#ChurchToo: How Purity Culture Upholds Abuse and How to Find Healing* (Minneapolis: Broadleaf Books, an imprint of 1517 Media, 2021).

35. Ruth Everhart, *The #metoo Reckoning: Facing the Church's Complicity in Sexual Abuse and Misconduct* (Downers Grove: InterVarsity, 2020).

36. Rachael Denhollander, *What Is a Girl Worth?* (Carol Stream: Tyndale House, 2019).

37. "Who Is Larry Nassar?," *USA Today*, https://www.usatoday.com/pages/interactives/larry-nassar-timeline/.

38. Allison, *#ChurchToo*, 26, 32, 182.

39. See Bradley R. Entner Wright, *Christians Are Hate-Filled Hypocrites—and Other Lies You've Been Told: A Sociologist Shatters Myths from the Secular and Christian Media* (Minneapolis: Bethany House, 2010).

40. Jeffrey M. Jones, "Belief in God in U.S. Dips to 81%, a New Low," *Gallup*, June 17, 2022, https://news.gallup.com/poll/393737/belief-god-dips-new-low.aspx.

41. Jeffrey M. Jones, "U.S. Church Membership Falls Below Majority for First Time," *Gallup*, March 29, 2021, https://news.gallup.com/poll/341963/church-membership-falls-below-majority-first-time.aspx.

42. Jeffrey M. Jones, "How Religious Are Americans?" *Gallup*, March 29, 2024, https://news.gallup.com/poll/358364/religious-americans.aspx.

43. Natasha Crain, *Faithfully Different* (Eugene: Harvest House, 2022), 17-33.

44. See, for example, Aaron M. Renn, *Life in the Negative World* (Grand Rapids: Zondervan, 2024).

CHAPTER 3—WOKENESS AND CONTEMPORARY CRITICAL THEORY

1. Bradley A. Levinson et al., *Beyond Critique* (Boulder: Paradigm Publishers, 2011), 26.
2. Stephen Eric Bronner, *Critical Theory: A Very Short Introduction* (New York: Oxford University Press, 2011), 2.
3. Karl Marx, *The German Ideology*, 1845, https://www.marxists.org/archive/marx/works/1845/german-ideology/ch01b.htm.
4. See Jacob P.K. Gross, "Education and Hegemony: The Influence of Antonio Gramsci," in Levinson et al., *Beyond Critique,* 51-79.
5. See Stephen Eric Bronner, *Critical Theory: A Very Short Introduction* (New York: Oxford University Press, 2011).
6. For more information on the relationship between critical legal studies and critical race theory, see Neil Shenvi and Timon Cline, "What if Critical Race Theory Were Just a Legal Theory? A Christian Critique," *Liberty University Law Review,* Vol. 17, Issue 3 (2022).
7. See, for instance, Tommy J. Curry, ""Shut Your Mouth When You're Talking to Me," *Georgetown Law Journal of Modern Critical Race Studies* 1, no. 3 (2011): 1-38.
8. For a short history of origins of CRT, see Khiara M. Bridges, *Critical Race Theory: A Primer*, Concepts and Insights Series (St. Paul: Foundation Press, 2019), 21-34.
9. See Richard Delgado and Jean Stefancic, *Critical Race Theory: An Introduction*, 3d ed. (New York: New York University Press, 2017), 20-24.
10. Gloria Ladson-Billings and William F. Tate, "Toward a Critical Race Theory of Education," *Teachers College Record: The Voice of Scholarship in Education* 97, no. 1 (September 1995): 47–68, https://doi.org/10.1177/016146819509700104.
11. Angela Harris, "Foreword," in Delgado and Stefancic, *CRT: An Introduction*, xv-xvi.
12. "Thinking Sex: Notes for a Radical Theory of the Politics of Sexuality," in *Deviations*, by Gayle S. Rubin (Durham: Duke University Press, 2012), 137–81, https://doi.org/10.1215/9780822394068-006.
13. Judith Butler, *Gender Trouble: Feminism and the Subversion of Identity*, Routledge Classics (New York: Routledge, 2006).
14. Judith Butler, *Undoing Gender* (New York ; London: Routledge, 2004), 218.
15. Kimberlé Crenshaw, "Demarginalizing the Intersection of Race and Sex," *University of Chicago Legal Forum*: Vol. 1989, Article 8, 1989, https://scholarship.law.columbia.edu/faculty_scholarship/3007.
16. Kimberle Crenshaw, "Mapping the Margins," *Stanford Law Review* 43, no. 6 (July 1991): 1241, https://doi.org/10.2307/1229039.
17. Crenshaw, "Demarginalizing the Intersection of Race and Sex."
18. Mari J. Matsuda, ed., *Words That Wound: Critical Race Theory, Assaultive Speech, and the First Amendment,* New Perspectives on Law, Culture, and Society (Boulder: Westview Press, 1993), 6-7.
19. See, for instance, Antonia Darder, Kortney Hernandez, and Kevin D. Lam, eds., *The Critical Pedagogy Reader*, 4th ed. (New York: Routledge, 2024).

20. Hannah McCann and Whitney Monaghan, *Queer Theory Now: From Foundations to Futures* (London: Bloomsbury Academic, 2022).

21. David J. Connor, Beth A. Ferri, and Subini A. Annamma, eds., *DisCrit: Disability Studies and Critical Race Theory in Education* (New York: Teachers College Press, 2016).

22. Dan Goodley, *Disability Studies: An Interdisciplinary Introduction*, 3d ed. (Thousand Oaks: Sage Publications, 2024).

23. Özlem Sensoy and Robin J. DiAngelo, *Is Everyone Really Equal? An Introduction to Key Concepts in Social Justice Education,* 2d ed. (New York: Teachers College Press, 2017), 44.

24. Sensoy and DiAngelo, *Is Everyone Really Equal?*, 73.

25. See, for example, José Medina, *The Epistemology of Resistance* (Oxford: Oxford University Press, 2013).

26. Ijeoma Oluo, *So You Want to Talk About Race* (New York: Seal, 2019), 15.

27. "16 Bridge-Building Tips for White People," *Be The Bridge,* 2019, https://bethebridge.com/docs/16Tips.pdf.

28. Mary McClintock, "How to Interrupt Oppressive Behavior," *Readings for Diversity and Social Justice,* eds. Maurianne Adams et al. (New York: Routledge, 2000), 483.

29. See Neil Shenvi and Pat Sawyer, "What Are We To Make Of 'Queers For Palestine'?" *Substack—Reality's Last Stand,* February 12, 2024, https://www.realityslaststand.com/p/what-are-we-to-make-of-queers-for/.

30. Sam Dorman, "NYT reporter, in now-deleted tweet, claims there's 'a difference between being politically black and racially black,'" *Fox News,* May 23, 2020, https://www.foxnews.com/media/nikole-hannah-jones-politically-racially-black.

31. "Best practices for sex and gender diversity in medical education," *American Medical Association,* https://www.ama-assn.org/system/files/cme-issue-brief-sex-gender-medical-education.pdf.

32. "APA Resolution on Gender Identity Change Efforts," *American Psychological Association,* February 2021, https://www.apa.org/about/policy/resolution-gender-identity-change-efforts.pdf.

33. Chase Strangio and Gabriel Arkles, "Four Myths About Trans Athletes, Debunked," April 30, 2020, https://www.aclu.org/news/lgbtq-rights/four-myths-about-trans-athletes-debunked.

34. See, for example, Figure 9.1 of Eduardo Bonilla-Silva, *Racism without Racists* (Lanham: Rowman & Littlefield, 2014), 228.

35. Robin J. DiAngelo, *White Fragility: Why It's so Hard for White People to Talk about Racism* (Boston: Beacon Press, 2018), 29.

36. Margaret L. Andersen and Patricia Hill Collins, eds., *Race, Class, and Gender: An Anthology* (Belmont: Wadsworth, 1992), 5.

37. Carl R. Trueman, *The Rise and Triumph of the Modern Self: Cultural Amnesia, Expressive Individualism, and the Road to Sexual Revolution* (Wheaton: Crossway, 2020), 369.

38. Shaun R. Harper, Lori D. Patton, and Ontario S. Wooden, "Access and Equity for African American Students in Higher Education: A Critical Race Historical Analysis of Policy Efforts," *The Journal of Higher Education* 80, no. 4 (July 2009): 392, https://doi.org/10.1080/00221546.2009.11779022.

39. Sonia Michelle Cintron et al., "A Pathway to Equitable Math Instruction," May 2021, https://equitablemath.org/wp-content/uploads/sites/2/2020/11/1_STRIDE1.pdf.

CHAPTER 4—THINKING WELL, THINKING BIBLICALLY

1. C.S. Lewis, *God in the Dock: Essays on Theology and Ethics*, ed. Walter Hooper (Grand Rapids: Eerdmans, 2002), 272-273 (emphasis in original).
2. Watts, "In Smithsonian Race Guidelines...," *Newsweek*, July 17, 2020.
3. See, for example, Christina Hoff Sommers, "Wage Gap Myth Exposed—by Feminists," *American Enterprise Institute*, November 4, 2012, https://www.aei.org/articles/wage-gap-myth-exposed-by-feminists/.
4. Nicholas Shackel, "The Vacuity of Postmodernist Methodology," *Metaphilosophy* 36, no. 3 (April 2005): 295-320, https://doi.org/10.1111/j.1467-9973.2005.00370.x.
5. The website boysvswomen.com/ shows the stark differences between high-level male and female athletic performance.
6. Greg Lukianoff and Jonathan Haidt, *The Coddling of the American Mind* (New York: Penguin Press, 2018), 25-26.
7. Ibram X. Kendi, *How to Be an Antiracist*, 1st ed. (New York: One World, 2019), 9.
8. Ibram X. Kendi, *Stamped from the Beginning: The Definitive History of Racist Ideas in America* (New York: Nation Books, 2016), 2, 11.
9. "Fatal Force," *Washington Post*, July 15, 2024, https://www.washingtonpost.com/graphics/investigations/police-shootings-database/.
10. Quoted in Mark A. Noll, *The Scandal of the Evangelical Mind* (Grand Rapids: W.B. Eerdmans, 1994), 202.

CHAPTER 5—CHALLENGING CONTEMPORARY CRITICAL THEORY

1. Peter Blood, Alan Tuttle, and George Lakey, "Understanding and Fighting Sexism: A Call to Men," in Margaret L. Andersen and Patricia Hill Collins, eds., *Race, Class, and Gender: An Anthology* (Belmont: Wadsworth, 1992), 139-140.
2. Peggy McIntosh, "White Privilege and Male Privilege," in Margaret L. Andersen and Patricia Hill Collins, eds., *Race, Class, and Gender: An Anthology* (Belmont: Wadsworth, 1992), 72.
3. Robin J. DiAngelo, *White Fragility* (Boston: Beacon, 2018), 149-150.
4. Matthew George Easton. "Entry for Justice," *Easton's Bible Dictionary*, https://www.biblestudytools.com/dictionaries/eastons-bible-dictionary/justice.html.
5. Mary McClintock, "How to Interrupt Oppressive Behavior," in *Readings for Diversity and Social Justice*, eds. Maurianne Adams et al. (New York: Routledge, 2000), 483.
6. Paul Butler, "Racially Based Jury Nullification," in Richard Delgado and Jean Stefancic, eds., *Critical Race Theory: The Cutting Edge*, 3d ed. (Philadelphia: Temple University Press, 2013), 282-290.

7. Ibram X. Kendi, *How to Be an Antiracist* (New York: One World, 2019), 18.
8. Thomas Sowell, *Discrimination and Disparities* (New York: Basic Books, 2019), vii, 7.
9. Özlem Sensoy and Robin J. DiAngelo, *Is Everyone Really Equal? An Introduction to Key Concepts in Social Justice Education*, 2d ed. (New York: Teachers College Press, 2017), 29-30.
10. Kristin Kobes Du Mez, *Jesus and John Wayne: How White Evangelicals Corrupted a Faith and Fractured a Nation*, 1st ed. (New York: Liveright Publishing, a division of W.W. Norton, 2020).
11. Beth Allison Barr, *The Making of Biblical Womanhood: How the Subjugation of Women Became Gospel Truth* (Grand Rapids: Brazos Press, 2021).
12. Jonathan Wilson-Hartgrove, *Reconstructing the Gospel: Finding Freedom from Slaveholder Religion* (Downers Grove: IVP, 2018).
13. Joseph R. Barndt, *Becoming an Anti-Racist Church: Journeying toward Wholeness*, Prisms (Minneapolis: Fortress Press, 2011).

CHAPTER 6—RACE

1. Derrick Bell, *Faces at the Bottom of the Well: The Permanence of Racism* (New York: Basic Books, 1992), ix.
2. See, for example, Eduardo Bonilla-Silva, *Racism without Racists*, 4th ed. (Lanham: Rowman & Littlefield, 2014).
3. Richard Delgado and Jean Stefancic, *Critical Race Theory: An Introduction*, 2d ed. (New York: NYU Press, 2012), 104.
4. Khiara M. Bridges, *Critical Race Theory: A Primer* (St. Paul: Foundation Press, 2019), 116 (emphasis in original).
5. Ijeoma Oluo, *So You Want to Talk About Race* (New York: Seal, 2019), 216-217.
6. William J. Barber II, "The Racist History of Tipping," *Politico*, July 17, 2019, https://www.politico.com/magazine/story/2019/07/17/william-barber-tipping-racist-past-227361/.
7. Andrea Freeman, "The Unbearable Whiteness of Milk: Food Oppression and the USDA," *U.C. Irvine L. Rev.* 1251 (2013), https://scholarship.law.uci.edu/cgi/viewcontent.cgi?article=1113&context=ucilr.
8. Scottie Andrew and Harmeet Kaur, "Everyday words and phrases that have racist connotations," *CNN*, July 7, 2020, https://www.cnn.com/2020/07/06/us/racism-words-phrases-slavery-trnd/index.html.
9. Sabrina Strings and Lindo Bacon, "The Racist Roots of Fighting Obesity," *Scientific American*, June 4, 2020, https://www.scientificamerican.com/article/the-racist-roots-of-fighting-obesity2/.
10. *United States v. Bhagat Singh Thind*, 261 U.S. 204 (1923), https://supreme.justia.com/cases/federal/us/261/204/.
11. Bobby Duffy et al., "Love thy neighbour? Public trust and acceptance of the people who live alongside us" (King's College London, 2023), https://doi.org/10.18742/PUB01-130.
12. Zach Goldberg, "America's White Saviors," *Tablet*, June 5, 2019, https://www.tabletmag.com/sections/news/articles/americas-white-saviors.

13. For a longer discussion of ethnic identity and solidarity that grew out of historical oppression, see Shenvi and Sawyer, *Critical Dilemma*, 346-349.

14. L.J. Zigerell, "How racial groups rate each other," *lgzigerell.com*, March 25, 2021, https://www.ljzigerell.com/?p=9002.

15. L.J. Zigerell, "Black and White Discrimination in the United States: Evidence from an Archive of Survey Experiment Studies," *Research & Politics* 5, no. 1 (January 2018), https://doi.org/10.1177/2053168017753862.

16. Merriam-Webster, s.v. "oppression," accessed January 1, 2025, https://www.merriam-webster.com/dictionary/oppression.

17. LeBron James, Twitter post, May 6, 2020, https://x.com/KingJames/status/1258156220969398272.

18. Kevin McCaffree and Anondah Saide, "How Informed Are Americans About Race and Policing?," *Skeptic Research Center*, February 20, 2021, https://www.skeptic.com/research-center/reports/Research-Report-CUPES-007.pdf.

19. "Fatal Force," *The Washington Post*, July 15, 2024, https://www.washingtonpost.com/graphics/investigations/police-shootings-database/.

20. "Mapping Police Violence," https://mappingpoliceviolence.us/.

21. "Expanded Homicide Data Table 1," *FBI: UCR*, https://ucr.fbi.gov/crime-in-the-u.s/2019/crime-in-the-u.s.-2019/tables/expanded-homicide-data-table-1.xls.

22. Neil Shenvi, "Race and Police Violence: Looking at the Data," *Shenviapologetics.com*, May 31, 2020, https://shenviapologetics.com/race-and-police-violence-looking-at-the-data/.

23. Erika Harrell and Elizabeth Davis, "Contacts Between Police and the Public, 2018—Statistical Tables," *Bureau of Justice Statistics*, December 2020, https://bjs.ojp.gov/content/pub/pdf/cbpp18st.pdf.

24. "Non-Fatal Civilian Injuries in Police Interventions," *University of Illinois—Chicago School of Public Health*, https://policeepi.uic.edu/trends-in-non-fatal-civilian-injuries/.

25. Danielle Davis and Christopher Cairns, "Emergency Department Visit Rates for Motor Vehicle Crashes by Selected Characteristics," *National Center for Health Statistics*, April 2023, https://www.cdc.gov/nchs/products/databriefs/db466.htm.

26. Lydia Saad, "Black Americans Want Police to Retain Local Presence," August 5, 2020, https://news.gallup.com/poll/316571/black-americans-police-retain-local-presence.aspx.

27. "Detroiters' Views on Crime and Policing," *Detroit Metro Area Communities Study*, Summer, 2021, https://detroitsurvey.umich.edu/wp-content/uploads/2021/09/DMACS-Detroiters-views-on-crime-and-policing_2021_09_14-1.pdf.

28. Linda Balcarová et al., "On the Robustness of Black Americans' Support for the Police: Evidence from a National Experiment," *Journal of Criminal Justice* 92 (May 2024): 102186, https://www.sciencedirect.com/science/article/abs/pii/S0047235224000357.

29. Martin Luther King Jr., "Remaining Awake Through a Great Revolution," commencement address, Oberlin College, Oberlin, Ohio, June 1965, https://www2.oberlin.edu/external/EOG/BlackHistoryMonth/MLK/CommAddress.html.

30. Alli Coritz, Jessica E. Peña, Paul Jacobs, Brittany Rico, Joyce Key Hahn, and Ricardo Henrique Lowe Jr., "Census Bureau Releases 2020 Census Population for More Than 200 New

Detailed Race and Ethnicity Groups," *U.S. Census*, September 21, 2023, https://www.census.gov/library/stories/2023/09/2020-census-dhc-a-race-overview.html.

CHAPTER 7—GENDER

1. Material in this section was adapted from Neil Shenvi and Pat Sawyer, "Feminism as a Critical Social Theory," *Eikon*, Volume 6, Issue 1, Spring, 2024, 41-50.
2. Elizabeth Cady Stanton, *The Woman's Bible—Part 1* (New York: European Publishing, 1895), 14.
3. Deborah Cameron, *Feminism* (Chicago: University of Chicago, 2019), 8.
4. Kathy Davis, "Intersectionality as Buzzword: A Sociology of Science Perspective on What Makes a Feminist Theory Successful," *Feminist Theory*, 2008, vol 9, issue 1, 67.
5. bell hooks, "Feminism: A Movement to End Sexist Oppression," in *Readings for Diversity and Social Justice*, 239-40.
6. "The worldwide war on baby girls," *The Economist*, March 4, 2010, https://www.economist.com/international/2010/03/04/the-worldwide-war-on-baby-girls.
7. Juliany González Nieves, "When We Were Not Women" in *Discovering Biblical Equality*, eds. Ronald W. Pierce and Cynthia Long Westfall, 3rd ed. (Downers Grove: InterVarsity, 2021).
8. Steven Pinker, *The Blank Slate: The Modern Denial of Human Nature* (London: Penguin, 2003), 435-439.
9. Leonard Sax, "How Common Is Intersex? A Response to Anne Fausto-Sterling," *The Journal of Sex Research* 39, no. 3 (August 1, 2002): 174-178, https://doi .org /10.1080/00224490209552139.
10. See additional discussion in Shenvi and Sawyer, *Critical Dilemma*, 230-232.
11. Kate Ng, "Transgender father Stefonknee Wolscht leaves family in Toronto to start new life as six-year-old girl," *The Independent,* December 11, 2015, https://www.the-independent.com/news/world/americas/stefonknee-wolschtt-transgender-father-leaves-family-in-toronto-to-start-new-life-as-a-sixyearold-girl-a6769051.html.
12. For an extended treatment, see, for example, John Piper, *Recovering Biblical Manhood and Womanhood* (Wheaton: Crossway, 2021).
13. Hollie McKay, "Critics slam MSNBC host's claim that kids belong to community, not parents," *Fox News*, April 9, 2013, https://www.foxnews.com/entertainment/critics-slam-msnbc-hosts-claim-that-kids-belong-to-community-not-parents.
14. Reta Ugena Whitlock, "Getting Queer: Teacher Education, Gender Studies, and the Cross-Disciplinary Quest for Queer Pedagogies," *Issues in Teacher Education,* Vol. 19, no. 2 (Fall 2010): 82.
15. David Gabbard, endorsement of William Pinar, ed., *Queer Theory in Education*, Studies in Curriculum Theory (Mahwah: L. Erlbaum Associates, 1998).
16. Kay Tisdall, *Critical Childhood Studies: Global Perspectives* (London: Bloomsbury, 2023), 42-43.
17. Ibid., 122.
18. Annamarie Jagose, *Queer Theory: An Introduction* (New York: NYU Press, 1996), 70-71.

19. Paul David Tripp, *Parenting: 14 Gospel Principles That Can Radically Change Your Family* (Wheaton: Crossway, 2024), 166.
20. Andrew T. Walker and Carl R. Trueman, *Faithful Reason: Natural Law Ethics for God's Glory and Our Good* (Brentwood: B&H Academic, 2024), 28-29.
21. Melissa Moschella, *To Whom Do Children Belong? Parental Rights, Civic Education, and Children's Autonomy*, first paperback edition (Cambridge: Cambridge University Press, 2017), 14, 20.
22. Ibid., 20.
23. Ibid., 38.
24. Emily Joy Allison, *#ChurchToo: How Purity Culture Upholds Abuse and How to Find Healing* (Minneapolis: Broadleaf Books, an imprint of 1517 Media, 2021), 103-104.
25. "Prevention," *nsvrc.org*, accessed December 22, 2024.
26. "Healing Justice Practice Spaces: A How-To Guide," *MeToo Movement*, December 18, 2014, https://metoomvmt.org/wp-content/uploads/2020/05/Healing-Justice-Practice-Space_TOOLKIT.pdf .

CHAPTER 8—SEXUALITY

1. Lauren Rowello, "Yes, kink belongs at Pride. And I want my kids to see it," *The Washington Post*, June 29, 2021, https://www.washingtonpost.com/outlook/2021/06/29/pride-month-kink-consent/.
2. Jon Brown, "San Francisco Pride Parade features public nudity around kids, 'Fetish Zone' with urine," *Christian Post*, July 1, 2024, https://www.christianpost.com/news/san-francisco-pride-parade-features-public-nudity-around-kids.html.
3. Sam Killerman, "The Genderbread Person," *itspronouncedmetrosexual.com*, https://www.itspronouncedmetrosexual.com/genderbread-person/.
4. Trans Student Educational Resources, 2015. "The Gender Unicorn," http://www.transstudent.org/gender.
5. Trans Student Educational Resources, 2015, "The Gender Unicorn," http://www.transstudent.org/gender.
6. Caroline Lowbridge, "The lesbians who feel pressured to have sex and relationships with trans women," *BBC*, October 26, 2021, https://www.bbc.com/news/uk-england-57853385.
7. Sara Ahmed, *Queer Phenomenology: Orientations, Objects, Others* (Durham: Duke University Press, 2006), 78.
8. Annamarie Jagose, *Queer Theory: An Introduction* (New York: NYU Press, 1996), 70-71.
9. Timothy Keller and Kathy Keller, *The Meaning of Marriage: Facing the Complexities of Commitment with the Wisdom of God* (New York: Dutton, 2011), 266.
10. Keller and Keller, *The Meaning of Marriage*, 270.
11. Keller and Keller, *The Meaning of Marriage*, 259.
12. The Nashville Statement, August 29, 2017, https://cbmw.org/the-nashville-statement/.
13. Rosaria Champagne Butterfield, *Five Lies of Our Anti-Christian Age* (Wheaton: Crossway, 2023), 80.

14. Jonathan Griffin, "India Willoughby: Is it discriminatory to refuse to date a trans woman?" *BBC*, January 12, 2018, https://www.bbc.com/news/blogs-trending-42652947.
15. Hannah Barnes, "Inside the collapse of the Tavistock Centre," *New Statesman,* March 20, 2024, https://www.newstatesman.com/politics/health/2024/03/inside-the-collapse-of-the-tavistock-centre.
16. Joshua Cohen, "More Cautious Approach to Gender-Affirming Care Among Minors," *Forbes,* June 14, 2023, https://www.forbes.com/sites/joshuacohen/2023/06/06/increasing-number-of-european-nations-adopt-a-more-cautious-approach-to-gender-affirming-care-among-minors/.
17. Hilary Cass, *Independent review of gender identity services for children and young people: Final report*, April 2024, https://cass.independent-review.uk/wp-content/uploads/2024/04/CassReview_Final.pdf.
18. Marshall Kirk and Hunter Madsen, *After the Ball: How America Will Conquer Its Fear and Hatred of Gays in the 90s* (New York: Plume, 1989).
19. Andrea Ganna et al., "Large-Scale GWAS Reveals Insights into the Genetic Architecture of Same-Sex Sexual Behavior," *Science* 365, no. 6456 (August 30, 2019): eaat7693, https://doi.org/10.1126/science.aat7693.
20. Niklas Långström et al., "Genetic and Environmental Effects on Same-Sex Sexual Behavior: A Population Study of Twins in Sweden," *Archives of Sexual Behavior* 39, no. 1 (February 2010): 75–80, https://doi.org/10.1007/s10508-008-9386-1.
21. Mary-Anne Enoch, "Genetic Influences on the Development of Alcoholism," *Current Psychiatry Reports* 15, no. 11 (November 2013): 412, https://doi.org/10.1007/s11920-013-0412-1.
22. "Gender Dysphoria," *Mount Sinai*, https://www.mountsinai.org/health-library/diseases-conditions/gender-dysphoria.
23. Abigail Shrier, *Irreversible Damage: The Transgender Craze Seducing Our Daughters* (Washington, DC: Regnery, 2020), 107.

CHAPTER 9—REACHING OUT

1. Neil Shenvi, *Why Believe? A Reasoned Approach to Christianity* (Wheaton: Crossway, 2022).
2. Jonathan Haidt, *The Anxious Generation* (New York: Penguin Press, 2024).
3. For example, John Stonestreet, "When Bad Ideas Get Loose," *Breakpoint*, September 30, 2019, https://breakpoint.org/breakpoint-when-bad-ideas-get-loose/.
4. Helen Pluckrose, *The Counterweight Handbook* (Durham: Pitchstone Publishing, 2023), 95-105.
5. Andrew T. Walker, "Christians Volunteering Pronouns?," *EPPC*, October 31, 2022, https://eppc.org/publication/christians-volunteering-pronouns/.
6. Helen Pluckrose, *The Counterweight Handbook* (Durham: Pitchstone, 2023).
7. Christena Cleveland, *God Is a Black Woman*, 1st ed. (San Francisco: HarperOne, 2022).
8. Love L. Sechrest, Johnny Ramírez-Johnson, and Amos Yong, eds., *Can "White" People Be Saved? Triangulating Race, Theology, and Mission*, Missiological Engagements (Downers Grove: IVP Academic, 2018).
9. Robin J. DiAngelo, *White Fragility: Why It's So Hard for White People to Talk About Racism* (Boston: Beacon Press, 2018), 149-150.

CHAPTER 10—WHAT NOW?

1. Martin Luther King Jr., "Speech at Illinois Wesleyan University" (1966), https://www.iwu.edu/mlk/page-4.html.

2. Neil Shenvi, "Race and Police Violence: Looking at the Data," *Shenviapologetics.com*, May 31, 2020, https://shenviapologetics.com/race-and-police-violence-looking-at-the-data/.

3. "A Resolution to Support Equity in Education," *The NC State Board of Education*, June 8, 2020, https://simbli.eboardsolutions.com/Meetings/Attachment.aspx?S=10399&AID=224836&MID=7233.

4. Neil Shenvi, "North Carolina Considers Using Public Schools To Discriminate In The Name Of 'Equality,'" *The Federalist*, August 24, 2020, https://thefederalist.com/2020/08/24/north-carolina-considers-using-public-schools-to-discriminate-in-the-name-of-equality/.

5. "Where Do Americans Stand on Abortion?" *Gallup*, July 7, 2023, https://news.gallup.com/poll/321143/americans-stand-abortion.aspx.

6. "2020 Democratic Party Platform," July 27, 2020, https://democrats.org/where-we-stand/party-platform/.

7. "The 2024 Republican Party Platform," https://prod-static.gop.com/media/RNC2024-Platform.pdf.

8. bell hooks, *Feminism Is for Everybody: Passionate Politics* (Cambridge: South End Press, 2000), 6, 26.

9. Emily, "Feminism—A Process," *Planned Parenthood*, March 11, 2019, https://www.plannedparenthood.org/planned-parenthood-delaware/blog/feminism-a-process.

10. See her book, Katy Faust and Stacy Manning, *Them Before Us* (New York: Post Hill Press, 2021).

11. "DPS Board of Education Monthly Meeting," *YouTube*, August 24, 2023, https://www.youtube.com/live/e7y9KPEThdw?t=2415s.

12. Ryan King, "Supreme Court affirmative action case showed 'astonishing' racial gaps," *New York Post*, June 29, 2023, https://nypost.com/2023/06/29/supreme-court-affirmative-action-case-showed-astonishing-racial-gaps/.

13. Hohn Cho, "Affirmative Action…or Unbiblical Partiality?," *shenviapologetics.com*, June 30, 2023, https://shenviapologetics.com/hohn-cho-affirmative-action-or-unbiblical-partiality/.

14. "Students for Fair Admissions, Inc. v. University of North Carolina," *SCOTUS Blog*, June 29, 2023, https://www.scotusblog.com/case-files/cases/students-for-fair-admissions-inc-v-university-of-north-carolina/.

15. "1 in 6 Hiring Managers Have Been Told to Stop Hiring White Men," *Resume Builder*, November 7, 2022, https://www.resumebuilder.com/1-in-6-hiring-managers-have-been-told-to-stop-hiring-white-men/.

16. Jen Christensen, "Judge gives grandparents custody of Ohio transgender teen," *CNN*, February 16, 2018, https://www.cnn.com/2018/02/16/health/ohio-transgender-teen-hearing-judge-decision/index.html.

17. Daniel Payne, "Indiana Catholic Couple Asks Supreme Court to Hear Transgender Child Custody Case," *NCRegister*, February 16, 2024, https://www.ncregister.com/cna/indiana-catholic-couple-asks-supreme-court-to-hear-transgender-child-custody-case.

18. Emily Washburn, "Indiana Family Loses Custody of Son Over Religious Beliefs; Supreme Court Won't Hear Case," *Daily Citizen,* March 25, 2024, https://dailycitizen.focusonthe family.com/indiana-family-loses-custody-of-son-religious-beliefs-supreme-court-wont-hear-case/.
19. Mahmoud et al., "Appellant's Opening Brief," United States Court of Appeals for the Fourth Circuit. No. 23-1890, October 11, 2023, https://www.aclu.org/wp-content/uploads/2023/11/Opening-Brief-Tamer-Mahmoud-v.-Monifa-McKnight.pdf.
20. Erin O'Donnell, "The Risks of Homeschooling," *Harvard Magazine,* May-June 2020, https://www.harvardmagazine.com/2020/04/right-now-risks-homeschooling.
21. Kerry McDonald, "5 Things I Learned Debating the Harvard Prof Who Called for a 'Presumptive Ban' on Homeschooling," *Cato Institute,* June 22, 2020, https://www.cato.org/commentary/5-things-i-learned-debating-harvard-prof-who-called-presumptive-ban-homeschooling.
22. C.S. Lewis, *The Screwtape Letters* (New York: HarperOne, 2013), 137-138.
23. James Lindsay, "What Is the Woke Right?," *newdiscourses.com,* October 28, 2024, https://new discourses.com/2024/10/what-is-the-woke-right/.
24. Konstantin Kisin, "Tucker Carlson and the Woke Right," *konstantinkisin.com,* February 17, 2024, https://www.konstantinkisin.com/p/tucker-carlson-and-the-woke-right.
25. For examples within the "Christian nationalist" movement, see Neil Shenvi, "What Is the 'Woke Right'?," *shenviapologetics.com,* June 10, 2024, https://shenviapologetics.com/what-is-the-woke-right/.
26. See, for example, Rita Abrahamsen et al., *World of the Right: Radical Conservatism and Global Order* (New York: Cambridge University Press, 2024).
27. "WHO COVID dashboard," *World Health Organization,* July 7, 2024, https://data.who.int/dashboards/covid19/deaths.
28. C.S. Lewis, *The Weight of Glory and Other Addresses* (San Francisco: Harper, 2001), 46.

ACKNOWLEDGMENTS

I owe debts of gratitude to many people who made this book possible.

First and foremost, the book was inspired by all the fans of *Critical Dilemma*, who urged us to write a follow-up. Thank you for your encouragement and support.

As usual, my family played a crucial role in this book's completion. In addition to being a wonderful mother and doctor, my wife is an ever-supportive spouse who was willing to overlook the piles and piles of books on the study floor for months on end. My children worked and played diligently as the manuscript went from an idea to an outline to a rough draft to a reality. You have made my life rich and joyful. I love you all.

My small group has been a tremendous blessing to me for the last 15 years. It has supported and sustained my spiritual life, reminding me that thinking carefully about questions of culture and worldview—though important—is only a small part of what it means to be a Christian.

This book's title emerged from a brainstorming session with a devout and brilliant math graduate student at Duke whom I've had the pleasure of knowing and mentoring for over a year. Thomas, I appreciate all our conversations and look forward to many more to come.

As usual, Bob, Steve, Becky, Lindsay, and Sherrie at Harvest House did a wonderful job with editing, designing, marketing, and resolving countless logistical details of which I have remained blissfully ignorant. Thank you for all your hard work.

And to Jesus Christ. Nothing in my hand I bring. Simply to the cross I cling.

—Neil

To the readers of *Critical Dilemma*, your strong appreciation and thoughtful responses have led to this volume.

To my dear wife, Wendy, your constant support and unyielding belief in me has made all the difference.

To my awesome kids, Hannah, Patrick, and Nicholas, a dad could not be more proud or more thankful.

To my friend and pastor, Tony Diana, you embody 1 Thessalonians 5:11; your faithful encouragement over 30 years has been life-giving.

To my brother, the late David Fox, your deep appreciation of *Critical Dilemma*, your testimony of its life-changing impact, and your enthusiastic promotion of my work has been a notable, humbling encouragement. Rest now, brother, in the presence of your Savior.

To all the Harvest House team, especially Bob, Steve, Becky, Lindsay, and Sherrie, I can't thank you enough for all your efforts. What a wonderful experience working with you.

Finally, to my Lord and Savior, Jesus Christ, the fountain of all wisdom and knowledge, my only hope, my everything.

—Pat

ABOUT NEIL SHENVI

Neil Shenvi has an AB in chemistry from Princeton University and a PhD in theoretical chemistry from UC Berkeley, where he wrote his dissertation on quantum computing. While at Berkeley, Neil became a Christian through attending church with his future wife and reading C.S. Lewis. After graduating, he worked as a research scientist at Yale University and Duke University on topics ranging from surface science to electronic structure theory. His book *Why Believe?: A Reasoned Approach to Christianity* was a *Christianity Today* Book of the Year finalist in 2023 in the Apologetics and Evangelism category. He is the coauthor with Pat Sawyer of *Critical Dilemma: the Rise of Critical Theories and Social Justice Ideology*, which was named *World* magazine's 2023 Book of the Year. He is widely recognized for his writings on critical theory, which have been published by *The Gospel Coalition*, *Eikon*, *Ratio Christi*, *The Federalist*, *American Conservative*, *The Journal of Christian Legal Thought*, and *The Liberty University Law Review*. In his free time, he enjoys reading, playing video games, and going to the gym. He is married and has four children. He can be reached on X (formerly known as Twitter) at @NeilShenvi or through his website www.shenviapologetics.com.

ABOUT PAT SAWYER

Pat Sawyer has a BA in psychology from UNC-Chapel Hill, an MA in communication studies from UNC-Greensboro, and a PhD in educational studies and cultural studies from UNC-Greensboro. His dissertation examined social justice and higher education in the context of neoliberalism. Pat is a faculty member at UNC-Greensboro and a member of Heterodox Academy. He is a regular speaker in the academy and has presented his scholarship at a number of conferences in the United States, Canada, and the United Kingdom. Pat has been published in peer-reviewed and editorial board-reviewed journals, edited academic books, and a number of popular outlets, including *The American Conservative*, *The Gospel Coalition*, and *The Federalist*. He is coauthor of *Disney as Doorway to Apologetic Dialogue* (Moral Apologetics Press, Fall 2023). Pat is on the editorial board of the peer-reviewed education journal *Philosophy*, Theory, and Foundations in Education. Prior to the academy, Pat worked in the financial and banking sectors for 17 years. He is married and has three children. He can be reached on Twitter at @RealPatSawyer or through his website at patsawyer.org.

ALSO BY NEIL SHENVI AND PAT SAWYER

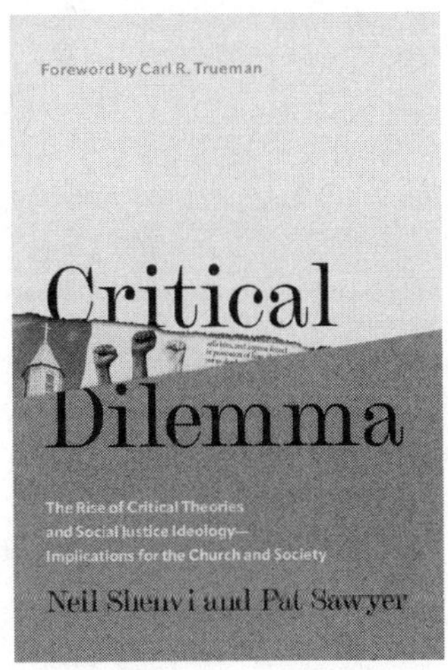

WHERE ARE CRITICAL THEORY AND THE SOCIAL JUSTICE MOVEMENT TAKING US?

Critical theory and its expression in fields such as critical race theory, critical pedagogy, and queer theory are having a profound impact on our culture. Contemporary critical theory's ideas about race, class, gender, identity, and justice have dramatically shaped how people think, act, and view one another—in Christian and secular spheres alike.

In *Critical Dilemma*, authors Neil Shenvi and Pat Sawyer illuminate the origins and influences of contemporary critical theory, considering it in the light of clear reason and biblical orthodoxy. While acknowledging that it can provide some legitimate insights regarding race, class, and gender, *Critical Dilemma* exposes the false assumptions at the heart of critical theory, arguing that it poses a serious threat to both the church and society at large.

Drawing on exhaustive research and careful analysis, Shenvi and Sawyer condemn racism, urge Christians to seek justice, and offer a path forward for racial healing and unity while also opposing critical theory's manifold errors.